irrationality

stuart sutherland

Stuart Sutherland, born in 1928, was Professor of Psychology at the University of Sussex where he founded the Laboratory of Experimental Psychology.

A prolific columnist and contributor to the *Observer*, the *New York Times* and the *Daily Telegraph*, he is best known for his iconoclastic book *Irrationality*, which was first published in 1992, and *Breakdown*, his candid and movingly personal account of his manic depression. He died in 1998.

Breakdown will be reissued by Pinter & Martin in 2009.

irrationality

stuart sutherland

pinter
&
martin

PINTER & MARTIN

Irrationality

First published by Constable and Company 1992
This edition published by Pinter & Martin Ltd 2007
Reprinted 2007, 2008, 2009

ISBN 978-1-905177-07-3

British Library Cataloguing-in-Publication Data
A catalogue record for this book is available from the British Library

Set in Sabon

Printed and bound in Great Britain by
Athenaeum Press Ltd, Gateshead, Tyne & Wear

This book has been printed on paper that is sourced and
harvested from sustainable forests and is FSC accredited

Pinter & Martin Ltd
6 Effra Parade
London SW2 1PS

www.pinterandmartin.com

contents

preface

Pace Aristotle, it can be argued that irrational behaviour is the norm not the exception. In order to demonstrate this, I have provided many startling examples of irrationality in everyday life and in the activities of the professions. It turns out that the decisions of doctors, generals, engineers, judges, businessmen and others are no more rational than those made by you or me though their effects are often more calamitous.

However, the real proof of the prevalence of irrationality comes from the massive amount of research on the topic undertaken over the last thirty years by psychologists. Their discoveries – unlike those of cosmologists – are as yet scarcely known to the general public. Although I have not myself worked directly on the topic, I became fascinated by the ingenuity of their experiments and by the light they throw on the workings of the mind. This book integrates the many factors that have been shown to cause irrational behaviour, including social and emotional biases as well as the many quirks of thought produced by such failings as not taking account of negative cases or being too swayed by what first comes to mind. Many of the experimental findings are so surprising that the reader's credulity may well be strained: almost all of them have, however, been replicated many times. To stave off the sceptical reader, there is a rather daunting list of sources, which needs to be consulted only by those lacking faith in my veracity or desiring to pursue specific issues in more detail.

I have tried to make clear to the layman work that is often hard to follow in the technical journals; for the most part I have avoided mathematical and statistical concepts, but of necessity a few elementary ones are introduced and explained towards the end of the book.

This is not a 'Do-it-Yourself' book on how to think, but I have ventured to place a few hints at the ends of chapters. Readers may learn to avoid some of the many snares that beset their thought processes – always provided they are already sufficiently rational to want to be more so, a desirable aim if there is any truth in Oscar Wilde's remark, 'There is no sin except stupidity.' If Oscar Wilde is right, irrationality is too important a subject to be taken seriously, a dictum that I have occasionally obeyed. Although I do not consider myself any more rational than anyone else, I beg readers not to inform me of any errors they detect in this book: it was hard enough synthesising the voluminous literature on irrationality without being told that the end product is itself irrational.

In deciding what generic pronoun to use I faced a dilemma. The use of masculine pronouns might offend feminists, but since in almost all cases the pronoun refers to someone acting irrationally, I decided it was safer to use the generic masculine: the reader is welcome to infer that I consider women more rational than men. Finally, I salute all those whose work I have pillaged: they are acknowledged in the notes at the end of the book.

Stuart Sutherland
Sussex University
August 1992

acknowledgements

I am grateful to Nicholas Bagnall, Colin Fisher and Phil Johnson-Laird for helpful comments on drafts of the manuscript. I am deeply indebted to Julia Purcell both for her comments and for her encouragement. I thank my daughters Gay and Julia Sutherland for help in preparing the index and notes. I am especially grateful to my secretary, Ann Doidge, for her speed, accuracy and patience in placing successive drafts on a word processor and for her ability to read my handwriting, which is more than I can do myself. I also thank Cambridge University Press and David Eddy for giving me permission to reproduce Tables 3 and 4.

1 introduction

Taken all in all, rationality has had a good press. Hamlet declared, 'What a piece of work is a man! How noble in reason!' Thomas Huxley, a fervent exponent of rationality, went much further: 'If some great Power would agree to make me always think what is true and do what is right, on condition of being turned into a sort of clock, and wound up every morning before I got out of bed, I should instantly close with the offer.' Whether or not rationality is as desirable a gift as Huxley believed, it is certain that people exhibit it only sporadically if at all. Consider, for example, how you would answer the following questions.

Which is more likely – that a mother with blue eyes has a daughter with blue eyes or that a daughter with blue eyes has a mother with blue eyes? Are there more words beginning with the letter 'k' than with 'k' as a third letter? Is an interview a useful selection procedure? Smoking increases the risk of lung cancer by a factor of ten and of fatal heart disease by a factor of two: do more smokers die of lung cancer than of heart disease? Are you a better than average driver? Could you be persuaded to give potentially lethal shocks to someone as part of a psychological experiment? Do more people die of strokes than of accidents? Which is more dangerous, cycling or riding the Big Wheel? Consider two maternity hospitals, one averaging forty-five births a day, the other fifteen: in which hospital is it more likely that on any given day 60 per cent of births will be boys? Is it always beneficial to reward people for performing a task well?

Unless you have been put on your guard by the title of this book, some of your answers to these simple questions are likely to be irrational, as indeed were some of mine when I first encountered them. Moreover, if you answered all of them, you were certainly irrational, since some contain insufficient information to warrant an answer: the inability to suspend judgement is one of the most prevalent aspects of irrationality.

Most people, like Aristotle, who defined man as 'a rational animal', believe that unless demented almost everyone is at least for the most part rational: of course their friends and acquaintances are less rational than they are themselves, but nonetheless they too are on the whole rational. Such beliefs have not always been held in the Western world, let alone in the East where mystic thinking is still prevalent. True, Aristotle's views were typical of classical times, but belief in human reason largely evaporated in the Dark Ages, to be replaced by the view that people should act on faith and perhaps to a lesser extent emotion. It was Descartes who revived the notion that man both is and should be a rational being: he should act according to the evidence of his senses and his power of reasoning, a thesis that led to the humanist tradition still persisting today. Man has no need of divine inspiration, his reason is sufficient unto itself. Until recently philosophers, psychologists and economists took it for granted that for the most part men act rationally.

The eminent philosopher, Gilbert Ryle remarked, 'Let the psychologist tell us why we are deceived, we can tell ourselves and him why we are not deceived.' In other words he took rationality as the norm or, if you like, he took it for granted: he believed that only acts that depart from rationality need to be explained.

Ryle led a cloistered life in Magdalen College, Oxford, an environment in which it is perhaps not too difficult to act rationally, but Sigmund Freud, who interacted in Vienna not with desiccated academics but with neurotic patients and with his often equally neurotic colleagues, shared Ryle's approach. He assumed that rational behaviour is the norm: he therefore attempted to explain only acts that are irrational, particularly dreams, neurotic symptoms, and slips of the tongue. His explanations are an attempt to show that once the unconscious processes underlying behaviour, particularly the conflict between the libido and the superego, are understood, all these apparently irrational acts are in reality rational: they allow the libido satisfaction in disguised form. The defence mechanisms that conceal the fulfilment of the libido's wishes from the superego are unconscious but entirely rational. The miser hoarding money that he will never use is not really irrational: he is gratifying himself by fulfilling an infant desire to retain his faeces.

Again, until about twenty years ago economics was almost completely based on the concept of the rational man. *Homo economicus* was pictured as having a set of preferences for different goods: he would trade off price against preference and buy whatever was most cost-effective for him. The businessman was also supposed to function with complete rationality: he would produce the goods that made the most profit and the price he set was that which would maximise profits. The possibility that businessmen might be lazy, stupid, inefficient or in search of a peerage was rarely discussed. We shall see that classical economists were wrong about both buyer and producer.

My purpose is to demonstrate that people are very much less rational than is commonly thought and to set out systematically the many reasons why this is so. Nobody, including I need hardly say myself, is exempt. I shall demonstrate the prevalence of irrationality partly by describing some of the many psychological experiments recently carried out on the subject and partly by giving some examples, often startling, both from everyday life and from the professions. Everybody is irrational some of the time, and the more complex the decisions to be taken, the more irrational they are. It might be thought that the main cause of irrational behaviour is that emotion clouds judgement. Although this is a factor, it is not the most important. There are many inherent defects in the ways people think and it is mainly these that will be examined here.

Irrationality can only be defined in terms of rationality, so one must ask what it is to be rational. Rationality takes two forms. Rational thinking leads to the conclusion that is most likely to be correct, given the knowledge one has. Rational decisions are more complicated, since a decision can only be evaluated if we know its objective: a rational action is the one that, given the person's knowledge, is most likely to achieve his end. Rationality can only be assessed in the light of what a person knows: it would be foolish for anyone who had a minimal acquaintance with astronomy to try to reach the moon by climbing a tree, but the same behaviour on the part of a small child might be entirely rational even if somewhat misguided. It is important to distinguish irrationality from ignorance, which also exists on a large scale. In 1976 40 per cent of American citizens thought that Israel was an Arab country, while today in Britain one in three thirteen-year-old children think the sun goes round the earth.

No attempt will be made to characterise in detail the nature of rational thought. In general it consists of detecting regularities in the world and applying them to predict the future or to infer hitherto unknown aspects of the present or past. Underlying it, is one of philosophy's most striking paradoxes. Rational thought, including all scientific thought, is based on the assumption that there are laws governing the world and that these laws remain constant over time – they will be the same in the future as in the past. This assumption cannot be justified: it is no good arguing that as far as we can tell the laws have remained constant in the past and therefore will stay the same in the future since this involves the very assumption that we are trying to prove. I shall ignore this need for an act of faith, for I am concerned with concrete instances of rationality and irrationality and most people can tell the difference, at least when it is pointed out to them.

A distinction should be drawn between irrationality and error. To be irrational an action must be performed deliberately. But a mistake that is made involuntarily is not irrational, though it is an error. In adding up two columns of figures we may forget to carry one, thus creating an accidental error.

Neither rational thinking nor rational decision-making necessarily leads to the best outcome. Had you lived before Australia was discovered, you would have been justified in concluding that all swans were white, but you would have been wrong: you had an insufficient knowledge of the fauna of the Antipodes. Again, were someone to offer to pay you £1,000 if a coin comes down heads, while you have to pay out £100 if it comes down tails, it is rational to take the bet, provided that one of your aims is making money and you are not too worried about losing a friend. But the coin may come down tails: although your decision was rational, it did not have good consequences. In one of his short stories, Saki presents a nice instance of a rational conclusion that turned out to be wrong. While eating his breakfast, a small boy informed his elders and betters that there was a frog in his bread and milk. Despite his detailed description of the markings on its skin, they claimed that was quite impossible. Although their conclusion – given their state of knowledge – was entirely rational, much to the small boy's satisfaction, they were wrong. As he explained, he had put the frog there himself. Taking the most rational decision, then, does not necessarily ensure the best outcome, because in human affairs there is almost always an element of chance. But over a lifetime chance tends to even out, and if you want to achieve your ends to the greatest possible extent, you had better take the rational decision as often as you can even though on occasion a different decision would have led to a better result. It is possible that by pointing out the ways in which people err, this book may help readers to take better decisions more often, but as will be discussed in the final chapter that may be too much to hope.

I have stressed that what constitutes a rational decision depends upon one's knowledge. There is a rider to this. If one has reason to believe one's knowledge is insufficient, then it is rational, particularly in the case of important decisions, to seek out more evidence: unfortunately, as we will see, when people do so, they usually act in a wholly irrational way, since they only seek evidence that will support their existing beliefs.

* * *

There are rational means to achieve an end, but one can ask whether there is such a thing as a rational end. There are certainly some irrational ones. For example, most people would think it irrational to pursue an end that is impossible to achieve: the standard example – flying to the moon – is now out of date. In addition, it is irrational to have conflicting ends. You cannot consistently strive to make your partner happy and to exploit her as much as possible. Perhaps a further form of irrationality is that few people bother to think out their goals in life and their order of priorities. They act spontaneously, and although this may be endearing or irritating depending on one's viewpoint, it can lead to irrational actions: that is to say, had they thought before acting, they might have acted in a way more likely to achieve their ends.

Philosophers have discussed at great length the ultimate goal, if any, of mankind, but they have reached no consensus, for that is the nature of philosophy. To be rational, a goal for mankind must be one that everyone could follow without conflict. Three plausible candidates are the survival of the human race, the greatest happiness of the greatest number and the pursuit of knowledge. None of them withstands scrutiny. If alien beings who were kinder, more intelligent and in every way superior to us landed on the Earth carrying a virus that we knew would wipe all of us out and if the only alternative to extinction were to kill them, we would undoubtedly do so: but that could be seen as a parochial and selfish act. In these circumstances some people might want to take into account goals other than the survival of the human race. As to happiness, how is it measured? How does one offset one person's misery against another's joy? The pursuit of knowledge sounds very glorious, but why is it better than everyone striving to be good athletes or excellent chess players? Moreover, it could be self-defeating, since the unwise use of its technological spin-offs could result in there being nobody left on Earth to know anything. In thinking about ultimate goals, we are beyond the realm of rationality. A given goal can only be defended in terms of a superior goal: one cannot as the saying goes 'get an "ought" from an "is"'. In Pascal's words, 'The heart has its reasons that reason knows not of.' Hence, ultimate goals cannot be defended: by their nature they have no superior goals in terms of which they can be justified. In practice, it may be doubted if anyone has systematically pursued any such ultimate goals.

We are born with a set of 'biological drives', like hunger, thirst, sex, and the avoidance of pain, as well as with more elusive but still powerful motives like curiosity, or the urge to dominate or to belong to a group. The presence of such drives tends to make us put ourselves first. It can be and indeed has been argued that this is irrational. People are not fundamentally different from one another: my neighbour may be more or less intelligent, witty or handsome than I am, but he shares the same biological make-up, feels the same pain, and has similar joys and sorrows. Rationally I should put his happiness on a par with my own. Unfortunately this claim does not hold up. A person may argue that his own experience – his own pains and pleasures – are unique: only he can experience them. A person can even, without inconsistency, be a solipsist, that is he may believe that only he exists and that the outside world is a figment of his imagination: hence he is entitled to put himself first.

One must distinguish between rationality and morality: attempts to justify morality on a rational basis have always foundered. Most people adopt a compromise position: while putting their own happiness first, they make more or less strenuous efforts to take that of others into account. The rationality of ends will not be further considered: we shall be concerned only with the irrationality of the means.

Some readers may protest that some of the instances of irrationality that follow are not really irrational at all. Certainly there are several borderline cases. First, much irrationality arises through not taking enough time to think things through. But someone may feel quite satisfied with a decision and believe that any gain made by more prolonged thought would not be commensurate with the extra time and effort involved. In the limit, a manager taking a complex decision could spend so much time thinking of all its ramifications that the firm went bankrupt before he had made his mind up. The manager who took a quick decision that was not optimal could not be accused of irrationality, provided he had made the best use of the time available to him. On the other hand, many people not under time stress make bad decisions because they do not take account of all the relevant factors. Saving the effort of hard thinking may be sensible over trivial decisions, but as will be shown it is always irrational and often calamitous when complex and important decisions are taken, as in business, medicine or politics.

Second, because we can only hold a small number of ideas in our minds at any one time, in making complex decisions people do not combine all the relevant factors. One way round this problem is to use pencil and paper to set out the pros and cons of different actions and it is irrational not to do so. Charles Darwin in his autobiography claims to have used this method – as it happens with success – in order to decide whether to marry: not many are likely to emulate him when taking this particular decision – one could argue that there are too many unknowns.

Third, as I shall demonstrate towards the end of this book, taking the best decision whether in a court of law or in everyday life may often involve the use of concepts drawn from elementary statistics. Few people have these tools to rational thinking at their disposal. I shall argue, however, that many of the mistakes that arise through neglect of elementary mathematics are so blatant that they must be counted as irrational.

Fourth, many organisations fail to achieve their proper goals because they are structured in ways that encourage selfish behaviour in their members. The selfishness of the members, however immoral, is not irrational, but the organisation as a whole functions irrationally in the sense that it fails to use the best means to achieve its ends.

Fifth, people often distort their thoughts about reality in order to make themselves feel more comfortable or happier. One instance is wishful thinking, in which a person has an irrational belief that something he wants will happen or that some aspect of himself or herself is better than in fact it is. Such thinking is universal. Self-deception can also help to make people happy. The sadistic schoolmaster who believes that he beats small boys for their own good rather than to indulge his own erotic desires is deceiving himself. Both wishful thinking and self-deception may contribute to a person's happiness and to this extent they are a rational means to an end. But I have defined irrationality as coming to conclusions that cannot be justified by one's current knowledge and in so far as someone distorts his view of the world or of himself he is thinking irrationally. We are so constructed that in order to gratify ourselves we sometimes hold irrational beliefs: the fact that they do so gratify us does not make them any less irrational.

In short, we will treat as irrational any thought process that leads to a conclusion or a decision that is not the best that could have been reached in the light of the evidence, given the time constraints that apply. This is admittedly setting very high standards for rationality, but I will in fact be mainly concerned with decisions and judgements that are unequivocally irrational because they arise from systematic and avoidable biases in thinking. Our main concern will be to demonstrate and discuss such biases, which are surprisingly common and which can have very pernicious consequences. A discussion of whether completely rational behaviour is always desirable must wait until the final chapter.

* * *

Not only are we victims of our instincts and self-serving desires, we are also governed by the state of our bodies, particularly of our brains. I shall not discuss the effects of brain injuries or severe mental illness on rationality, but it may be worth giving two bizarre examples. There is a small area in the middle of the right-hand side of the brain which produces a curious effect if an epileptic focus develops there. In such a focus the nerve cells from time to time all fire together: when they do so, they cause an epileptic seizure. A focus in this particular area can render the person highly religious, and cause him to avoid sex in any form and to give up all addictions such as smoking and alcohol. Remarkably, when the focus is removed the person goes back to his previous existence: he may become an atheist, and return to cigarettes, alcohol and the pursuit of sex. It may be that the form the Christian religion has taken was in part caused by St Paul suffering an epileptic attack on the road to Damascus.

Again, schizophrenia has devastating effects on rationality. The patient may believe his thoughts are being controlled or monitored by some outside agency or he may believe he is Napoleon or Jesus Christ. Some schizophrenics take everything literally so that when walking down a corridor with a sign on a door saying, 'Please knock', they always knock as they pass.

As a matter of fact, psychologists know very much less about irrational behaviour caused by mental illness or by brain damage than they do about the common or garden irrationality to which every one of us is prone, and with which we are here concerned. The errors that will be described are made by most people, but not necessarily by all. The reader who gives the wrong answer to some of the problems that will be posed may console himself with the thought that he is not alone. Remember that you know that this book is about irrationality and hence are likely to be on your guard: you may well not fall into the irrational booby traps that are set. But in almost all cases, when the questions are put to unsuspecting people who have not been forewarned, they do fall, usually heavily.

Many of the examples used come from medicine. The reader should not run away with the idea that doctors are any more irrational than anyone else. Their failings are simply better documented than those of journalists, civil servants, historians, engineers, generals, judges and – regrettably – psychologists: follies committed by all these experts appear in this book. Although the figures drawn from medicine on mortality rates, the diagnostic power of different tests and so on were correct at the time the studies described were undertaken, they are not necessarily correct now, for medical techniques are constantly improving. For our purposes, it is the state of knowledge at the time a decision was made that is important, for a doctor can only be shown to have acted irrationally in the light of his existing knowledge.

In describing psychological experiments, I have used almost no technical terms, but there are three that will recur. A *subject* is a person on whom an experiment is conducted. Usually, subjects are volunteers, but they may be university students dragooned into 'volunteering' by their professors or told that acting as a subject is an essential part of their course. Moreover, people sometimes become subjects without knowing they are doing so. The experimenter may arrange a craftily staged car accident and observe who walks by on the other side of the street and who goes to help, or people may rashly attend a group whose purported object is losing weight, but whose real aim is more sinister. These days, considerable circumspection is needed in order to avoid falling prey to the social psychologist's greed for subjects.

The second term is *stooge*, also called an accomplice or a confederate. The stooge either acts as though he were a subject, thus deceiving the real subjects taking part, or he assumes some other predetermined and false role. The stooge is instructed by the experimenter to act and speak in a particular way in order to record the effects on the real subject's behaviour. Stooges are likely to pop up all over the place. The waitress who spills a bowl of soup on your lap, the shop assistant who gives you the wrong change or the chap sitting by you in the theatre who shouts 'Fire', all may just be stooges. There is no known defence against the stooge, but in all these circumstances you should keep an eye open for a professorial-looking figure with a notebook, lurking in the background.

Almost all psychologists make it a policy to *debrief* their subjects. The word as used in psychology has almost the opposite meaning from that given it by the military: at the end of an experiment, the subject is told what it was all about, particularly when deception has been used. If, as often happens, the subject has been induced to do something shameful or has performed very badly on a test, he is told that he is no worse than anyone else and sent off with a reassuring pat on the head. The debriefings with which we shall be concerned are mainly those that occur half-way through an experiment in order to discover what effect such debriefing will have on the subjects' subsequent performance.

Many of the studies reported here involve deception, for psychologists, particularly social psychologists, are not without guile. Such deceptions may make readers uneasy. I have no view on this myself: the best that can be said is that if a subject is fooled into behaving shamefully in an experiment, he or she might learn something from the experience. Many experimenters report that their subjects all thanked them afterwards for an interesting and salutary experience, but then they would, wouldn't they?

It is common to end introductory chapters by giving a blow-by-blow summary of the remaining chapters. Since I have no intention of easing the reader's life by obviating the need to read on, I give no such summary here. However, as some guidance to the book's organisation, Chapter 2 deals with the most prevalent reason for errors in thinking, which plays a role in many of the other mistakes detailed later in the book. The next seven chapters cover the social and emotional causes of irrationality, while Chapters 10 to 19 deal with errors produced simply by our inability to think straight. The next two chapters describe some ideal methods of manipulating evidence that if used would, at least in theory, produce conclusions that were the best possible in the light of the evidence: the results obtained by such methods are compared with those arrived at by intuition, which is shown to be seriously lacking. Chapter 22 is a résumé of some of the errors already discussed, showing how they explain the widespread but irrational belief in the paranormal. The final chapter examines the deeper causes of irrationality in terms of our evolutionary history and the nature of our brains and also considers what if anything can be done to promote rationality – as it turns out, no easy task; I end by raising the question 'Is rationality really necessary – or even desirable?'

2 the wrong impression

The leading part in the film *Jaws* was a man-eating shark. The screening of the film caused a sharp drop in the number of swimmers off the coast of California, where the occasional shark is to be found near the beaches. It has been calculated that the risk of swimmers being snapped up by a shark is very much less than the risk of their being killed in a road accident while on the way to the coast. People do not take account of the true facts – they go upon what makes the deepest impression, or on what first comes to mind.

As a further illustration, consider these two questions: 'Are there more words with "r" as the first letter than with "r" in the third position?' 'Are there more words beginning with "k" than with "k" as the third letter?' Unless you sense that there is some sort of trick being played, you are likely to answer yes to both questions. But you would be wrong – there are more words with 'r' or 'k' in the third position than there are words beginning with each letter. The mistake is made because words, both in dictionaries and in our minds, are arranged by their initial letter. It is easy to retrieve from memory words beginning with 'r', like 'roar', 'rusty' and 'ribald', but much more difficult to recover words like 'street', 'care' and 'borrow', despite their greater frequency. Lest you think this experiment is unfair because nobody could know the answer without counting up words in a dictionary, here is a variant on it in which knowledge is not involved. The question is, 'Are there more words ending in "-ing" than ending in "-n-" (that is, having "n" as the penultimate letter)?' Most people think that '-ing' endings are more common, but in fact '-n-' must be more frequent since all '-ing' endings have 'n' as the penultimate letter in addition to many other words (like 'fine'). People can recall words ending in '-ing' more readily than those ending in '-n-' and they do not stop to go through the simple argument outlined.

Judging by the first thing that comes to mind is called the 'availability error'. I have made it the first error to be described because it permeates all reasoning and, as we shall see throughout the rest of the book, many other specific errors are in reality just further instances of it. Suppose you are thinking of buying a car and you mention it to a friend. He gives you a glowing account of his own car. Deeply impressed, you rush out to buy the same model, only to find that it is totally unreliable and has an outrageous thirst for petrol. The immediacy and salience (availability) of his description have made you forget all the statistics to be found in consumer magazines. You have also committed a second common fallacy, which will be discussed later: no matter how good your friend's car is, it may or may not be representative of that model in general. No two cars of the same type perform equally well and he may simply have been lucky with his.

There are dozens of experiments demonstrating faulty reasoning caused by the availability error. In one extreme case, subjects first had to learn a list of words (a task much beloved by psychologists). The words were the same for all subjects, except that those for one group included four terms of praise – 'adventurous', 'self-confident', 'independent' and 'persistent'. For a second group, they included four disparaging words – 'reckless', 'conceited', 'aloof' and 'stubborn'. After learning the words, all the subjects read a short story about a young man who had several dangerous hobbies, thought well of his abilities, had few friends, and rarely changed his mind once it was made up. Finally they were asked to evaluate him. Although it was made clear that the previously presented list of words had no connection whatsoever with the man in the story, those who had learned the favourable adjectives thought much better of him than those who had learned the unfavourable ones. The words were in their minds (available) at the time they read the story and hence had coloured their interpretation of it. If items such as the words learned in this experiment can affect subjects' interpretation of something completely unconnected, how much more strongly are people likely to be affected by aspects of a situation that are highly salient and are closely connected with whatever is being judged?

In order to expound the next experiment it is necessary to explain a fiendish game, known as 'The Prisoner's Dilemma'. It is based on the following scenario. Two people are in gaol for a crime they are thought to have committed together. The governor tells them that the length of their sentence will depend, in a rather complicated way, on whether or not they confess to the crime. The sentences are as follows:

1. If one confesses and the other does not, the one who confesses goes free, while the other gets twenty years in gaol.

2. If neither confesses, they will each be given a two-year sentence.
3. If both confess, they will each spend five years in gaol.

The dilemma facing the prisoners is whether or not to confess – they are in separate cells and neither knows what the other will do. The best outcome is if neither confesses, because the combined length of time they spend in gaol is only four years. But not confessing is dangerous since if the other prisoner confesses, the one who does not spends twenty years in gaol.

The game is not as far removed from real life as might at first appear. In the long run it would clearly be beneficial for all countries to reduce the emissions of carbon dioxide, the principal cause of the greenhouse effect, the results of which may prove disastrous. On the other hand, such reduction is expensive: it entails using fewer fossil fuels to produce energy or using less energy. If all countries agree to a reduction, all will benefit. But if a few refuse (as the USA is at the moment doing) but most agree, those refusing will benefit both by saving the costs of reducing the emissions and by the reduction in the size of the greenhouse effect caused by other countries reducing emissions. To give a more mundane example, people have to decide whether surreptitiously to water their gardens in a drought. If everyone did so, the water supply might be exhausted and the effects would be disastrous for all. On the other hand if just a few people act in this antisocial way, they will benefit at the expense of a small loss to the community. These situations exactly parallel the Prisoner's Dilemma, a game which is often used by psychologists to measure people's willingness to collaborate. Making the choice that if made by both leads to the minimal loss to the two combined is known as 'collaborating', the other choice is 'defecting' – if made by one person, it leads to a large loss for the other if he collaborates.

The game has produced endless speculation among philosophers because it is unclear what is the rational thing to do. Until recently the puzzle has remained insoluble. Even if your opponent has collaborated for some time, you never know when he will defect, thus landing you with a substantial penalty if you are collaborating. Interestingly, there is now an indication of the best way to play the game. A strategy is any rule adopted by a player for a number of rounds against the same opponent, for example, 'Always defect', or 'Defect randomly half the time, collaborate on the other half'. In a recent study, a large number of different strategies were proposed by mathematicians and others. These strategies were tested against one another on a computer. The best strategy, that is the one that maximised the player's gains against any of the other strategies tested, turned out to be 'Collaborate on the first round and then copy whatever the opponent did on his last move'. This strategy punishes the opponent for defecting and rewards him for co-operating. Its success is particularly interesting since it suggests that behaving altruistically (on some occasions) can secure the highest possible gain for the person doing so: altruistic behaviour, whose existence has long puzzled evolutionary theorists, can therefore help to achieve one's own ends, and hence survival. Although in real life the Prisoner's Dilemma rarely occurs in the same form more than once, it occurs over and over again in different forms. Hence the strategy outlined is still likely to be the best.

In experiments, monetary rewards or penalties are substituted for gaol sentences, if only in order to make it easier to find volunteers as subjects. The 'prisoners' are usually faced with two buttons – call them 'C' and 'D' for 'co-operating' and 'defecting'. They are given rules such as:

If they both press C, they receive £5 each.
If one presses C and the other D, the first is fined £10 and the second receives £10.
If both press D, they are each fined £1.

In the experiment with which we are concerned here, one group of subjects was exposed to a touching radio programme about someone who had given a kidney to a complete stranger in need of a transplant, while the other group listened to an account of some particularly vile human behaviour, to wit an urban atrocity. Pairs of subjects were then asked to play Prisoner's Dilemma. Those who had listened to the touching story of the kidney transplant collaborated much more than did those who had heard about the atrocity, although the stories had absolutely nothing to do with the game they were playing. Once again, recent experiences even when they are irrelevant can make people behave more or less selfishly.

Here is a rather different but equally irrational example of faulty judgement directly caused by the availability error. Subjects were read lists of names of men and women, some of them fictitious, some the names of famous people. All were called by both their Christian name and surname, so the sex of each was obvious. Each list contained approximately half female and half male names, and the subjects had to judge whether there were more men's or women's names. When the men were all famous, like Winston Churchill or John Kennedy, and the women were not well known, subjects thought there were more men than women, and vice versa when the women were famous and the men unknown. Names of important people made more impact (were more available) than those of unknown people and the judgements were based on this factor rather than on the actual frequency of men and women in each list.

Before discussing what makes material available, it is worth considering some examples of the availability error being craftily put to use in real life. The organisers of lotteries give maximum publicity to past winners, and of course say nothing about the great majority who have won no prizes. By publicising winners, they make winning foremost in the minds of potential buyers of tickets and hence make them believe that they are more likely to win than they really are. Similarly the rattling of coins disgorged from a fruit machine is intended to call people's attention to the possibility of winning money: the machine maintains a steadfast silence at other times.

People's tendency to base their judgements on what is available is manipulated by shopkeepers throughout the world and also by otherwise respectable publishers. Would you be more likely to buy a book costing £5.95 or one costing £6.00? The important figure is the number of pounds: it is therefore more available than the pence and people seize on it, disregarding the fact that in the case quoted there is only a difference in price of 5p.

One may ask what makes something 'available'. The experiments already cited show that recently presented material is available, but it has also been found that anything that produces strong emotion, that is dramatic, that leads to the formation of images and that is concrete rather than abstract is also readily available. A murder committed by a Muslim or Japanese will receive far more coverage in the newspapers than one committed by John Smith: it is more dramatic, less of an everyday occurrence and hence more available. Moreover, people are likely to have stronger emotional feelings about Muslims and Japanese than about John Smith.

A massive amount of work has been done on images, which affect all aspects of our mental life. If someone has to learn to pair one word with another, for example to say 'car' when given the word 'dog', he learns much faster if he is told to form an image connecting the members of each pair, for instance, by imagining a dog sitting in a car. Moreover, people have an amazing capacity to remember pictures. After being shown 10,000 photographs just once they can correctly recognise almost all of them a week later. This is in marked contrast to the very poor memory for isolated words. Later in the chapter, I shall illustrate the power of images to evoke irrational responses by their use in advertising.

There have been several experiments showing that concrete material is more available than abstract material. One was again based on the Prisoner's Dilemma. The subject's partner in the game was not a real partner. The moves made by the 'partner' were in reality made by the experimenter and consisted of a prearranged proportion of co-operating and defecting moves. In one condition, subjects learned what move their partner had made by watching which of two lights flashed. In the other, they were passed a handwritten note through a slit. One might think that this would make little difference to how they thought of their partner, but in fact it made a great deal. When notes were passed the subjects saw their partners' moves as being made much more deliberately, that is they saw them as intending to co-operate or defect. Moreover, they showed more trust in a partner who made co-operative moves when notes were passed than when communication was made by the lights, for they made more co-operative moves themselves in the former case than in the latter. Similarly, they distrusted a defecting partner more in the condition with notes than in that with lights. It is extraordinary that whether a light is flashed or a note passed should make such a difference to people's behaviour: the note is a concrete reminder that they are dealing with a real person, who is more or less trustworthy.

The availability error is responsible for a large number of irrational judgements in real life. Do you regard fairgrounds as dangerous? Certainly most people do. There is the Big Wheel with its carriages turning precariously in the air, the roller-coaster with its frightening bends and changes of speed, the Octopus subjecting you to massive centrifugal force while rocking you violently to and fro, and many other machines moving in a variety of contortions. Yet most people (including myself until I learned the facts) are wrong. According to a report of the British Health and Safety Committee, if you cycle on main roads for an hour you are forty times as likely to be killed as if you spend the same length of time riding fairground machines, and you are seven times as safe on them as when driving a car. Fairground accidents are of course dramatic and well publicised: they are 'available'. It is also known that people grossly overestimate the chances of dying a violent death, for example, in an air crash or in street riots. In one study it was found that people think they are twice as likely to die of an accident as from a stroke; in fact forty times as many people die of strokes as from accidents. The reason for this false belief is that, although most people die in their beds, air crashes and violence are constantly reported in the media and are highly dramatic: they are therefore 'available'.

Not only do people hold irrational beliefs about the frequency of violence, but they are driven by their beliefs to wholly irrational actions. In 1986 the number of Americans visiting Europe as tourists showed a sharp drop. They had been scared away as a result of a few much-publicised plane hijackings and possibly by the American bombing of Libya. But they had failed to take account of the less-publicised prevalence of violent crime in the US: in fact Americans living in cities put themselves at greater risk of meeting a violent death by staying at home. Exactly the same irrational refusal to fly occurred during the Gulf War.

Sometimes the availability error does seemingly drive people to act rationally. In California the number of insurance policies taken out against earthquakes increases steeply after a quake, but then drops gradually until the next one. But even this behaviour is not really rational since whether you take out insurance should depend not on when the last earthquake was but on the probability of earthquakes in the future. Again, after Mrs Ford and Mrs Rockefeller developed breast cancer, large numbers of American women rushed to the hospitals to have diagnostic tests. They had hitherto been completely unmoved by government warnings that they should have tests at regular intervals.

There is a more everyday example of the effects of availability, which is familiar to everyone who drives. A driver who has just passed an accident almost invariably slows down. The accident makes available the possibility that he too will crash: unfortunately the effect wears off within a few miles. The sight of a police car has the same result.

The availability error is just as common in the professions as in everyday life. It is known that a doctor who has recently seen a number of cases of a particular disease becomes more prone to diagnose that illness in patients who have not got it. This would of course make sense in the case of contagious diseases, but the mistaken diagnoses occur even in non-contagious ones such as appendicitis. The same kind of error afflicts stockbrokers who on seeing the market going up recommend their clients to buy, and to sell when it goes down. Statistically, there is little or no connection between rises and falls one day and the next or even one week and the next, but the mere fact that shares have risen prompts people to buy them. The correct strategy is the opposite of that commonly used, namely, to buy at troughs and sell at peaks, though it is not easy to implement. Nor can high-level managers be exempted. They are likely to be influenced by a conversation they had at lunch or by a stray item read in a newspaper rather than using all the evidence at their disposal and even better seeking new information when it is needed.

Statistics are abstract and pallid. For this reason most people ignore them. The knowledge that smoking increases the risk of lung cancer tenfold has little effect. People who give up smoking usually do so only when an isolated dramatic event occurs, for example, if they develop pneumonia and are told by their doctor that it could have been caused by cancer, or if a close friend dies of lung cancer. It might be thought that the reason why smoking has decreased more in doctors than in the general population is that they are intelligent people and that they know the figures on deaths caused by smoking: moreover, they presumably want to set a good example to their patients. A large-scale survey of doctors showed that this picture is considerably idealised. Smoking has dropped most dramatically in those doctors who have been most exposed to the effects of smoking, for example, chest physicians and radiologists. It has dropped considerably less in consultants in other specialities and in general practitioners. Even for doctors the statistics on cigarette smoking do not have the same immediacy as the sight of someone dying as a result of the habit.

It is often said that first impressions are the most important. The saying would appear to conflict with the 'availability error', since that would suggest that what happened *last* would be uppermost in the mind and therefore most important. Before resolving this paradox, some of the evidence for the importance of first impressions should be examined.

One of the first experiments on the topic was run in the USA by Solomon Asch. He asked subjects to evaluate a person simply on the basis of a list of six adjectives describing him. They might be told that he was 'intelligent, industrious, impulsive, critical, stubborn and envious'. Other subjects were given exactly the same six words but in the opposite order, 'envious, stubborn, critical, impulsive, industrious and intelligent'. All subjects were then asked to fill in a rating sheet in order to evaluate the person. For example, they had to indicate how happy they thought he was, how sociable he was, and so on. The subjects who heard the first list, which began with favourable adjectives, evaluated the person considerably more highly than did those given the list beginning with the derogatory words. This effect – being more heavily influenced by early than by late items – is called the 'primacy error'. There are two possible explanations for it.

First, in the Asch experiment, when subjects heard the first words, perhaps they began to build a mental picture of the person. They then tried to make subsequent words fit in with this picture. A subject who had heard that the person was intelligent and industrious might think of 'impulsive' as meaning spontaneous and regard it as quite a good thing, whereas someone who had first heard the adverse words 'envious' and 'stubborn' might think 'impulsive' meant acting rashly and without thought.

The alternative explanation is that while people are absorbing material, their attention may begin to wander and therefore they are more influenced by the first items they receive than by later ones. An ingenious experiment suggests that this explanation cannot be correct. Subjects watched a stooge attempting to solve thirty anagrams in succession. The stooge, who knew the answers, always solved exactly half the anagrams, but he would deliberately solve many anagrams early on and very few later or he would solve many of the later ones but few of the early ones. Subjects were subsequently asked how many anagrams had been solved by the person they had been watching. When more anagrams had been solved early on, they thought that more had been solved in total than when more had been solved towards the end. This is just another example of the importance of early impressions, but the clever part of the experiment was that the subjects were told to guess after each anagram whether the person they were watching would solve the next one. They must have been paying attention throughout, because their guesses changed as the number of anagrams solved changed: at times when many anagrams were being solved, they tended to think that the next one would be, but when few anagrams were being solved they would guess that the next one would not be. Although they were therefore clearly paying attention throughout, the subjects still thought that more anagrams in total were solved if the soluble ones came mainly at the beginning than if they came towards the end. Hence, lack of attention to later items is not the cause of the primacy error.

These experiments and many others suggest that beliefs are formed by first impressions: later evidence is interpreted in the light of these beliefs. There is, however, no conflict between the primacy error and the effect of recency on availability. The primacy error occurs because when connected material (such as a newspaper article or lecture) is presented, the interpretation of the later material is coloured by the earlier. The recency effect, on the other hand, occurs when material is not connected; under these circumstances, we tend to be influenced by what we have seen or heard most recently.

The primacy error can be regarded as one form of the availability error: the early items are immediately available in our minds when we encounter the rest. In making a judgement it is not the actual items that matter so much as the meaning we attach to them and that meaning can be altered by the first material we encounter, particularly if it is relevant to the remainder. This error is itself related to another bias in thinking that will be discussed in a later chapter, which will show that for a variety of reasons people cling tenaciously to their existing beliefs and make every effort to avoid discovering that they might be wrong.

The primacy error has important effects in everyday life. If you first encounter someone when he happens to be in a bad mood, you are likely to be prejudiced against him, even if he subsequently behaves more pleasantly. It has been demonstrated that interviewers form an impression of the candidate within the first minute or so and spend the rest of the interview trying to confirm that impression. If you are writing a book, make sure that the beginning is really good: it may be remarked parenthetically that few people ever finish a book so for the most part it would make little difference if the last chapter were mere gobbledegook. If you are writing examination papers, be sure to produce a really good first paragraph. And if you are a doctor diagnosing a patient, make every effort to take as much account of the symptoms you discover *last* as of those you discover first.

Also related to the availability error is the halo effect. If a person has one salient (available) good trait, his other characteristics are likely to be judged by others as better than they really are. Handsome men and women tend to be rated highly on intelligence, athletic prowess, sense of humour and so on. In fact physical appearance has little to do with such other characteristics: there is a small correlation between being handsome and being intelligent but it is not enough to account for the mistakes people make in their judgements. There is, incidentally, the opposite effect, which is known as the devil effect. The presence in an individual of one salient bad trait, like selfishness, can lower people's opinion of all his other traits: he tends to be seen as more dishonest and less intelligent than he really is. An extreme example occurred when I was serving on a jury, trying a case of rape of a minor. One of my fellow jurymen began the proceedings by remarking about the defendant, 'I don't like the look of him. We should find him guilty.' People influenced by the halo effect are completely unaware that they are biased by it.

One of the most extraordinary consequences of the halo effect occurs in blackjack. If in a casino the dealer's first upward card is an ace, any player may 'insure', that is he may make a side bet of up to half his original stake: if the dealer gets a blackjack, the player receives twice the value of his side bet, otherwise he loses all of it. A simple calculation shows that (unless he has counted cards) the player will lose on average 7.7 per cent of the money staked as 'insurance'. Yet Willem Wagenaar showed that in a Dutch casino most players sometimes insure and more than 12 per cent always insure. He concludes that the only explanation for this irrational behaviour is that they were deceived by the name 'insurance' into thinking that this was the most prudent course of action.

The halo effect has other pernicious consequences. In one study, the same examination scripts were rewritten twice, once in good handwriting and once in bad handwriting. They were then given to two sets of examiners: each saw all the scripts with half written badly and half well. They were all told to disregard the handwriting and to mark purely on the content. On average the scripts in good handwriting received considerably higher marks than those in poor writing. A similar experiment had an even more horrifying result. When the same essay was shown to examiners bearing a surname and either a male or female Christian name, it received higher marks when the examiner thought it was written by a man.

The halo effect has been put to good (or bad, depending on your point of view) use by the advertising industry for many years. A can of orangeade bearing the name 'Sunblessed' conjures up visions of oranges ripening under a Mediterranean sun and the effect may be enhanced by depicting luscious trees bearing large brightly coloured oranges. And why not throw in a beach for good measure? To the potential buyer the attributes suggested by the name and the picture rub off on the contents of the can and he has every expectation that it will taste delicious whether or not it does. As a matter of fact it is likely to taste better than it really is because he brings to it a set of expectations – juicy, ripe oranges and a holiday atmosphere – which will influence the way it actually tastes. For most products, however, the name and the packaging are irrelevant, except in so far as they signify that the maker has enough sense to choose a good advertising or packaging agency.

Although the halo effect has been known for seventy years, it is remarkable how little notice is taken of it. Only recently have most university examination papers been submitted by number rather than by name, a device that university administrators render worthless, since they usually number the papers in alphabetical order, presumably under the misapprehension that the examiners can't count. One of the most damaging ways in which the halo effect is ignored is the almost universal prevalence of the interview as a means of selection, whether for hospital staff, university students, army officers, the police, civil servants, or whomsoever. I will demonstrate later that the great majority of selection interviews are useless, and may indeed lower the chances of selecting the right candidate. Part of the reason is the halo effect: the interviewers are too influenced by comparatively trivial but salient aspects of the interviewee, which affect their judgement of his or her other characteristics.

One might think that in a scientific subject, the halo effect would not occur. Unfortunately this is not so. When a scientist or more usually several scientists submit a paper to a learned journal, a decision has to be taken on whether to accept it. Normally, the paper is sent off to two or three referees, who are chosen as experts in the usually rather narrow field covered by the paper. The editor decides whether to publish it on the basis of their reports. In 1982, two psychologists published an account of a revealing trick. They selected from each of twelve well-known journals of psychology one published article that had been written by members of one of the ten most prestigious psychology departments in the US, such as Harvard or Princeton: in consequence, the authors were mostly eminent psychologists. Next, they changed the authors' names to fictitious ones and their affiliations to those of some imaginary university, such as the Tri-Valley Centre for Human Potential. They then went through the articles carefully and whenever they found a passage that might provide a clue to the real authors, they altered it slightly, while leaving the basic contents unchanged. Each article was then typed and submitted under the imaginary names and affiliations to the very same journal that had originally published it.

Of the twelve journals, only three spotted that they had already published the article. This was a grave lapse of memory on the part of the editors and their referees, but then memory is fallible; however, worse was to come. Eight out of the remaining nine articles, all of which had been previously published, were rejected. Moreover, of the sixteen referees and eight editors who looked at these eight papers, every single one stated that the paper they examined did not merit publication. This is surely a startling instance of the availability error. It suggests that in deciding whether an article should be published, referees and editors pay more attention to the authors' names and to the standing of the institution to which they belong than they do to the scientific work reported. You might think that such bias by referees could not occur in a really rigorous subject like physics. But a review of bias, based on 619 articles published in journals of physics, concludes that 'access to publication may sometimes be easier' if you are 'part of the current in-group of well-known physicists' – surely a most delicate way of putting the point.

There are a number of explanations for the lapses over the psychology articles. I shall assume that they should all have been published, but it does not affect the argument; as far as human irrationality goes, the editors had either made a mistake by agreeing to publish originally or they made a mistake by not agreeing to publish subsequently.

The referees and editors could have acted as they did for either or both of two rational reasons. First, the research reported might already have been published by other workers in the two years since the original papers came out. Scrutiny of the referees' reports revealed that this was not the reason: none of them rejected the papers because the findings were not new. Second, it could be argued that workers from a good institution would be more careful in collecting their data and less prone to fraud than those from an unknown institution. This is an implausible reason, if only because some psychologists at good institutions owe their eminence to successful fraud. It is unlikely to have caused the rejection of the papers by unknown authors, since the referees made detailed criticisms of various points in the papers, many of which appear to have been valid. They criticised the statistics used and made remarks like 'The theoretical organization . . . seems loose and filled with . . . undocumented conclusions' or 'It is all very confusing.'

The most likely explanation is that both the original acceptance and the subsequent rejection occurred for irrational reasons. The first words a referee or an editor sees on reading an article are the authors' names and the name of their institution. If these are prestigious, he will be biased towards interpreting the paper in the best light possible; if they are not, he is probably going to look for flaws and to be more sensitive to what is wrong than to what is right. Here, then, is a dramatic demonstration of the availability error combined with the primacy and halo effects.

Everyone is irrational some of the time and in particular everyone is susceptible to the availability error. I give a final striking example, this time to do with publishers. In 1969, Jerzy Kosinsky's novel *Steps* won the American National Book Award for fiction. Eight years later some joker had it retyped and sent the manuscript with no title and under a false name to fourteen major publishers and thirteen literary agents in the US, including Random House, the firm that had originally published it. Of the twenty-seven people to whom it was submitted, not one recognised that it had already been published. Moreover, all twenty-seven rejected it. All it lacked was Jerzy Kosinsky's name to create the halo effect: without the name, it was seen as an indifferent book. Once again, the publishing industry is no more irrational than any other and despite the Kosinsky episode probably does not deserve Colin Haycraft's remark, 'If you can't live, write; if you can't write, be a publisher; if you can't be a publisher, be a literary agent; and if you can't be a literary agent, God help you.'

moral

1. Never base a judgement or decision on a single case, no matter how striking.
2. In forming an impression of a person (or object) try to break your judgement down into his (or its) separate qualities without letting any strikingly good or bad qualities influence your opinion about the remainder. This may seem cold, but it is important in situations, such as interviews or medical diagnoses based on a range of symptoms, where the judgement may seriously affect the person being judged.
3. When exposed to connected material, suspend judgement until the end: try to give as much weight to the last item as the first.
4. Try to avoid obtaining information that would bias you: for example, in judging whether an article or a book should be published, remain ignorant of the author's name until you have formed your own opinion of the work.
5. If you happen to be a publisher, check your back list on receipt of an MS: you don't want to publish the same book twice.

3 obedience

In the early 'sixties, Stanley Milgram advertised in a local newspaper for subjects to take part in an experiment at Yale University. Despite the meagre payment ($4) offered, he secured hundreds of people from all walks of life – postmen, teachers, salesmen, labourers and so forth. On arriving at the laboratory they were told they were to take part in an experiment investigating the effects of punishment on learning. Each subject was introduced to a stooge and it was explained that one of the two would be required to teach the other a simple task.

The subject and the stooge drew lots from a box containing two slips of paper to decide who should be the teacher and who the pupil. With the guile that has become the hallmark of the social psychologist, the experimenter had written 'teacher' on both slips so that the subject thought he had been selected at random to be the teacher. The pupil's task was to learn to associate one word with another, for example he might have to learn to respond 'box' to the word 'blue'. The teacher would read out the word 'blue' and then four other words like 'sky, ink, box, lamp' and the pupil – that is the stooge – had to press one of four buttons to indicate which of the set of four were correct. There were of course many pairs of words to be learned.

The teacher was in the next room to the pupil, but could see whether he had made the right response from which of four lights came on. Before the pupil began learning the words, the teacher watched him being strapped into a chair. The experimenter said that this was to prevent him moving too much when electric shocks were delivered, and added, 'Although the shocks can be extremely painful, they cause no permanent tissue damage.' In the teacher's room was a shock generator, with switches each labelled with a voltage running from 15 to 450. In addition, under different groups of switches was a verbal description of the shock intensity, for example, 'Slight

Shock', 'Strong Shock', 'Danger: Severe Shock'. A buzzer sounded whenever one of the switches was depressed. The subject was told that he must give a shock every time the pupil made a mistake and he was to increase the level by one step after each successive mistake. Whenever he demurred about increasing the shock level, the experimenter would urge him to continue, using such phrases as, 'The experiment requires that you continue' or 'You have no other choice, you must go on.'

Of course no shocks were actually delivered, but the stooge who was supposed to be receiving them would scream and groan when the 75-volt shock level was reached and for higher levels would yell to be let out or shout that he couldn't stand the pain. Beyond 330 volts he remained silent and no longer gave answers, though the teacher was told to shock him for not replying.

Appallingly, in the first experiment twenty-five subjects out of forty continued delivering shocks until they reached the highest level – 450 volts, marked 'Danger: Severe Shock'. None of the others stopped at 'Moderate Shock' and several went to 'Extreme Intensity Shock'.

Milgram rang many changes on this experiment, the results of which were as dismaying as those of the original one. Perhaps surprisingly, just as many women subjects gave maximum shock levels as men. It may be that although in general women are more tender-hearted than men, they are also more obedient to authority (as witnessed by women's lower crime rate): these two tendencies may have roughly balanced one another out. When subjects were placed in the same room as the pupil the number going to the highest shock level was reduced to one in four, presumably because such proximity brings home to the subject the consequences of what he is doing – another example of 'availability'. Possibly such proximity also makes the subject feel he is in the same group as the stooge and in a different one from the remote experimenter, thus giving him more allegiance to the former and less to the latter. Finally, when, after giving the initial instruction, the experimenter left the room and was not there to bully the subject into continuing with the shocks, only nine out of forty went to the highest level, though that is bad enough; even when subjects were left entirely free to decide the maximum shock level themselves without any pressure whatsoever, one went to the highest.

One might think that the subjects had realised that this was just a game and that in fact no shocks were being delivered. Unfortunately this is not true. Many of them became extremely nervous in the course of the experiment. They sweated and trembled, and begged the experimenter to allow them to stop. All of the subjects' protocols tell the same story. On reaching the maximum shock level one said to the experimenter, 'What if he's dead in there? I mean, he told me he can't stand the shock . . .', but he still went on to administer a further 450-volt shock. Another said, 'I was really concerned with that man in there. Worried he'd had a heart attack. He said he had a bad heart.' Others stolidly delivered shocks according to orders without any sign of emotion. Milgram's description of one of these reads, 'The scene is brutal and depressing: his hard, impassive face showing total indifference as he subdues the screaming learner and gives him shocks. He seems to derive no pleasure from the act himself, only quiet satisfaction at doing his job properly. When he administers 450 volts, he turns to the experimenter and asks, "Where do we go from here, Professor?" His tone is deferential and expresses his willingness to be a co-operative subject, in contrast to the learner's obstinacy.'

Although when they were debriefed, in order to save face it was in their own interests to tell the experimenter they had realised it was a put-up job and no shocks were being delivered, almost none of them did so. When followed up some years later, many of the subjects claimed they had learned something valuable from their experience. Here are two typical responses: 'This experiment has strengthened my belief that man should avoid harm to his fellow men even at the risk of violating authority;' 'When I was a subject in 1964, though I believed that I was hurting someone, I was totally unaware of why I was doing so. Few people ever realise when they are acting according to their own beliefs and when they are meekly submitting to authority . . .' So the habit of obedience is so ingrained that people can act out of it without even knowing they are doing so.

Milgram's results are not limited to America: the experiment has been repeated in Munich, Rome, South Africa and Australia, in all of which places even more subjects went to the highest shock levels than at Yale.

What made so many decent and law-abiding American citizens administer, at least so they believed, 450-volt shocks to wholly innocent people? The answer is obedience to authority. When the experimenter leaves the room on a pretext and delegates the supervision of the experiment to a stooge having no real authority, the number of people giving maximum shock levels drops by a third, though that is still 20 per cent of those tested.

Obedience to authority is instilled in us from birth – obedience to our parents, to our teachers, to our bosses and to the law. Moreover, it is a prerequisite for the functioning of any organised group. Aeroplane pilots must cede authority to ground traffic control if there is not to be chaos in the skies. Both in a small group and in the large and complex societies that exist today, someone has to lead and others have to follow, though the person who leads in one situation may be a follower in another. We are systematically taught to respect authority figures and not to bring them into disrepute. Many of the subjects in Milgram's experiments may have felt it would be rude not to obey the experimenter's commands and not a little embarrassing.

In the United States – far more so than in Britain – professors, perhaps particularly professors in a scientific subject, are seen as authority figures. They are also seen as being credible so that the initial reassurance that the shock could not inflict permanent tissue damage may have been believed by some of the subjects, though judging by their protests by no means all. Nevertheless, of those that went to the most extreme levels of shock none were in doubt that they were inflicting severe pain simply at the experimenter's behest.

In these experiments there were no sanctions for failure to comply: the subjects were volunteers and could have walked out of the laboratory whenever they chose. In many everyday life situations – in the army, the police force, and even in business – there are penalties for disobedience. When such sanctions are present, unthinking obedience must surely be even greater than in Milgram's experiments. He believes that the tendency to obey and to conform is the explanation for why so many otherwise decent Germans committed atrocities in the Second World War.

There are other experiments on the power of authority, each with the same outcome. In one study, a telephone call was made to a nurse by someone claiming to be a doctor in the hospital whom she had never met. He told her to give a patient a 20 mg dose of a drug called Aspoten (in reality a placebo), adding that she must give it immediately because he wanted the drug to take effect before he saw the patient, when he came to the ward. He added that he would sign the prescription then. Despite the fact that he had ordered twice the maximum dose set out on the label and that there was a rule that no nurse should administer a drug before the doctor had signed the prescription, 95 per cent of the nurses approached complied. Such is the power of authority. In another real-life experiment, a pleasant-looking man boarded a London tube, went up to a stranger and said, 'Would you please give me your seat?' Almost everyone approached stood up to let him sit down. If you have sufficient nerve, you should have no difficulty in getting a seat on a bus or train no matter how crowded.

There is an interesting case related to obedience, where two (or more) people have responsibility but one has authority over the other. The respect for authority may make the junior person hesitate to express his own views or observations. This has led to several commercial aircraft crashes, in which the co-pilot believed that the pilot was making an error but did not dare say so. Again, in a study of a British obstetric ward, it was found that 72 per cent of Senior House Officers would not voice disagreement over a course of treatment to a more senior doctor. In these cases the extreme respect for authority is clearly misguided.

Of course people do not always obey commands. Indeed they may react by doing the opposite of what they are told to do if they resent the command. Although there has been little experimental work on this problem, it seems likely that people will react adversely to being told what to do if the person giving the orders does not have the authority to do so, if the orders are issued in a crass way, if there is no penalty for disobedience, and if the person strongly disapproves of what he is asked to do.

A well-known instance of obedience leading to predictable disaster is the Charge of the Light Brigade in the Crimean War. Lord Raglan, the aristocratic but doltish British commander, sent a message by aide-de-camp ordering 'the cavalry to advance rapidly to the front . . . to prevent the enemy carrying away the guns'. In the valley in front of the Light Brigade was a battery of Turkish artillery; in the hills on either side of the valley were more Turkish guns and also riflemen. To obey the order as it stood would mean the destruction of the Light Brigade since they would be under fire from the front and both sides. Moreover, it was sheer folly for cavalry to attack artillery without infantry support. Nevertheless, despite their doubts, the cavalry commanders obeyed the order to the letter. With extreme bravery, the troops carried out the charge with parade-ground precision. Of the 700 who took part, fewer than 200 returned. Lord Raglan subsequently blamed the cavalry commander for failing to ascertain the enemy's disposition and to summon other troops to his aid. The episode raises the question of whether there are circumstances under which a military order should be disobeyed.

The more general question of when it is rational to disobey authority is difficult. It would clearly be folly to drive on the right-hand side of the road in Britain or on the left in America. Although an arbitrary rule has been imposed by authority, chaos would ensue if drivers broke it. But what about taking marijuana, a drug that is probably no more harmful than cigarettes at least in its long-term effects? If one believes that the law as it stands is an encroachment on individual liberties, surely it is rational to break it – provided of course the chances of being caught are sufficiently low. In fact, many people do defy the law. The better-off may avoid paying income tax or may feel no guilt at smuggling goods through customs, while the poor may obtain social security under false pretences. But in these cases, there is no acknowledged authority figure standing over them. There is nobody visible whom it would be embarrassing to disobey. In practice, most people think it rational to defy a bad law or an evil government so long as they can get away with it. The popular rising in Peking that took place in 1989 met with plaudits from the West: there is a point at which it is not only rational but desirable to disobey. But surely this point was reached in Milgram's experiments: after all, many subjects thought they were in danger of killing their pupils, all for the sake of a psychological experiment.

Although more than obedience is at issue, Milgram's results throw some light on the wholly irrational acts of mass destruction that have characterised much of this century. One thinks of the senseless bombing of Dresden at a time when the war was nearly won, which was ordered by Bomber Harris and sanctioned by Churchill; of the Nazi extermination of the Jews; of the American use of napalm against civilians in Vietnam; and of the American massacre of civilians, including women and children, at My Lai. The execution of these atrocities depended for the most part on the irrational obedience of ordinary people and in the light of Milgram's results one can only say, 'There but for the grace of God go I.' In all these instances, nobody was in any doubt about the horrifying consequences of his behaviour. So why did they act as they did?

First, all these actions were performed by people who had received a strong training in obedience from military or paramilitary organisations. They had been systematically taught not to question orders. Second, the initial order is usually given by someone removed from the situation, who does not have to see the victims – the appalling consequences of the order are therefore not 'available'. General Haig, who was responsible for the pointless deaths of hundreds of thousands of his own troops in the First World War, could not bear to enter a military hospital where the consequences of his continual blundering were apparent. According to Norman Dixon, Eichmann and Himmler, both of whom sent millions of Jews to their deaths, became physically ill when shown the effects of their orders. In the case of bombing or artillery fire even the final act is performed by someone who does not witness its results. They are ignored because they are not 'available'. Third, in all these instances, disobedience would have brought heavy penalties. Fourth, the groups against whom these atrocities were committed were in all cases out-groups – Germans, Jews and Vietnamese (or 'gooks' as the US soldiers called them). Fifth, in some of the cases every effort had been made to

downgrade and vilify the members of the out-group. From the early
'thirties Hitler had put up a barrage of propaganda reviling the Jews;
in the concentration camps the toilet facilities were deliberately kept
wholly inadequate so that the inmates who went to the gas chambers
were not merely dirty but covered with faeces. It is easier to kill someone if you regard him as sub-human.

Sixth, people who believe they must always obey orders tend to
exculpate themselves by denying even to themselves that they have
any personal moral responsibility. This is plain from some of
Milgram's protocols in which subjects asked the experimenter if *he*
would take full responsibility for what was happening. If one does
not feel responsible for one's own actions, the usual feelings of guilt
and shame that arise from hurting others are absent: the damage is
someone else's fault.

Finally, and perhaps most important of all, as we have seen from
Milgram's protocols, acting out of obedience is often an automatic
habit: people obey without even being aware that obedience is the
cause of their actions. If obedience is unquestioned and habitual,
there is no possibility of deciding whether it is rational: that would
require thought.

Several of the factors listed play a role in conformity and in the
attitudes within and between social groups: they will be expanded in
the next two chapters, which demonstrate the powerful effects they
exert.

moral

1. Think before obeying.
2. Ask whether the command is justified.
3. Never volunteer to become a subject in the Psychological
   Laboratory at Yale.

4   conformity

Obedience is behaving in the way dictated by a figure of authority, conformity is behaving in the same way as one's equals. It is often rational to conform to social norms. You go through a red traffic light at your own peril and unless you happen to be dining in an Arab country, loud belching at table is unlikely to increase your own or anyone else's enjoyment of a dinner party. Nevertheless, the desire to conform, of which on most occasions we are not even aware, can lead to highly irrational behaviour.

Imagine that you have volunteered to be a subject in a psychological experiment. You are taken into a room containing a semicircle of nine chairs and are placed in a seat next to someone sitting at one end. The other seats soon fill up and the experimenter explains that the subjects' task is to judge the lengths of lines. The group is shown two cards: the first has a single line and the second three lines, one of which is exactly the same length as the line on the first card while the other two are quite clearly bigger or smaller. For example, the first card might have an 8-inch line, and the other lines of 6, 8 and 10 inches. The experimenter explains that you each have to pick the line on the second card that is the same length as the single line on the first. It is so obvious which is the correct line that you probably feel he must be a bit barmy – he is after all a psychologist. He asks members of the group to call out their judgements in turn starting from the subject furthest away from you. To your amazement, none of the other members of the group pick the correct line: they all select the same incorrect one. The question is, what do you say when it comes to your turn?

In fact, all the other people in the semicircle were stooges: they had been told what answer to give by the experimenter. There were many different groups, each of which saw eighteen different pairs of cards: on six of these presentations the stooges chose the correct line, but on the other twelve they all picked the same wrong line.

The question remains, if you were a subject in this experiment, what would *you* do? In fact, only one quarter of the subjects trusted the evidence of their senses sufficiently to pick the right line on all of the twelve trials on which the others made a false judgement. Three-quarters picked the wrong line at least once and most did so many times. Some deliberately distorted their judgements, believing the majority were wrong but not being prepared to contradict them; others were not sure whether the majority were right or not and thought there might be something wrong with their own eyesight; while some were completely convinced the majority were right. Moreover, most of the subjects who were *not* influenced by other people's judgements became extremely nervous and hesitant.

The experiment, originally performed in the US by Solomon Asch, has been repeated several times with the same basic results, though the number of subjects announcing the wrong response has usually been slightly less. There are several possible reasons for this. Perhaps America was a particularly conformist country in the McCarthy era when the experiment was first performed. Or perhaps with the passage of time the exposure of students to psychological experiments has been so great that they have become suspicious of the experimenter's tricks. However, when the three lines on the second card are almost the same height as one another so that it is difficult to decide which is the right one, nearly everyone is affected by the false responses given by the stooges. What is particularly interesting is that almost every subject tested in this situation has subsequently claimed not to have been influenced by the judgement of the majority: they conformed to it without even realising they were doing so. People often conform through habit just as they obey through habit.

It has been found that when it is obvious which is the right line, if just one of the stooges gives the correct response, very few subjects make a mistake. This may be because part of the motive for going along with the majority is fear of rejection: the evidence that one other person is not rejected for responding correctly may persuade the subject that he has nothing to fear by making the same response himself. In a further twist to his experiment, Asch asked subjects to write down their judgements in confidence; although many were still influenced by the majority, more gave correct answers than in the previous experiments.

Asch's findings demonstrate that people tend to conform to the behaviour of others whether they know they are making a mistake by so doing or whether they are unaware both of their mistake and of the social pressure that has induced them to make it. To distort one's judgements through conformity, without knowing one is doing so, is irrational, as is much everyday conformity. Consider a trivial example. In Britain there is a conventional reluctance to talk to strangers: in consequence many people endure railway carriages that are either freezing or far too hot because they are too embarrassed to ask another passenger to close or open the window. One can often observe two passengers sitting opposite one another, both shivering with cold because neither has the temerity to close the window. Embarrassment results from failure to conform, whether intentionally or accidentally. But while it is wrong to offend others, does it matter what a stranger thinks of one, particularly over so trivial a matter as regulating the temperature in a train?

Of more importance, the effects of conformity on beliefs and attitudes are the more injurious because people tend to associate with others who have similar beliefs to themselves. It will be shown in a later chapter that the only way to substantiate a belief is to try to disprove it. But because like mixes with like, people are rarely exposed to counter-arguments to their more deeply held convictions, let alone to counter-evidence. Their beliefs conform to those of their associates: hence, there is little possibility of eliminating persistent errors.

It is known that any decision that is publicly announced is more likely to be executed than one taken privately. People are afraid of looking foolish, if they do not stick to a decision made in public, but they readily backslide if the decision has been taken in private. It is partly because political decisions are public that politicians are so extraordinarily reluctant to change their mind, even when – as, for example, in the case of the introduction of the poll tax in Britain – the initial decision was clearly wrong. Since no one is always right, the willingness to change one's mind in the light of new evidence is a sign of rationality not weakness.

In several studies, undertaken by advertising agencies, a group of strangers was gathered together and harangued about the virtues of a particular product. At the end of the session they were asked either to say out loud or to write down in privacy whether they intended to buy the product in question. Those who declared in front of everyone else that they would buy were much more likely to do so than those who wrote it down in secret.

In a more formal study, an experimenter purporting to belong to the local gas company interviewed house-owners telling them that he was investigating the extent to which they could reduce energy consumption. He discussed various ways in which they could conserve energy and explained that the results would be published in a local

newspaper. Half the subjects were told that if they agreed to co-operate, their names would appear in the article; the other half were told
that they would remain anonymous. All agreed to take part, and
signed a form to that effect, which either stated that they gave consent for their names to be published or that their names would not
appear. A few months later the amount of gas used in centrally heating each house was recorded. The respondents who had agreed to
their names appearing had used much less gas than those who had
been randomly selected to remain anonymous.

This phenomenon lies behind the success of such organisations as
Weight Watchers and Alcoholics Anonymous. A public commitment
to lose weight or give up alcohol is much more effective than a private decision. Social approval for doing something desirable but difficult is helpful, while disapproval of failure can lead to a feeling of
shame.

The effect of public commitment has been demonstrated many
times, but a realistic study on married women living in Yale
University takes it a step further. All the women selected for the study
were strongly in favour of disseminating information about birth
control. Half of them signed a public petition urging that information
on this topic should be given to pupils at the local high school. No
approach was made to the other half. The next day half the women
who had signed and half of those who had not been asked to sign
received a highly persuasive leaflet giving a list of reasons why
teenagers should *not* be given information on birth control (it would
promote promiscuity, the decision to give such information should be
made by the parents and so on.) A day or so later, someone (needless
to say one of the experimenters) called to ask each woman to undertake volunteer work for a group formed to promote the spread of
information on birth control. There was evidence that the leaflet that
argued against giving teenagers information on birth control really
was persuasive: of the women who had *not* signed the petition (and
who were therefore not publicly committed to the dissemination of
information to adolescents) fewer agreed to take part in the voluntary
group than of those who had not received the leaflet.

Exactly the opposite effect occurred in women who *had* signed the
petition. Half of the women who had both signed and received the
leaflet agreed to join the group, while only one in ten of those who
had signed but had *not* received the leaflet agreed. In other words, the
women who had publicly announced their commitment by signing
reacted very strongly against the leaflet. Instead of reducing their
commitment, its message, which was counter to their views, actually
increased it. Once someone is strongly committed to a belief (in this

case by announcing it publicly), contrary arguments may only serve to increase its strength: when people's beliefs are challenged, they may become even more convinced that they are right, a phenomenon known as the 'boomerang effect'. This effect is, at least partly, caused by their need to justify a commitment from which they feel they cannot escape. In short, the leaflet increased the commitment of women already pledged to providing information about birth control, because they had to prove to themselves that despite its counter-arguments they had done the right thing by signing the petition.

There is clearly considerable irrationality at work here. All the women started out with the same attitudes, but after reading the other side of the case, those who were not publicly committed weakened their views slightly whereas those who were publicly committed developed even more extreme views.

Unthinking conformity to current habits can lead to great evil. One thinks of the strange and unpleasant customs that evolved in English public schools: fags were made to burn their fingers at the fire while making toast for their seniors or were thrashed on a whim. Although several other factors including obedience were at work, conformity to the appalling group norms of Nazi Germany played a part in the atrocities committed there. It also at one time maintained the strange custom of settling disputes by duelling. Those who duelled had the physical courage to do so, but lacked the moral courage to decline because they were scared of being thought cowards by their friends: they had to conform. Many evil actions performed under the guise of a faith, like the burning of heretics, were at least partially motivated by conformity. When the customs of a society are good, conformity can of course have a beneficial effect, but they are seldom wholly good. Most people conform rather than thinking out for themselves which customs are worth following and which are not.

As a more trivial example of the injurious effects of conformity, consider women's fashions, in which the combination of a desire to conform and a desire to excel can lead to some dismaying end products. Fashion trends are usually set by a group that others admire; depending on the era, it may be the Royal Family, film stars or even – in the 'sixties when obeisance was paid to youth – the young. Those who lead fashion usually want to differentiate themselves from the multitude that follows them. As the hoi polloi catch up, the leaders try to stay ahead by exaggerating the current fashion and a competition ensues in which each exaggeration is in turn emulated by others. This can produce such injurious articles as the stiletto heel, the tight corset, and the crinoline (itself a revival for the third time of the far-thingale). The desire to conform on which the cycle of fashion is based is for the most part irrational. No one achieves any of the other attributes of film stars or society women by copying the way they dress. Nevertheless, the extreme and irrational outcomes to which fashion sometimes leads are produced less by individual irrationality than by the interaction of factors operating within the group, partic-ularly by the influence of conformity and competitiveness.

I have discussed fashion in women's clothes as an example, but many of the same considerations apply to fashions in painting, music, poetry, buildings, and men's clothes. Although the last have in recent years not run to extremes, it must have been irksome to wear the large codpieces of the sixteenth century. Once again there was a desire both to conform and, among the leaders, to stay ahead.

People conform, then, both to the attitudes of the groups to which they belong and to those of society as a whole. There are two other cases – conformity to the behaviour or attitudes of a single person whom one respects and conformity to the behaviour of a crowd of like-minded strangers.

Copying the behaviour of a 'model' can be beneficial. It is known that young children learn mainly by modelling their behaviour on that of their parents, a tendency that is almost certainly inborn. Spoken language is learned almost entirely by imitation: parents rarely correct their children's grammar or their misuse of words, they only correct when the child says something that is false. All children have innate mechanisms that enable them to infer how to talk cor-rectly from the limited samples of speech to which they are exposed. A six-month-old infant who sticks out his tongue in response to see-ing the same gesture made by his parent is performing a remarkable feat. The child has never seen his own tongue, yet he is able to con-nect his parent's gesture with it and respond accordingly.

It has been repeatedly found that a message from an expert or from someone of high credibility is far more persuasive than the same mes-sage from a source of low credibility. For example, in one study sub-jects were given articles on preventive medicine and told they were either from reputable medical journals or were translations from *Pravda*. Not surprisingly, the very same articles changed their atti-tudes far more when they thought they came from the reliable med-ical source. When an expert stays within his sphere of expertise, it is rational to have faith in him, or perhaps one should say some faith, for experts are often wrong, sometimes disastrously. Unfortunately, however, people can be reputable in ways that have no bearing on the message they transmit. A declaration from a baseball star to the effect that he uses such and such a hair cream has a large effect on sales. Although baseball players may be expert on the pitch, they are (with few exceptions) as little known for the refinement of their hair styles as for their sartorial elegance.

In this instance conformity to the baseball player's views stems from people's tendency to see all attributes of a person consistently. The unacknowledged reasoning is that since he's a good baseball player he must have good judgement about hair cream and about any other product he is paid to promote. This is just another example of the halo effect. There is, however, a second reason why it is irrational to be persuaded by advertisements in which an expert promotes a product. Even when the winner of the Wimbledon women's finals is shown drooling over a Whizzbang racquet, it does not mean she approves of it; it only means she has been paid to approve. Yet such is the irrationality of tennis players that they rush to invest in a Whizzbang.

I have dealt with conformity to society as a whole and to the attitudes of a prestigious individual. I now turn to conformity in crowds, which can give rise to three kinds of extreme behaviour – panic, violence and religious conversion.

Suppose you are in a cinema sitting about ten yards from the nearest exit and you notice that a fire has broken out. Everybody rises to their feet. Do you rush for the exit, pushing past and possibly trampling on other people? Or do you calmly wait your turn to get out, hoping that an orderly queue will form? The situation is analogous to the game of Prisoner's Dilemma already described. If everyone behaves in an orderly way, the maximum number will be saved, though some sitting furthest away from the exits may lose their lives. If most people do not panic, the minority rushing for the exit may save their own lives at the expense of others. If everyone panics, then many lives will be lost. Unless there is some person in authority present, many people are likely to panic, partly because they are trying to save themselves and partly because for two reasons panic spreads. If you see someone else pushing his way to the exit, you are likely to feel that that is unjust and licenses you to do it yourself. Moreover, in a crowd any strong emotion seems to spread to more and more of its members. Fear is contagious: so are tears. If others feel panic, you come to feel it too. Nevertheless, most such panics are irrational, if only because the ensuing mêlée often reduces the chance of survival for everyone present.

Panic can be reduced by the presence of authority figures. There have been few panics in aircraft crashes, mainly because the crews are trained to exercise a calming influence. Again, panic is rare on the battlefield although the level of fear could hardly be higher: in a study of American troops in the Second World War, it was found that immediately before battle, one in four of them vomited and one in five lost control of their bowels. The prolonged training and the influence of officers and NCOs, and – perhaps as important – the desire to conform to their own group's ideals and not to let their comrades down, all exercise a restraining effect on soldiers despite the extreme fear.

Few people indulge in systematic and pointless violence on their own, but from the lynch mobs of the deep South in America to the supporters of British football teams, it is not uncommon in crowds. Perhaps there is no fun in committing solitary mayhem. The disgusting lynchings of black men in America's Southern states, which often involved not merely killing but gratuitous torture, had a point, at least in the eyes of the perpetrators, namely, to subdue blacks. But the wanton violence of football supporters seems pointless. It is largely limited to crowd behaviour for a variety of reasons, including the abrogation of responsibility produced by being part of a crowd. The de-individuating effect of crowds is reasonably well documented: the crowd gives its members a feeling of anonymity – nobody can know just who did what. This was demonstrated in an experiment in which subjects were encouraged to give electric shocks to a stooge. Those who were dressed in laboratory coats and hoods, thus remaining completely anonymous, gave more shocks than those who were normally dressed and whose names were known. No shocks were in fact given, but the stooge pretended that he was being shocked.

Other reasons for crowd violence include the tendency for hostile emotions to spread; the desire to exhibit machismo to impress other members of one's group; the desire to lead by being the first to perform an outrage; and the desire to reforce the identity of one's own group by attacking other groups. The escalation in violence is also produced by the leaders trying to stay ahead, while others conform (as in the case of fashion). But perhaps as important is the licence provided by noticing that other members of the crowd are not observing the conventional values of the larger society. There have been many studies showing that people copy deviant behaviour in others, ranging from a pedestrian walking across the street against a red traffic light (which is illegal in many American states) to various forms of aggression. Provided the behaviour is not punished, others will imitate it. After all, 'If he can get away with it, why can't I?'

A third effect to which crowds are conducive is religious conversion. Conversion *per se* is not necessarily irrational, but it is surely folly to be converted solely because one is in a crowd of whom some are of the faith. How many of those who were swayed by Billy Graham would have become ardent Christians through solitary meditation on the Gospels? And how many would have been converted if they had just had a chat with Billy Graham on his own? Once again, the crowd promotes contagious emotion and conformity.

Both Graham and others of his ilk use more techniques of persuasion than mere mass hysteria. They also employ public commitment and a gradual slide in degree of commitment, a technique that will be dealt with later. Having harangued his audience about securing redemption through religious conversion in order to reduce the guilt and shame that all of us feel from time to time, he asks those who are ready to bear witness to step on to the platform: there they testify to their past sins and announce publicly that they are joining the religious movement, reinforcing their decision by signing a pledge. Having been through all this, it takes a firm-minded nonconformist to backslide and by so doing earn the disapproval of his new-found friends. The gullibility of people in such situations is such that many American evangelists have become extremely rich at the expense of their naïve flocks: in North Carolina Jim Bakker received $158 million in donations, of which at least $4 million, ostensibly donated to Christ, went into his own pocket. Thanks to his flock's irrationality, he enjoyed a flamboyant lifestyle, even providing air-conditioning in his dogs' kennels. He is now serving a forty-five-year prison sentence.

The influence of one's equals can sometimes operate in a different but equally undesirable way. The decision whether to go to the help of a stranger in trouble is often a difficult one. If he is badly hurt and you have no medical knowledge, you may make matters worse; if it turns out he does not need help after all, then it will be embarrassing, indeed it may even be embarrassing if he does need help both because you may not be able to give it and because of a reluctance to speak to strangers; if he has been attacked, there is a danger that anyone going to his assistance will also be attacked; people squeamish about the sight of blood or other injuries will have to brace themselves to approach; and perhaps most shaming of all, in this day and age it may well turn out to be one of those nefarious social psychologists pretending to be hurt and you are likely to look extremely foolish. At the very least the helper will lose some of his valuable time. Here are two well-recorded cases from real life.

Late one night in 1964 a young woman called Kitty Genovese was walking in New York from the spot where she had parked her car to her apartment. She was attacked by a man with a knife and screamed. Lights went on in the building and the attacker drove off, only to return to stab her again. He drove away once more, which gave her the chance to crawl to the door of her building. But he returned for a third assault, which killed her. The whole incident lasted half an hour and was observed by thirty-eight people from their windows. Not one intervened and not one called the police.

The second case is even better known. On the lonely road from Jerusalem to Jericho, a man was attacked by robbers and severely beaten. A priest happened to be walking that way, but he passed by on the other side of the road, as did a Levite. There followed a Samaritan, who 'was moved with compassion and came to him and bound up his wounds', subsequently carrying him to an inn where he paid the innkeeper to look after him. It is likely that the priest and the Levite passed by on the other side because the closer one is to someone in trouble the more difficult it becomes to resist helping and because it may have enabled them to deny to themselves that they had any responsibility for or duty towards the unfortunate man.

One might expect that out of the thirty-eight people who witnessed the killing of Kitty Genovese, there would be at least one who, if not as noble as the Good Samaritan, would take the trouble to go to the telephone and call the police. Why did the Good Samaritan act so differently from them? The answer is known.

Experiments have shown that when several people witness an event requiring intervention, each feels less responsibility than if he is on his own. In one study, the subjects, who were first-year students, were told they were to discuss the difficulties of settling down to university life. They could hear but not see one another. The number of subjects present varied from one to four and in addition there was always a stooge pretending to be a real student. During the conversation, the stooge revealed that he was prone to epilepsy and shortly afterwards feigned an epileptic attack. When there was only one genuine subject present, 85 per cent of the students reported to the experimenter. When there were two or five real subjects, only 62 per cent and 32 per cent respectively reported it. Clearly each thought it was someone else's responsibility to intervene.

The effect has also been demonstrated in an amusing study that was even closer to real life. Two experimenters went into a liquor store in New York State and, while the shopkeeper was in a back room, walked off with a crate of lager, saying, 'They'll never miss this.' They chose the time of their thefts so that on each occasion there were either one or two genuine customers in the shop. After the lager had been taken, the shopkeeper, who was in the know, returned to the counter. If the customers – the involuntary subjects – did not report the theft immediately, he asked what had happened to the two men. The theft was reported 65 per cent of the time by customers who were alone in the shop, but only 51 per cent when there were two customers. If each individual customer had behaved in the same way regardless of how many were in the shop, one would expect that with two customers the theft would have been reported 87 per cent of the time by one or the other: clearly, if each customer had not been inhibited by the presence of the other, there would have been a higher percentage of reports from two than from one. In short, when more than one person is present it becomes much less likely that a given individual will intervene in a criminal act.

There are several other studies on what is called 'the bystander effect'. All had the same basic result, but some additional findings were obtained. For example, people come to the aid of a woman in trouble more often than they do if it is a man; and they try to help members of their own race more than members of other races. An apocryphal but bizarre example of the bystander effect is the story of the two sociologists who walked past a man who had been attacked and left bleeding in a ditch. One said to the other, 'We must find the man who did this – he needs help.'

Before leaving this phenomenon, it is worth analysing why it is irrational. People fail to help others when there is more than one possible helper present partly because, by not taking action, they are conforming to the others' inaction. Of course they may feel that it would be embarrassing to intervene, but embarrassment itself arises from a failure to conform. In addition it is possible that they feel they do not need to help because someone else will. But anyone stopping to reflect would realise that if he thinks someone else will help and therefore does not help himself, the other person may feel the same way with the result that no help will be forthcoming. Moreover, the abrogation of responsibility because there are others present to take action cannot be the whole story. In the case of the theft of beer, there were two people present neither of whom reported the theft, although each could see that the other was not reporting it. Each was conforming to the other's behaviour.

moral

1. Think carefully before announcing a decision publicly: you will find it harder to change.
2. When you embark on a course of action from which you do not want to relapse, announce it to as many people as you can.
3. Ask yourself whether you are doing something merely because others do and if so, ask whether it really furthers your own ends.
4. Don't be impressed by advice from someone you admire unless he is an expert on the topic in question – and even if he is, remember that experts are often wrong.
5. Don't be stampeded by the behaviour of a crowd into acts you would not commit in calmer moments.
6. Don't fail to go to someone's assistance because there are others present who might – or might not.
7. Recall that, 'If you can talk with crowds and keep your virtue . . . You'll be a man, my son.'

5 in-groups and out-groups

With the exception of Groucho Marx, men are essentially clubable animals whether they join the Garrick, or follow Arsenal or the Red Socks. Rotarians or members of the local tennis club gather together because they have common interests, in both senses of the word. They may join a club because it is likely to further their career, as being a Rotarian is reputed to do; because they enjoy indifferent claret and conversation as in the case of the Garrick; or because they want to take part in some sport or game, like chess, that requires two or more to play. Or they may find themselves part of a 'minority group' like Jews, blacks, or paradoxically women. Group membership brings many benefits – a feeling of belonging, a sense of cohesion, assistance in the pursuit of common goals and the receipt of favours from other members. People usually belong to groups whose attitudes are similar to their own, thus ensuring support for their own beliefs. In the terms of the psychologist's trade, any group to which a person belongs is an in-group, those to which he does not belong are out-groups.

The previous chapter dealt with the ways in which a person's behaviour tends to conform to that of any group of which he is a member. Belonging to a group, however, has other and more complicated consequences. The interaction between its members has some remarkable effects on their attitudes and on their behaviour towards other groups.

The individual conforms to the group, but something considerably more surprising happens to the group as a whole. From the ground already covered, one might expect that the attitude of each member would drift towards the mid-position held by the rest of the group. In practice, if the members' attitudes are biased in one direction, simply by interacting together their attitudes become even more biased in the same direction. This was nicely demonstrated in a real-life study undertaken at Bennington, one of the most prestigious women's colleges in the US. The prevailing political ethos there has always been liberal, but it was found that the students became more liberal the longer they stayed. This suggests that the members of a group do not merely move towards the group norm: if there is a prevailing attitude in the group, it becomes accentuated in its members.

Bennington College is of course fairly large, and its students do not take group decisions. In our society the most important decisions are usually taken by small groups, colloquially known as committees, or as someone put it 'bodies that take minutes and waste hours'. It is important to consider whether such small groups are likely to take more rational decisions than their members acting independently. In the first experiment on this question, individuals were given a description of a risky action that could be disastrous. For example, they might be told to imagine that they were thinking of investing all their spare money in a company that is fighting for a government contract. If it succeeds, they would multiply their money by a factor of 1,000; if it fails, it would go bankrupt and they would lose everything. If the chances were a million to one in favour of success, probably most people would invest. In order to measure how much risk each was prepared to take, subjects were asked individually what odds they would need to make the investment. The degree of risk each subject would take can be gauged by the odds he would accept – the lower the acceptable odds, the higher the acceptable risk. Twelve different kinds of risk were put to each individual. After each had independently given the acceptable odds, they discussed the risks as a group in order to reach joint agreement about the acceptable odds. The group as a whole opted for much lower odds than the individuals – in other words, the group was prepared to take a greater risk than its members acting separately (a phenomenon known as the 'risky shift'). This effect has been replicated more than a hundred times: in many of these studies, the risk was rather more realistic, for example, the possibility of receiving a strong electric shock balanced against the possibility of a monetary reward.

The finding that group attitudes are more extreme than those of individuals is not limited to the acceptance of higher risks. One study measured the attitudes of individual French high school pupils to President de Gaulle and to Americans. They then had a discussion on each topic and had to come to an agreement on their attitudes. Needless to say, the individuals' attitudes to de Gaulle were in general highly favourable, while those to Americans were moderately unfavourable. But the agreed attitude after group discussion was even more favourable to de Gaulle and even less favourable to Americans. Once again the attitudes of the group were more extreme than those of the individual.

This phenomenon occurs for several reasons. First, the members want to be valued by the group: if the group attitude lies mainly in one direction, its members may try to obtain the approval of the others by expressing extreme attitudes in the favoured direction (compare the success of the stiletto heel); they may suppress arguments going in the other direction; and they may be prepared to be more extreme in the group, particularly over the risky shift, because, as we have seen, membership of a group reduces individual responsibility. Several studies have shown that in addition to taking more extreme decisions than individuals, the members of a group are more confident about the correctness of the group's decisions than about that of their own. Such faith in group decisions, which in general are worse than those made by individuals, presumably arises from the feeling of solidarity given by the group. If all or most agree, they are unlikely, the members feel, to be wrong.

Irvin Janis, following George Orwell, has called the tendency for the attitudes of a tightly knit group to become extreme 'Groupthink'. According to him, the members may develop an illusion of invulnerability coupled with extreme optimism; they ignore inconvenient facts; their belief in their own morality may lead them to commit immoral actions as a means to an end; they hold stereotyped views of rival or enemy groups whom they regard as evil or weak; individual members attempt to silence dissent from others in the group; each member suppresses his own doubts in order to conform; there is an illusion of unanimity resulting from this suppression; and finally, they protect other members by concealing information not in line with the group's views. Two further points are worth making. First, when a leader picks an advisory committee, he is unlikely to select either people who have very different views from himself or people who are more intelligent or more powerful in discussion than himself. The point cannot be proven, but to maintain their self-esteem leaders are likely to surround themselves by acolytes, thus exacerbating the tendencies already mentioned. Second, when a committee has a leader, the members will want to please him, particularly if he can influence their careers: this can be particularly pernicious, for the more the members agree with the leader, the more extreme his own attitudes are likely to become and hence the other members make even more extreme statements. It is a characteristic vicious circle.

Janis points out that when President Kennedy was discussing the Bay of Pigs operation with his advisers, Arthur Schlesinger was initially opposed to it. Robert Kennedy took Schlesinger aside and said, 'The President has made his mind up. Don't push it any further. Now is the time for everyone to help him all they can.' One of the dangers of being at the head of an organisation, whether as a prime minister, managing director, general or professor, is suffering from lack of criticism. Mrs Thatcher had little or no capacity for self-criticism, a defect that she exacerbated by dismissing from office those rash enough to disagree with her. President Reagan, on the other hand, was aware of his colleagues' reluctance to criticise him. In his autobiography he writes, 'In any top position, you risk becoming isolated. People tell you what you want to hear and are reluctant to tell you about somebody who might not be pulling his weight or doing something hurtful to your administration. Not many people close to you are willing to say: "You're wrong."' Although there is no experimental evidence, it seems clear that a person who receives too much adulation is likely to lose the capacity for self-criticism and hence to make inflexible and wrong decisions. Beerbohm Tree remarked, 'The only man who wasn't spoiled by being lionised was Daniel.'

Janis gives several further examples of his principles at work, including President Johnson's decision to escalate the war in Vietnam, taken with the support of his advisers but despite intelligence reports that the war could not be won. The interplay of the factors operating within a group is further illustrated by the accounts of the battles of Arnhem and of Pearl Harbor given in later chapters.

Committees, then, clearly have their dangers: in particular they are likely to go to extremes. But, as we shall see, one of the problems from which individuals suffer is that instead of thinking of all possible courses of action they tend merely to stick to the one that first comes to mind. One might expect a committee of people who held disparate views to produce and carefully consider more alternative actions and more reasons for and against each than would a single individual. The only systematic work on this problem has been on brain-storming, where a task requiring creativity is set, such as thinking of a good title for a brief plot. The answers given are assessed by a panel of judges. The results of these experiments are inconclusive: sometimes a brain-storming group comes out with a better answer than an individual, on other occasions it does worse.

All that can be concluded is that it is irrational both to suppress criticism and to form committees of people who think alike, even though to be effective they must share a common goal. If committees so often come to less rational decisions than an individual, one may ask why they are so popular, for it is well known that 'Nobody takes a decision on his own unless it is impossible to form a committee.' The reason for the prevalence of committees may be that they are 'safe' – the responsibility for taking a decision is diffused among several people and nobody need feel much guilt if it turns out to be wrong. Although the members of committees share decision-making, it has been found that most of them believe they have contributed far more to it than they have. When a committee member is asked how much of the time during the meeting he himself spent talking, he tends to overestimate grossly. This is just another form of the 'availability error'. Before speaking people will be busy thinking out what they are going to say: this is likely to stop them noticing others' contributions. They are, moreover, likely to remember what they have said much better than what others have said, partly because they have more emotional investment in their own contributions, partly because their statements will correspond to their own attitudes built up over many years.

In-groups strive to differentiate themselves from others. One method is to develop a distinctive appearance. In this respect, the punk with his or her bright green Mohican, leather gear and chains, and the skinheads with their shaven skulls are no different from members of the peerage with their ermine robes or academics with their mortar boards, gowns and brightly coloured hoods. Although, in the days of the overhead projector, academic gowns are no longer needed as a protection against chalk, they still ensure that spilling the gravy while his thoughts are on higher things will not soil the college fellow's ordinary clothes.

Wearing robes and uniforms stems partly from tradition and partly from our love of ritual. It is for the most part a comparatively harmless habit and may even provide onlookers with a quiet giggle. Its danger is that it may give people an inflated sense of their own importance and it is socially divisive. Uniforms are less prevalent in the US, a more egalitarian society than Britain. Moreover, wearing the dress of a particular profession distances a person from others and encourages him to behave in extreme and irrational ways. Would the judge who recently gave only an eighteen-month prison sentence to a man who had raped a woman, sodomised her and compelled her to have oral sex have been so lenient if he had been dressed in mufti and therefore identified himself more with ordinary citizens? Or would Judge Bertrand Richards have told a woman who had been raped that she was guilty of 'a great deal of contributory negligence for having hitchhiked'? It is hard to imagine anyone not wearing a wig making such asinine pronouncements.

These observations are supported by experiments. Subjects were encouraged to give (sham) electric shocks to a stooge. When they were dressed like nurses they became *less* aggressive than those normally dressed, while wearing Ku Klux Klan outfits made them very much more aggressive. It is of course irrational to allow one's behaviour to be influenced by the clothes one wears, but these experiments show that it is so influenced. If uniforms can have such strong effects in an experiment, how much more powerful is their influence likely to be on those genuinely entitled to wear them?

It should be added that some uniforms are entirely rational in that they serve a useful purpose: for example, it is sometimes important to recognise a person's occupation quickly. We need to be able to identify policemen, firemen and bus conductors, and their uniforms enable us to do so, while before pressing the trigger the soldier has to decide whether he is confronted by friend or foe.

Unfortunately there are more pernicious ways of achieving group cohesion than by adopting a distinctive appearance. Group members may come to despise, dislike or even hate other groups. The classic research on this topic was undertaken by Muzifer Sherif in the 'forties and 'fifties and had sensational results. Since he conducted experiments each year for several years, always with the same outcome, I have for convenience run together material from more than one study. The subjects were white middle-class Protestant American boys about twelve years old; they had no idea they were being studied, since they were invited to attend a summer camp and the experimenters passed themselves off as the camp director, counsellors, and even an odd-job man: social psychologists are nothing if not versatile. The boys were chosen from different schools and neighbourhoods so that none of them already knew one another. Initially they all lived in a single large bunkhouse.

After three days they had begun to form friendships and each was asked who were his special friends. They were then divided into two separate camps with friends allocated as far as possible to different camps. Although they still all ate together, each of the groups began to develop its own conventions. One called itself the 'Eagles', the other the 'Rattlers'. They stamped these names on their T-shirts, for even in those days other people's clothes were widely read. They began going to separate places to swim and each group developed its own slang. After a further four days, the boys were again informally asked who were their special friends. Their former friends had been abandoned, for now nine out of ten of the boys named as friends were within their own group.

In the next stage, the experimenter introduced competitive games between the groups, such as softball or soccer. The members of the team that won the series of games were each to be given a prize of a camping knife. At first the games were played in a reasonably good-natured way, but soon both teams became distinctly acrimonious. Accusations of being dirty players or cheats began to fly around, and the members of each group bumped, pushed and shoved those of the other as they queued for their food. Asked to rate the performance of individuals at the games, both groups rated their own members much higher than those of the other. One group attacked the other's camp at night, overturning beds and strewing their belongings around. They ended up by refusing to share the common dining-room. These experiments have been repeated many times both by Sherif and by others, always with the same result: indeed, it is said that one such experiment had to be stopped for fear of mayhem.

Parenthetically, it should be observed that these findings suggest that games played between different countries (or even between different towns in the same country), far from promoting amity between them, will only foster animosity. Even test matches bear this out, despite the fact that cricket is usually thought to be a gentlemanly game. Tests have created considerable ill-will between England and Australia, with allegations of cheating or lack of sportsmanship going back at least sixty years. In a recent series, the West Indies were alleged by the English to have forced a draw by playing very slowly, an unsportsmanlike trick that the West Indian umpire did nothing to stop. Subsequently the English accused him of extreme bias, whereupon the West Indians banned the radio broadcasts made for the BBC by an English commentator who had castigated the umpire's behaviour. Nor do international football matches seem to do much to foster camaraderie between the supporters of opposing teams. The violence and hatred between the followers of different countries' teams in the World Cup is notorious.

In view of all the evidence, which ranges from foul play and foul tempers at public school Rugby matches to dirty work across the chess board, it is extraordinary that many people still believe that competitive sport improves relations between the nationalities or groups to which the opposing teams belong. Maybe this false belief is caused by the connotations of the word 'game': it suggests something that should not be taken seriously. Too often, however, it is. As George Orwell remarked, 'Serious sport has nothing to do with fair play. It is bound up with hatred, jealousy, boastfulness, disregard of all rules, and sadistic pleasure in witnessing violence.'

Returning to Sherif, his research illustrates how easily hatred between different groups may arise. After all, the boys were all Americans, they were all white, and they all had the same religion.

Moreover, friends tended to be placed in different groups, which should have reduced group rivalry. The experiment is a perfect illustration of the sheer irrationality of disliking someone because he belongs to a different group. The cause of such hostility can in part be competition for a scarce resource (in this case the camping knives). But since in Sherif's experiments antagonism developed before the competitive games were introduced, this is not a complete explanation. It is likely that it is difficult to take pride in one's own group without regarding other groups as inferior.

In the final stage of his experiments, Sherif was able to reduce the antagonism between the groups. He did so by getting the boys to engage on tasks that required their combined efforts. The groups pooled their funds to buy a film of *Treasure Island* which they all wanted to see; he arranged for a lorry bringing supplies to get stuck, and the groups joined together to pull it out of the mud; again the camp water tank 'accidentally' sprang a leak, and they all helped to repair it. Taking part in such common tasks greatly reduced the antagonism and some friendships began to form between members of different groups. One is reminded of the friendliness between strangers of different classes and creeds that existed in Britain during the Second World War, a time when almost everyone was committed to the same overriding goal, the defeat of Germany. More recent evidence, however, suggests that engaging on a common task only decreases hostility between groups if their joint endeavours are successful: otherwise, they simply blame one another for the failure.

In real life, the rivalry between groups may be so irrational that each may try to do the other down even at its own expense. In an aircraft factory in Britain the toolroom workers received a weekly wage very slightly higher than that of the production workers. In wage negotiations the toolroom shop stewards tried to preserve this differential, even when by so doing they would receive a smaller wage themselves. They preferred a settlement that gave them £67.30 a week and the production workers a pound less, to one that gave them an extra two pounds (£69.30) but gave the production workers more (£70.30).

It is of course comforting to belong to a cohesive group. Most people like to be liked and most people would rather have their ideas supported by others than bear the doubts instilled by having them challenged. As we have seen, the need to value one's own group is part of the cause of prejudice against other groups: it is difficult if not impossible to think of one's own group as 'special' without thinking of other groups as in some way inferior. Such prejudice against out-groups is usually accompanied by the formation of stereotypes: Jews are seen as avaricious, blacks as lazy and so on. These stereotypes often have no foundation in fact: the English tend to regard the Scottish as mean, but more money is raised in street collections per inhabitant in Scotland than in England.

Before discussing the causes of stereotypes, one incorrect theory must be dispelled. It has been suggested that intolerance of other groups can be caused by too rigorous an upbringing, but this cannot be true, for there are often swift changes in tolerance. The German Jews were reasonably well tolerated in 1920 but within a few years they came to be not merely abused by the Nazi regime, but despised by much of the German population. There had been no marked change in methods of child-rearing.

There are a variety of reasons for the existence of stereotypes. Richard Nisbett and Lee Ross point out that not all stereotypes are detrimental: they apply to librarians, jockeys, professors, stockbrokers and so on. One reason for holding stereotypes is that they are convenient: we do not have to assess the individual case, we merely assume he or she conforms to the stereotype.

A second reason is that we tend to notice anything that supports our own opinions. We notice the Scotsman who is canny about money, but don't pay much attention to one that is generous.

Third, we notice the actions of members of a minority group much more readily than those of a larger group. They are conspicuous ('available') because they are rare. In the same way, bad behaviour is more noticeable than normal behaviour, so we will be particularly struck by a member of a minority group behaving badly. A notorious example comes from the days when women rarely drove. Whenever a woman made a driving error, men would glance at her and say, 'Oh God, there goes another woman driver.' Normal driving by women did not stand out and therefore was not noticed. Compelling evidence for the last two points will be given in later chapters.

Fourth, stereotypes can be self-fulfilling. If blacks are thought to be lazy, they find it hard to get jobs. In consequence they are seen idling around the streets, thus confirming the belief that they are lazy.

Fifth, some aspects of a stereotype may have a basis in reality. It seems likely that overall professors are more earnest than disc jockeys. But even if the stereotype has a foundation in fact, it is irrational to apply it to the individual case, for doubtless there are some serious-minded disc jockeys and the occasional flippant professor.

Sixth, it has been found that the difference between one set of objects and another becomes exaggerated when labels are attached to them. In a simple experiment, four short lines were each labelled 'A' and four slightly longer ones 'B'. People saw a bigger difference in the average length of the two sets of lines when they were labelled in this way than when no labels were attached. All groups about which stereotypes are formed are labelled by their names, and this may encourage us to see out-groups as differing more from ourselves than they in fact do.

Seventh, as we saw when discussing the halo effect, a person who has one salient quality may be seen as having other related qualities that he does not possess. This also applies to groups. Because some ethnic groups look different from whites, the latter are likely to believe that they differ radically in other ways.

Eighth, a small initial bias in the attribution of prejudicial characteristics to members of an out-group is likely to increase as a result of the social interaction within the in-group that was described at the beginning of the chapter. Moreover, once prejudiced beliefs have been accepted by a person, he may continue to act on them, even when he is not trying to impress members of his own group. A series of studies on prejudice against blacks was conducted in the 'seventies: the results were remarkable. If an American was confronted in public with a black who needed help, he would give it just as readily as to a white. If, however, he was in a situation where the help would not be observed, then he was far less likely to help a black than a white. This was discovered by leaving in a public place a stamped but unsealed envelope addressed to a university: sticking out of the envelope was an application form on which was a picture of the applicant. Whites more often went to the trouble of posting the application of another white than that of a black. These findings were made when, at least in middle-class circles, prejudice against blacks had been strongly disavowed. People therefore did not show their prejudice in public, but it still emerged if they were unobserved.

Finally, do-gooders can reinforce others' prejudices by accepting the very qualities that people are prejudiced about and attempting to explain them away. As Richard Nisbett and Lee Ross put it, when people argue that the laziness of blacks is due to the 'culture of poverty or the father-absent syndrome or anomie born of oppression and powerlessness', they are showing just as much prejudice as do people who believe in the laziness without attempting to explain it away.

For all these reasons, then, prejudicial stereotypes are common, powerful, and hard to eradicate: their irrationality is obvious. They both derive from hostility to outgroups and once formed support that hostility. But stereotypes not based on prejudice can lead to equally irrational thinking. In one experiment, subjects were given a list of sentences like, 'Carol, a librarian, is attractive and serious.' Each sentence gave a name, an occupation and two traits, one stereotyped (in this case 'serious'), the other not thought to be characteristic of the occupation ('attractive' – the prejudicial stereotype for women librarians is that they are mousy). When asked which traits had been used of which occupation, the subjects showed a marked tendency to recall the stereotyped traits and to forget the non-stereotyped ones. They thought that stewardesses had been described as 'attractive' but not that women librarians had been described in the same way, though they recalled that the latter were 'serious'. We remember what we expect to hear: in this case the stereotype governed the expectation.

This chapter has dealt with two related topics – the tendency for attitudes within a group to go to extremes and the development of prejudice towards out-groups. Such prejudice has probably caused more misery throughout human history than any other factor. It was partly responsible for the last world war: at the very least Hitler's in-group slogan 'Herrenvolk' helped to get the German people behind him and to support the Anschluss. It is possible that the dislike of out-groups is to some extent inborn and reaches back to our tribal history. That does not justify it nor does it necessarily mean that it is impossible to control.

moral

1. Whether you are a member of a committee or a golf club, be careful not to be carried away by the prevailing views. Consider and express counterarguments.
2. If you are forming a committee, ensure that different viewpoints are represented.
3. If you are the head of an organisation, try not to be affected by sycophancy.
4. Be wary of forming stereotypes, but if you do, remember that not everyone will neatly conform to them.
5. If you must wear uniform, wear that of nurses.

6 organisational folly

Anyone who has ever sat on a committee will have heard someone say, 'We can't do that: it will set a precedent.' This remark is wholly irrational. The proposed action against which it is directed is either sensible or not. If it is sensible, taking it will set a good precedent; if it is not sensible, the action should not be taken. Whether or not a precedent is set is therefore irrelevant: the decision should be made on its own merits. Moreover, outside courts of law, nobody need be bound by past decisions: the past is finished, it cannot be changed, and its only use is that it may sometimes be possible to learn from it. Following traditional practices is the easiest thing to do: to change anything usually requires hard thinking, which many find disagreeable, and the energy to overcome the inertia that characterises many large organisations, perhaps particularly in the public sector.

This chapter is an interlude. It considers the irrationality not of individuals but of organisations: and it is based on the assumption that a rational organisation will adopt the best means available of pursuing its ends. In practice this rarely happens because its members are often activated by greed or sloth and may put their own ends such as self-advancement or avoidance of risk before those of the organisation to which they belong. As a result the organisation as a whole acts irrationally. The design of an organisation should surely be such as to prevent as far as possible selfish behaviour on the part of its members but many organisations seem to be irrationally structured in ways that reward selfish behaviour rather than punish it. Although I will concentrate on organisational irrationality arising from self-serving motives, I shall also give a few examples of organisational irrationality stemming from insufficient or biased thinking.

To start with the public sector, in a brilliant book, *Your Disobedient Servant*, Leslie Chapman gave an account of how he tried to cut down waste in one part of the British Civil Service. He was Regional Director of the Southern Region of the Ministry of

Public Buildings and Works (subsequently renamed the Property Services Agency). This ministry was responsible for providing buildings and services to a range of government bodies including other departments of the Civil Service and the armed forces. He decided to take a look at wasteful practices in his own region. Among the discoveries made by the teams he set up were the following.

1. Little-used stores as large as aircraft hangars were lit by incandescent tubes. Whenever a tube burnt out, two men trundling a very high trolley went in to replace it. Since the loss of one or two tubes made very little difference to the lighting, he ordered that all dud tubes should be replaced in one periodic visit (for example, once every six months).
2. Such stores were heated to the same temperature as offices. He had the heating switched off and saw to it that if need be anyone entering a store was warmly clad.
3. He found that most of the stores were not needed and sold some off. Those that could not be sold, he pulled down for fear that someone would find a use for them.
4. He sold all but six of the cranes owned by the region and much other surplus equipment including concrete mixers and lorries. He had calculated that it was cheaper to hire such equipment for the short periods over which it was needed.
5. He sold tracts of surplus land, thus not only recovering their capital cost but abolishing the need to maintain them.
6. He discovered that the cost of storing and issuing a small item like a tap washer was about £3.00 (by 1972 prices). He forbade the storage of such items and instructed his staff to buy them from local shops when needed.
7. His region provided chauffeur-driven cars, which were used both by his own department and by other government organisations. He closed down the service. In future his staff had to drive themselves or, if the occasion really warranted, hire a limousine from a private company.
8. Finally, he discovered that it was much cheaper to contract out most of the work in the region than to employ direct labour. Accordingly, he halved the labour force, after gaining the consent of the unions and setting up a scheme to find jobs elsewhere for those made redundant.

As a result of Chapman's unusual initiative, the overall expenditure per annum in the Southern Region of the Ministry of Public Buildings and Works was slashed by one third from about £10 million to £6.5

million. The other six regions were informed of the methods he had used to effect these savings, but they made little effort to emulate him. Whereas he had saved a third of his budget, they subsequently saved on average only 8 per cent of theirs and none of them went about achieving savings in his systematic way, although he offered to lend them his own teams which had learned how to track down wastage.

Chapman was a determined man and tried to get something done about waste not only in the other regions of the Property Services Agency but in other areas of the Civil Service. The irrational complacency of that institution is reflected in the reply that Chapman received when he wrote to Sir William Armstrong, the then Head of the Civil Service. Armstrong (now best known for his equivocal remark that he had been 'economical with the truth') did not deign to reply himself, but a member of his staff sent a curt note: 'I write to acknowledge your letter . . . and enclosures to Sir William Armstrong. These have been read with interest. Yours sincerely . . .' Although Sir William and his office were clearly not interested in saving the taxpayer's purse, he was subsequently made a peer for his services to the nation. One member of the Civil Service once remarked that, 'The Civil Service is a self-perpetuating oligarchy, and what better system is there?' He may be right, but some may find this pronouncement rather startling.

Returning to Chapman, having left the Civil Service in order to write an excoriating book about its wasteful practices, he became a member of the Executive Board of London Transport, a public body funded in large part by the Greater London Council and the government. He again uncovered many monstrous examples of waste, including a large car pool, used to ferry both junior and senior managers to wherever their whim took them. It is small wonder that they preferred this method of transport to the discomfort, filth and delays of their own buses and tubes. The management did themselves well in other ways. The dining room for top managers was heavily subsidised and the general manager had an office that was 900 square feet in area. Chapman discovered that a saving of at least 30 per cent could be made on track maintenance: similar sums could be saved on other activities, for example on cleaning, by having the work done by outside labour rather than by London Transport's directly employed staff. And so on and on.

In the case of London Transport, Chapman made little progress because of the opposition of the rest of the board and particularly the chairman. He made numerous proposals for reducing waste, but they were all brushed aside. He was, moreover, removed from the board less than two years after joining it; he subsequently recounted his extraordinary experiences in a second book, *Waste Away*. If my brief account has not convinced the reader of the shameful and irrational waste that occurs in the British public sector, Chapman's books will. The wasteful practices of public bodies have no limits: Chapman gives many further examples, of which three of the more bizarre follow. Islington Council paid a firm £730 to weed 2 square metres of shrubbery. Liverpool Council paid two gas-light lighters and a mate more than £250,000 over an eight-year period: there were no gas lamps in Liverpool. In Leicestershire, the council deprived 200 physically handicapped children of their holiday by cutting their subsidy: they made up for this by increasing their Chairman's allowances by an amount that would have paid for the children's holidays four times over.

For our present purposes, the important question is why does such waste occur? There are many reasons.

1. As Chapman points out, in public bodies few individuals are clearly accountable to anyone else: decisions are taken for the most part in committees. We have already seen that in many committees the members attempt to ingratiate themselves with the chairman. They use arguments that support his views and may present a case that is even more extreme than his own, thus pushing his attitudes even further in the direction in which they already lie. These tendencies are likely to become even more pronounced when, as is often the case, the prospects, including promotion, of the other members are largely governed by the chairman. Most committees do not, therefore, provide a means to take rational decisions. They merely confirm or, worse, exacerbate the chairman's attitudes, while relieving him of accountability. But without accountability there is little incentive to put things right, except for the often unacknowledged duty that all civil servants owe to their countrymen who pay their salaries.

2. Chapman argues that promotion in the Civil Service is largely determined by seniority and that except in the most unusual circumstances a job is a job for life. Again this promotes inertia. Any changes involve risks and few people will take risks, unless they can see some benefit to themselves.

3. The structure of most public organisations actually encourages overspending. Promotion may depend on having a post with a given number of people under one, or on the amount of money handled. This is a direct incentive to indulge in wasteful practices.

4. In many public organisations, the sum of money allocated to one sector in a given year depends largely on its budget for the previous year. Nobody examines how that budget was actually spent

nor whether the spending was necessary. Again, this provides a direct incentive for waste, since it ensures that individual sectors of public (and some private) bodies will spend as much as possible rather than as little as possible. It is irrational to penalise departments that save money in one year by cutting their budget for the following one. There is no substitute for a careful scrutiny of how money is actually spent. Chapman has proved that this is possible and that large savings can be achieved.

5. Anyone who wants to change any aspect of an institution will undoubtedly put other people to considerable trouble: in the case of effecting economies there may also be a loss of jobs. Neither outcome is likely to be popular. Chapman has called attention to several cases in which, within London Transport, employees who tried to reduce costs were either sacked or threatened. The fear of losing one's job or of failing to gain promotion by rocking the boat is a strong disincentive for seeking economies.

6. Greed and the search for prestige also play a part. Both result in unnecessarily lavish facilities for higher management, like luxurious dining-rooms and chauffeur-driven cars. To the extent that a manager's prestige depends on the size of his budget and the number of people working under him, he is likely to inflate spending unnecessarily.

7. Chapman argues that the government bodies that investigate Civil Service departments are largely ineffective. Civil Servants are paid by the general public and have a duty to the public (as do borough and county councils). The press is a powerful weapon and if the waste that occurs were brought to its attention, it would rapidly be made public and willy nilly someone would have to do something about it. But unfortunately Britain is one of the least democratic countries in the Western world: the Official Secrets Act, which has recently been strengthened, forbids government employees to disclose without permission anything they have learned in the course of their duties. Local councils have rules for their employees that achieve the same end. In consequence, public bodies in Britain operate behind a screen of secrecy: their mistakes and their mismanagement are largely hidden from the public, to whom they should be accountable. The British government takes its obsession with secrecy to extreme limits. Information that directly affects the consumer is withheld: some of the many topics on which information is not available include tests of drugs and drinking water; hygiene in restaurants; the safety of pesticides; and the results of inspecting meat plants. Recently the government even suppressed a report by school inspectors on a project to train teachers in mod-

ern methods of improving pupils' ability to use the English language. Information is of course essential to the citizens of a democracy: without it they can neither determine rationally how to vote nor can they make sensible choices in their everyday lives. Secrecy has other knock-on effects: according to Amnesty, Britain has the worst record on human rights of any country in Western Europe, and this despite the fact that it is hard to believe that British citizens are any less humane than those of other countries.

There are two reforms that would improve the public services. First, make the way they are run accessible to all. Second, insist that everyone in public employment should use public services when available. If MPs and civil servants were compelled to travel by tube not taxi, to use the National Health Service not private medicine (taking their turn in the queue) and if their children had to go to state schools, we would see a rapid improvement in all these services. The situation in Britain can be contrasted with that in the US, a more democratic country, where it is possible not only to make public what goes on in government bodies (unless national security is endangered), but actually to subpoena these bodies for documents, which they are then legally compelled to produce. It is of course not the individual members of public bodies who are irrational – it is after all perfectly rational to be motivated by greed, ambition and sloth. It is the organisations that fail to achieve the ends for which they exist: they are therefore examples of corporate irrationality. Moreover, the irrationality could be reduced if public bodies were more rationally structured. They should be responsible to paid representatives of the general public who do not belong to the body in question; promotion should be earned not because it is 'Blogg's turn' but for advancing the ends of the organisation: dismissal, particularly of senior staff, should be much more common that it at present is; and the workings of the organisation should be accessible to the press and the public.

Corporate irrationality undoubtedly exists in the private sector, but I know of no such carefully documented account as that of Chapman's. Certainly the recently published Directors' Guide to Relocation Management reveals directors acting perhaps in their own best interests but not in those of their companies. In relocating their premises, one might expect them to take into account the rent per square foot, the ease of transport, the provision of raw materials (for manufacturing companies), and the availability of suitable employees. Not a bit of it. One firm moved to Nottingham because the town was thought to have more blondes per square foot than any other. Another consideration that was thought of importance was the length of the waiting lists at golf clubs. One firm sent out a search party not merely to find a town with a river but to count the number of swans upon it.

One gross abuse that has recently been much publicised is the high pay rises allocated to themselves by directors at a time when management was trying to persuade workers to accept rises at or just over the increase in the cost of living. According to the British Institute of Management, in 1990 the directors of British companies increased their salaries by an average of 22.7 per cent. Many went beyond this: for example, Mr Mick Newmarch, chief executive of the large British insurance group, the Prudential, received a 43 per cent increase, making his salary over £0.5 million. The company had not exactly prospered under his management, for it had just had to sell off at a loss of £340 million all the estate agencies it had recently bought; as a result the holders of Prudential policies had had their bonuses cut for the first time in fifty years. Despite the publicity it received, Mr Newmarch's pay rise was in fact quite modest compared to some. For example, in the same year Sir Ian MacLaurin received a rise of 330 per cent taking his salary to nearly £1.5 million. One might think that these rises could be justified by the value of the executives in question to the company. There is little evidence for this. Indeed MacLaurin's company, Tesco, had dropped its return as a proportion of assets in the year before his salary shot up. Such extreme selfishness on the part of management, which must have a deleterious effect on its relationship with employees, is not irrational. But the greed of executives causes companies as a whole to behave irrationally and the fact that companies are so structured as to allow such selfishness is in itself irrational. Rises in directors' pay might be more reasonable if they were determined by performance or had to be sanctioned by a postal ballot of all shareholders.

It is hard to say what motivates most takeover bids, but many seem to be governed by ambition on the part of executives. What is certain is that the shares of the company making the takeover almost invariably drop with good reason, for it has been found that after an acquisition, severe losses are usually made for four years and it takes on average eight years before any profit is made. An example of a particularly irrational takeover is that made by Staveley Industries in the late 1960s. They acquired Craven Brothers, a loss-making company engaged largely on making parts for steam engines, of which very few still existed.

This takeover suggests a refusal to face facts (the reasons for which will be set out in Chapters 10 and 11). It is worth giving a few more examples of irrationality in industry. Dimplex specialised in the manufacture of electrical storage heaters and oil-filled radiators. The oil crisis of 1974 doubled the cost of electricity over a four-year period. Not unnaturally people turned to cheaper forms of heating, mainly coal or gas. Rather than attempting to diversify their products, Dimplex continued to concentrate on electrical space heating. The chairman was blind to what was happening, and in 1975 announced that 'electricity will become the main source of energy within the home'. Even in 1977 he attributed his company's record loss in the previous half-year to the fact that customers were not 'aware that domestic heating by electricity has many advantages over heating by other fuels'. A few months later a receiver was appointed.

Another example of the irrational adherence to tradition is the transformer division of Ferranti's. The company had started with the making of high-voltage transformers and Sebastian and Basil de Ferranti, who held two of the three main executive posts, were, presumably for sentimental reasons, reluctant to sell or close down this division. Because – as a result of excess manufacturing capacity in the transformer industry – the demand for transformers had been overestimated, and because the Japanese could sell transformers in the world market at lower prices than Ferranti, the transformer side of the business was losing about £1.5 million a year by 1974. At that time the company as a whole was in a state of crisis, but it was saved when the government injected over £20 million. The transformer business was phased out, somewhat belatedly, in 1978. A study conducted by *Fortune* magazine found that over 50 per cent of American businessmen thought that following tradition was more important than making profits. Following tradition, as in the cases of Dimplex and Ferranti, may be the easiest course to take, but it is not always the wisest. The world moves on.

One way in which many firms, particularly small ones, seem to be woefully irrational is in failing to maintain financial control – that is, keeping a record of the inputs to and outputs from particular parts of the firm. For example, in 1976, Queensway Discount Warehouses, which sold furniture and carpets, was losing money. Because proper records had not been kept it was impossible to determine which of its twenty-seven branches were profitable and which were not.

Here are two final examples, both caused by a lack of forethought so extreme that it is hard to believe. The R. F. D. Group Ltd, makers of life-saving equipment such as parachutes, decided to move its factory from Belfast to Newcastle. It had overlooked the fact that most of its skilled employees did not want to leave Ulster. As a result the factory was never more than one third full. Finally, a furniture company had its maintenance division in Norwich and its manufacturing division in Dundee. In consequence, a van had to be sent from Norwich to Dundee in order to change some light bulbs. The last two instances suggest that managers should be educated in geography, but one may doubt whether even this would eradicate their persistent irrationality.

In dealing with the private sector, it has only been possible to give scattered examples of irrationality, for I know of no detailed account such as Chapman provides for one branch of the Civil Service. It seems certain that businessmen are given to exaggerated hopes – in the US three out of four new small businesses become bankrupt within four years, whether through bad luck or bad management.

The members of all professions sometimes behave irrationally, but the irrationality of financial advisers is matched only by that of their clients. Most investors are apparently unaware of their ineptitude, but it is well documented in David Dreman's highly readable *Contrarian Investment Strategy*, which is the source of most of what follows. It has been shown in dozens of separate studies that advisers on equities consistently do worse than the market they are in, even before making allowance for any fees they charge. The same applies to the managers of pension funds, of unit trusts, and of the portfolios of insurance companies. The main reason for their poor performance is probably that they follow the herd, rather than anticipating it. They buy when prices are high and sell when prices are low. As for their wretched clients, in deciding what to buy they would do better to stick a pin in Stock Exchange listings than to follow their loss-making advice or to buy unit trusts. A couple of examples may help to drive the point home. At a conference of 2,000 institutional investors held in New York in 1970, a poll revealed that the delegates' favourite stock was National Student Marketing, one of the most fashionable stocks of the time. Within six months it had dropped from $120 to $13. The following year they proceeded to give a further demonstration of their expertise by choosing airlines as the industry that would perform best over the following year: in fact airline stocks fell by 50 per cent at a time when the market as a whole was rising.

Two main methods of forecasting the future values of shares are used. The first sounds sensible. The investment analyst determines the prospects of companies by breaking their operations up into individual segments. For example, in analysing an insurance company, he might examine separately the earnings, recent growth and so on of life, car, house and contents insurance, and he might further try to break down these different kinds of insurance by the region of the insurers. Some of the information he requires may not be divulged by the management and much of what is divulged may be inaccurate. He will also have to take into account the prospects of competing companies. Having obtained all this information he must put it together, but this is impossible for three reasons. The first is the limitation of the human mind, which cannot systematically use vast amounts of information to come to the right conclusion: the analyst suffers from information overload. The second is that for the reasons set out in Chapter 20 he has no means of knowing how to put it together correctly. Finally, chance plays a large part in the fortunes of a firm and it is impossible to allow for this: no matter how efficient a firm, its performance may slump as a result of a strike or of a general recession. For whatever reason, financial advisers using this method do worse than the market they are in. In 1974 thirty-six investment advisers were asked to pick their five favourite stocks. There was a large degree of consensus, but when the performance of the most favoured ten stocks was examined over the two-year period 1972-73, it was found that the recommended stocks had dropped by 27 per cent more than the average fall during the declining market then prevailing.

A second way of predicting the future of stocks is known as 'chartism'. It can be applied either to the stock market as a whole or to individual shares. The value of the share is plotted on a graph and the analyst looks for trends. He tries to spot such features as a 'primary trend', whether up or down, neglecting small dips or minor peaks. Unfortunately for the chartist, it has been conclusively demonstrated by mathematical analysis that changes in share prices are completely random: they cannot possibly be predicted from examining past records. Although as a result of these findings, the number of chartists has dropped, there are many who persist in taking this useless approach.

The continued resort to investment analysts both by the general public and by large firms with money to invest is a puzzle, since they are known to be worse than useless. It is as though a doctor were to be paid for prescribing drugs that were worse for the patient than ones selected at random. Analysts differ from civil servants and businessmen in that the latter two produce corporate irrationality by their own selfishness and irrationality, whereas investment analysts fail at their job because they follow the herd. By buying stocks that are in fashion and selling ones that are out of it, they ensure that they are always a move behind the game.

7 misplaced consistency

People strive to maintain consistency in their beliefs, often at the expense of the truth. One example is the halo effect, which has already been described. If a person has some salient (available) trait that is good, it tends to colour the way in which all his other characteristics are seen. In other people's eyes they are distorted to fit in with the one estimable trait. People are unwilling to accept that others may be a mixture of good and bad: they try to see them as a consistent whole.

The halo effect operates even when someone has no vested interest in seeing another person or object as wholly good (or wholly bad), but the effects of the drive for consistency become even stronger when someone has made a large investment in anything. If a couple are looking for a house, they will examine several of the sort they want, or more likely the sort they can afford: they will find in each of them things they like, such as a well-fitted kitchen, and things they dislike, such as a cramped dining-room. They will of course be influenced in their appraisal of one part of the house by their attitudes to other parts (the halo effect), and will almost certainly be unduly influenced by their first impressions. Eventually, after a good deal of mental conflict they settle for a particular house and buy it. Apart from the time and effort expended in the search, they will have spent a great deal of money. If they are not to feel foolish, they must justify to themselves the commitment they have made, so after the house has been bought they tend to exaggerate what they formerly saw as its good points and to minimise its bad points. The well-fitted kitchen becomes the ideal kitchen and the cramped dining-room is now seen as rather cosy. The upgrading of the virtues of the house is partly caused by the drive for consistency. Most people think they take sensible decisions, particularly if they have put a lot of thought into something, and the better the house the more sensible the decision. There may be, however, a motivational factor at work: because it would be extremely upsetting to feel that a large sum of money had been misspent, the purchasers unconsciously set out to reassure themselves that they have done the right thing. Of course this is all quite irrational, since the purchase of a house does not make it either better or worse, even if subjectively it becomes more desirable.

These effects of taking a decision have been demonstrated many times: here are two examples. Teenage girls were shown a large selection of records and asked to give a score to each indicating how much they liked it. Each girl was then asked to choose between two of the records that she liked only moderately well and she received her choice as a gift. New ratings of these two records were then obtained and it was found that the record chosen was seen as considerably more attractive than originally, while the one rejected was liked much less than before.

The second study was on real life. Students nearing the end of a management course who had already visited firms at which they might work were asked to rate the three prospective jobs that they found most attractive. At this stage there was almost no difference in the rated attractiveness of these most favoured jobs. After the students had decided which one to take, but before they actually started work, further ratings were obtained. The jobs they had chosen were now thought to be markedly more attractive than before, while the ones they had rejected were seen as much less attractive. Having taken a decision, the students had to justify it to themselves: nobody likes to be wrong. Both studies demonstrate a further piece of irrationality. People tend to lower their opinion of anything they don't or can't get. This effect is much better known: it is 'sour grapes'.

Although the usual finding is that bolstering the attractiveness of an option occurs only after a choice has been made, there is some evidence that it may occur (equally irrationally) during the decision process itself. Women students in Australia who had volunteered as subjects were informed that the experiment was on the effects of unpleasant stimulation on the performance of an intellectual task. They had to decide whether to receive a foul-tasting substance or to be exposed to very unpleasant noise. They were told that both stimuli could produce unpleasant short-term effects like dizziness, headaches and nausea, and were asked to rate how unpleasant they thought each would be. Next, one group were told that before they chose they would be given more information about the effects of the bad taste and the noise, the others were told they would not learn anything further. A few minutes later they again rated the unpleasantness of the alternatives. There was no change in the group who were expecting the additional information, but there was quite a large change in the other group: in the initial ratings there had been little difference between the two options, but now this group saw the option for which they originally had a slight preference as much less unpleasant than the other one. In fact they later all chose the option for which they had raised their preference, but much to their relief they were not subjected either to the foul taste or the nasty noise. This experiment suggests that in some instances people may bolster the desirability of an option before they have committed themselves. Such a process not only helps them to take a difficult decision, but once again helps to convince them that it is the right one.

Someone who has bought a new car may boast about its acceleration, its manoeuvrability and its petrol consumption. Such boasts are often rightly taken as a sign of uncertainty. Who is he trying to convince? Bruno Bettelheim noted an extreme form of bolstering a decision. In Nazi concentration camps some of the prisoners identified with the guards. They accepted their appalling values, wore fragments of Gestapo uniforms, and imitated their behaviour to the point of assisting in the torture of their fellow prisoners. They had presumably given up all hope of resistance: they therefore decided on complete compliance and to bolster their faith in this decision came to accept the guards' values.

There are two ways in which regret rather than satisfaction may follow a decision. First, some investigators have found that for a brief period after a decision is made, people may actually regret it: they feel uncertain whether they have done the right thing. However, they then proceed to convince themselves that they have by overvaluing the benefits of their decision. Regret can occur in a second way. If the consequences of a decision are much worse than anticipated, they can no longer be glossed over. The house-buyer who on moving in finds his future home needs a new roof and is riddled with dry rot cannot disguise his mistake even from himself and, far from justifying his decision by ascribing imaginary virtues to the property, he is likely to acknowledge and to regret his error.

When a decision has to be reversed people often go to extreme limits to magnify in their minds its bad consequences. As far as I know there has been no experimental work on this, but Janis and Mann give a nice instance from Boswell's journals. In 1792 he began an affair with a beautiful young actress called Louisa. He fell so madly in love that he remained faithful to her, thus abandoning his usual practice of having casual sex with anyone who took his fancy. His friends could not believe his exaggerated account of her virtues. Six months later Boswell discovered he had contracted gonorrhoea: Louisa pleaded that although she had caught the disease a long time before meeting him, she was sure she had fully recovered. Boswell refused to believe her and described her as a 'dissembling whore'. His love for her turned to hatred: he vilified her and left her. To justify reversing a decision or an attitude that turns out to have been clearly wrong, it pays to represent its consequences in the blackest possible terms.

Another ploy is simply to forget the past, or anything that reminds one of it. Ex-lovers burn each other's photographs and many spouses who are left by their partner cannot bear to live in the same house because it provides so many reminders of the past. 'I'm gonna wash that man right out of my hair,' as *South Pacific* has it. Blackening the past is certainly irrational since it distorts the truth, but trying to forget seems a perfectly sensible way of dealing with it, unless it stops you learning something that could prevent you making the same mistake again as most people are prone to do.

The opposite of reversing an attitude is to allow it gradually to become more extreme. People often slide into a series of actions without stopping to take a conscious decision. Many criminals start by committing minor crimes which gradually escalate, and may wind up with armed robbery or murder. They might have been horrified by the thought of murder at the outset of their career, but by gradually progressing through crimes of increasing severity, at any one point their actions and attitudes remain roughly consistent with those immediately preceding. Much of our behaviour is governed by such an irrational slide. A woman buys a brand of perfume and happens to like it, possibly because she was in a good mood the first time she tried it. Buying it becomes a habit and she never tests another brand to see how it compares.

This human failing is exploited by, among others, insurance salesmen using the 'foot-in-the-door' technique. Once the door is opened they try to blandish their way into the house: if successful, they point out the virtues of insurance in general, discover the personal situation of the householder and then find – surprise, surprise – that they happen to have a policy that is tailor-made for him and remarkably cheap. Through these insidious steps the poor man winds up buying a policy he does not want and cannot afford. In this instance there is more at work than the slide from one step to another: embarrassment, which underlies much human irrationality, plays a considerable role. The householder may mistakenly feel that the insurance salesman has to earn a living, he has spent a great deal of time, he will be disappointed if he does not effect a sale, and anyway he seems a very nice chap. But consistency also plays a role: someone who has embarked on a course of action may feel he must continue with it to justify his initial decision.

Several experiments have documented the effectiveness of the slide in persuading people to do something they would not otherwise have done. In one study, Californian housewives were approached with a request to allow the erection of a small sign outside their house reading BE A SAFE DRIVER. Almost all of them agreed. In the second stage of the experiment, they and another group of women who had not been previously approached were asked if they would agree to the display of a very large and very ugly sign reading DRIVE CAREFULLY. Three-quarters of those who had permitted the first sign to go up agreed to the second request, whereas only one in six of the women being approached for the first time would allow their houses to be disfigured by this monstrous sign.

In human history, sexual seduction is perhaps the oldest form of the slide and is probably still the commonest: provided both partners enjoy the steps, it is perfectly rational, whereas being led by degrees to do something one initially disapproves of and may subsequently regret is clearly irrational.

It is often said that if something is hard to get, it becomes more attractive. This has been shown to be true, but only if someone voluntarily chooses to undergo the rigours of getting it. In an experiment close to real life, women were asked if they would like to take part in a discussion on the psychology of sex. One group was told that in order to overcome any shyness they must first undergo an experience that they might find distressing: they were asked to read obscene words and pornographic accounts of sexual activities. (The experiment was conducted at a time when young women might well have found this experience more distressing than most would today.) The second group were not asked to go through these curious preliminaries. At each discussion, all the women except the subject were stooges, who chatted in a desultory, inhibited and boring fashion about the sexual behaviour of animals. After listening to this tedious chit-chat, the genuine subjects were asked to evaluate the worthless discussion. Those who had been through the initiation ceremony thought it had been considerably more interesting than those who had not.

In an even more convincing study, overweight women were invited to take part in a new form of therapy for reducing weight. They were required to carry out various rather unpleasant tasks such as reading nursery rhymes aloud while the sound of their voices was played back to them after a short delay: this procedure induces stuttering and hesitancy and makes it very difficult to speak. Half the subjects performed tasks like this for five sessions, each of an hour. The other half had the same number of sessions, but each lasted only a few minutes. They were all weighed one year later. The first group, which had had to make far more effort, had lost on average 6.7 pounds, while the second had lost only .3 pounds. The so-called therapy was of course completely worthless and had no connection with weight loss, but the group which had put a lot of effort into it had to justify that effort to themselves: they therefore proceeded to lose weight.

There is a related form of irrationality that is even more extreme. People who have made a sacrifice (in money, time or effort) in order to do something tend to go on doing it even when they stand to lose more than they gain by continuing. Almost everyone reading these pages will at some time have paid money to see a bad film or a bad play. Despite excruciating boredom, people often refuse to leave even if the show is so bad that they would have paid a small amount of money to avoid seeing it at all. Thus, they irrationally suffer a double blow – they have spent money and they endure an hour or two's needless boredom. The sensible thing for them to do is to leave, which means they only suffer the monetary loss.

This case (and others like it that have been well documented experimentally) is slightly different from and more baffling than the ones so far discussed, for people may continue to watch a boring show even though they cannot delude themselves into thinking that the decision to attend was a good one. They are determined 'to get their money's worth': such refusal to cut losses whether occurring consciously or unconsciously is a common form of irrationality. People fail to sell shares that have dropped in value and have no prospects because they will have lost money, even if it is obvious that they will lose even more money by hanging on to them than by accepting the loss and investing elsewhere. And generals are notorious for persisting in the strategies on which they have embarked on after their futility is obvious. In the First World War, it became apparent, if only from the battle of Verdun, in which 800,000 lives were lost, that in trench warfare direct attacks were not only doomed to failure but would cost the attackers far more casualties than the defenders. Yet in the battle of the Somme, despite losing 57,000 men in the first few hours, General Haig continued to attack well-defended German positions with further appalling losses to his troops. In this case it was, of course, not Haig who suffered but his men. The reluctance to stop a project in which large funds have already been invested is revealed by a remark of Senator Denton when he was urging the US Senate to continue a waterway project that was clearly not viable. He said, 'To terminate a project in which $1.1 billion has been invested represents an unconscionable mishandling of taxpayers' dollars.' What he could not see was that to continue the work would represent an even more unconscionable mishandling.

The refusal to abandon a useless project in which a sum of money has been invested is known as the 'sunk cost error'. It is an extreme form of misplaced consistency. People simply are not willing to admit to themselves that they should not have laid out the money in the first place and continue to expend money and effort in the vain hope of salvaging something, even when it is clear that there is nothing to gain by so doing. As we shall see in later chapters, our inability to acknowledge our own errors even to ourselves is one of the most fundamental causes of irrationality.

There is an interesting variant of the sunk cost error that is also well documented experimentally. Suppose you go to the theatre to see a play. On arrival you discover you have lost your ticket. You put in a pathetic plea to the box office, but the stern custodian refuses to replace the lost seat. Since, however, the theatre is not full, she offers to sell you a ticket at the price you originally paid, say £15 (either you have found a very reasonably priced theatre or you are sitting in the gallery). You then calculate that if you buy another ticket it will have cost you £30 to see the play and you feel it just isn't worth it, so you go home. It has been shown experimentally that many people reason like this, but they are in error. You have already lost the money originally paid for the seat, and nothing can get it back. Hence if you were prepared to pay £15 originally, you should be prepared to buy a new ticket at the same price (assuming of course that you have not changed your mind about the excellence of the play in the mean time). Ask yourself whether you would be deterred from buying a ticket because you had lost a £20 note.

This mistake like the sunk cost error arises because people fail to realise that all that matters is their future gains and losses. The past is the past and is irrelevant. If at this moment I will lose by continuing an activity, I should discontinue it no matter how much I have already invested. If at this moment I would benefit by undertaking some activity (e.g. the theatre) I should not be put off by the fact that I have already lost some investment in it (the lost seat). All decisions should be based solely on the present situation: they should look to the future and ignore the past, except in so far as one can learn from it. All that can be learned in the two cases outlined is first not to buy tickets for bad plays and second to keep your ticket in a safe place, not by your kitchen sink.

Both the errors described can be regarded as arising out of misplaced consistency. In sunk costs errors, continuing an activity is consistent with having started it; in its variant, discontinuing an activity is consistent with not devoting more money (or effort) to it than usual.

There is a further related form of irrationality that is almost universal. Suppose someone buys a few cases of claret at £6 a bottle and five years later discovers their value has increased dramatically and they can be sold for £60 a bottle. Suppose further that he has a rule that he will never pay more than £10 a bottle for wine. It would appear that the logical thing for him to do is to sell the wine that has appreciated: it is in effect costing him £60 every time he opens a bottle (or approximately £2 a swig). Many, if not most, people do not sell: they argue to themselves that it is only costing them the £6 they paid for it, whereas in reality it is costing what they could get for it if it were sold. This curious mistake runs through the whole of everyday life. People are far less upset if they break an antique vase worth £1,000 if they bought it years ago for £1 than if they bought it the day before for £1,000. Yet its true value in monetary terms is the same in both cases – £1,000. It is hard to make sense of this particular piece of irrationality: perhaps the price paid for a commodity is more available than the money it would fetch if sold.

There is another common kind of consistency that is equally irrational. People who are persuaded to do something distasteful or immoral have to justify themselves by inventing a reason for having done it. If they are given a large reward for their action, that may be reason enough; they only have to justify themselves if the reward is not large enough to compensate for the distasteful act. In one of the first studies to reveal this phenomenon, subjects were required to spend twenty minutes turning pegs arranged in row after row. After performing this pointless and monotonous task, they were asked to tell the next subject (a stooge) that the task was very interesting in order to encourage her to take part. In return for lying to her, some were offered $1, others $20. All the subjects agreed to tell the lie. After they had done so, they were asked to evaluate the interest of the task. Those given the smaller reward rated it as much more interesting than those given the large one. Presumably the ones promised $20 thought that this was a good enough reason for telling a fairly venial lie, while those offered $1 could not use this excuse. They therefore pretended to themselves that the task was less dull than it actually was in order to reduce the extent of their lie.

In a subsequent experiment, the subject to whom the lie was told (the stooge) refused to do the task so that the lie had no deleterious effects. Both the high reward and the low reward subjects now rated the task at the same level of dullness. The latter group were able to exculpate themselves because their lie had been ineffective and therefore they did not have to underestimate how boring the task was. It has also been found that the effect does not occur if people think they have no freedom of choice about lying. People who were told that they must lie because it was a part of the experiment to which they had committed themselves by volunteering to be subjects did not underestimate the tedium of the task. If you do something under compulsion, there is no need to justify it.

It could be argued that in these experiments the subjects were not themselves deceived, but that they underestimated the monotony of the task simply in order not to look foolish in the eyes of the experimenter. A number of studies have examined this possibility. Most have made use of an ingenious device called the 'bogus pipeline'. The subjects are fitted with electrodes attached to the head and told that their brain waves will be recorded. The experimenter assures them that these recordings are much more powerful than a lie detector and will reveal with certainty whether they are telling the truth. The subjects were invariably American university students, whose misplaced faith in their professors is so great that one can assume they were fooled by this dodge. In most of these experiments the group getting the small reward continued to value the boring experience more highly than those getting a large reward. However, the difference tends not to be so marked, suggesting that the subjects both deceive themselves and also tend to lie to the experimenter in order to justify themselves.

moral

1. Beware of overrating the results of a choice you have made, particularly if it has cost you a great deal of time, effort or money.
2. Try not to move by small steps to an attitude or action of which you would initially have disapproved.
3. No matter how much time, effort or money you have invested in a project, cut your losses if investing more will not be beneficial.
4. Value any activity or possession at the price it is worth to you now,

regardless of the past.

5. If you are persuaded to do something distasteful, try not to minimise its unpleasantness in order to justify yourself.

6. Never allow an insurance salesman past your front door.

8   misuse of rewards
and punishment

At the end of the last chapter, I showed that giving someone a negligible reward (or no reward) for performing an unpleasant act makes the act seem less disagreeable than it really is. One can also ask what is the effect of a large reward on the perception of a *pleasant* task. The answer is unequivocal: it devalues the task in the eyes of those performing it. Nursery school children were provided in their playtime with brightly coloured Magic Markers and attractive drawing paper. Those who showed an interest in drawing were subsequently given the same apparatus in the classroom and encouraged to draw. One group was promised a glossy certificate for good drawing, while another was given no reward. Two weeks later the material was again provided and the children were told it was up to them whether they wanted to draw or not. The group previously given the certificate showed a marked decline in interest, while the other group drew as much as they had done in the previous two sessions. Presumably the children thought that drawing could not be of much interest in its own right if a reward was needed to make them engage in it.

This type of experiment has been repeated many times, with both children and adults, and with a variety of tasks, from solving puzzles to acting as voluntary teachers. The results have always been the same. Here is an example from a real-life situation. For twelve weeks eight students who wrote headlines for their university newspaper in two shifts were observed at work. The four students in one shift were paid $0.50 for each headline written, while the members of the other shift were not paid. In the last few weeks of observation, the unpaid shift wrote more headlines than the other one and more than they themselves had written in the first four weeks. The paid shift failed to improve their performance: presumably the monetary reward had devalued the task for them. In another study, 1,200 adults were asked if they would donate blood in a bloodsmobile. Many more of them not given a monetary incentive agreed to donate than of those offered

$10. This finding suggests that reward devalues any activity worth doing in its own right, not merely pleasurable activities.

There have also been studies on the effects of rewarding activities that are not intrinsically pleasurable. Many of these concern 'token economies': in some mental hospitals and other institutions, the inmates are sometimes given tokens for behaving well, for example, for dressing themselves properly, cleaning their teeth, not eating in a messy fashion, and so on. The tokens can be exchanged for privileges, like watching television or having a chat with a nurse. Such tokens often do help to induce better behaviour while the person is in the institution, but the behaviour reverts to its original level when they leave and reward is no longer available. Once outside the institution their behaviour is no better than that of patients not rewarded with tokens.

These experiments raise some fundamental questions about the role of reward. Both the psychologist and the layman tend to assume that if you want to get people to do something, rewarding them for it, whether by praise or sweets or money, is the best way to go about it. In the short run this may be true. But the experiments clearly demonstrate that, at least in the case of activities that are intrinsically pleasurable, people who are rewarded will engage in less of the activity after the reward is withdrawn than people who have never been rewarded. This goes against one major psychological theory of motivation which alleges that if people are rewarded for some activity, the desire to engage in it will eventually become autonomous: they will be motivated to perform that activity even without reward. Many laymen mistakenly think in the same way.

Before considering the irrational use of rewards in everyday life, it is necessary to introduce a caveat. Almost all the experiments run by psychologists have used forms of reward, like money or certificates, that have no natural connection with the task. However, to learn many tasks, it is necessary for the pupil to find out where he is right and where he is wrong. This sort of feedback, which in technical jargon is called 'knowledge of results', is often provided by the environment without human intervention. For example, nobody receives lessons in how to play darts – they somehow gauge how hard they have thrown the dart, observe whether it is above or below the target, and adjust further throws accordingly. Similarly, in driving an unfamiliar car, one learns how fast it is safe to take corners by registering the extent to which the car is thrown towards the outside of the bend.

There are, however, many kinds of skill, such as learning how to manipulate algebraic equations, in which knowledge of results has to be provided by another person (or nowadays in some instances by a computer program written by a person). The pupil simply could not learn unless he is told when he is correct and when he is wrong. When information of this sort is given, it has two quite separate functions. It will help the pupil to see how to improve his performance, but it will also be interpreted as praise for correct performance and blame for errors, that is as reward and punishment. In short, it is often impossible to teach a skill without appearing to be allocating praise or blame. It seems likely that pupils learn best when they interpret the teacher's remarks as helping them to improve their performance rather than as appraising them. Clearly the more specific are the teacher's comments on a piece of work, the more likely they are to be regarded as in the former category: specific comments are much more helpful than more general praise and blame.

All this raises the question of the extent to which working to please the teacher (or indeed anyone else) devalues the task in the eyes of someone performing it. It may be that praise functions in a different way from other rewards, like money, and does not have their undesirable effects and indeed this was supported in an experiment that found that praise for performing well did not devalue the task. There are two fundamental ways in which praise differs from material rewards. First, it can be internalised, that is, a person can praise himself for doing something well even in the absence of others: people derive satisfaction from their achievements and that is very like praising themselves. Nobody needs to be praised or to receive money for completing a crossword puzzle. Second, there are many tasks in which good performance will always elicit praise from others – from friends, relatives, or colleagues: for such tasks, there is no point at which the reward of external praise is likely to be cut off in the way that for many activities monetary rewards often cease after a time. These two points suggest that praise may have effects that are very different from those of other forms of extrinsic reward: it may become internalised and the occurrence of praise from others may continue to occur.

The above passage is a digression, but it is necessary to make clear that not all reinforcements, in particular praise and intrinsic rewards (self-praise), necessarily have damaging effects. Having made this caveat, we can proceed to examine the irrational ways in which rewards that have little to do with the reinforced activity are applied in everyday life.

Material rewards reduce the attractiveness of pleasurable activities and have little effect on less pleasurable ones once they have been withdrawn, and yet in the Western world education and many other activities are often based on such rewards.

The findings on the effects of reward call into question the practice of giving grades in schools. The child should be persuaded that reading and even algebra are worthwhile activities in their own right – whenever this is possible – or alternatively that they are a means to achieving one of the child's own superordinate ends. Curiosity about the world and the drive to manipulate it successfully are inborn in all mammals and are particularly strong in man's nearest relatives, monkeys and apes. The satisfaction of getting something right or of discovering something is itself a powerful reward, albeit one largely ignored by the behaviourist school of psychology.

The deleterious effects of extrinsic rewards other than praise have implications for all institutions, including hospitals, universities and factories. In most firms, employees are motivated largely by financial rewards which include not merely salaries or weekly pay, but bonuses, commissions and piece work. This system destroys the interest of the work in the eye of the employee, as was recognised by some in the US where Theory Y Management was introduced in the early 'sixties. This approach attempts to structure work in such a way that the employee will motivate himself by a desire to perform well. Where possible, the planning and execution of a job are combined. The employee is given as much participation in decisions as possible, since as we shall see there is a far greater commitment to actions freely chosen than to those that are not. Unfortunately this style of management is still rare in the US and even rarer in the UK. Although it is difficult or impossible to structure all jobs in this way, many can be and indeed in Japan are. The beneficial effects of this approach on productivity, efficiency and morale are well documented by experiments in factories, but whether through complacency or ignorance are largely ignored by British managers. All the evidence suggests that if workers are to perform well, they must be motivated by a pride in so doing, not by conventional sticks and carrots.

As to giving prizes, a curious habit that is endemic in our society, consider two incidents from the 1930s, which the reader can readily translate into contemporary practice. Here is a not atypical extract from a headmistress's speech following morning prayers. 'Now girls, I have an important announcement to make. It gives me great pleasure to tell you that Celia Blagworthy has been awarded the prize for knitting the longest muffler of the year. Will the assembly please give three rousing cheers? And now step forward, Celia Blagworthy.' Celia, blushing heavily, mounts the platform and is presented with a book, only to discover subsequently that she already owns it or that it is too boring to read. However that may be, the acclaim of her schoolfellows is reward enough. But how do you think Celia's friend, Monica Moonstopper, feels? She had after all knitted a muffler that was only half an inch shorter than Celia's masterpiece: indeed had a little more tension been applied to her own when it was measured, she might easily have won. Full of envy and disappointment, she retires to the lavatory where she is so overcome by tears that she misses a complete morning's lessons.

Meanwhile, the King of Sweden, playing the part of the headmistress, has just presented Celia's father, Professor Martin Blagworthy, with the most coveted award in science – a Nobel Prize. The citation states that it is for his 'epoch-making research on the eye of the black-crested toad', but it had been a close run thing and Monica's father, Dr Moonstopper, who had discovered almost everything there is to be known about the eye of the common frog, was so upset when he first heard the news that he threw away his Bunsen burner. He was unable to comfort himself with the reflection that in that year, as far as scientific circles were concerned, toads were in and frogs were out, for he bitterly blamed himself for his choice of species.

Boys' schools are just as bad as girls', but then so are most adult institutions. There are prizes for the best novel of the year (or rather the one that is thought best by a panel of judges, most of whom are so afraid of criticism that they dare not depart from conventional opinion), for the best new office building, for the best motor car, the best play, the best painting, the best journalist in each of about a dozen categories, the most enterprising company of the year, and for the best film, the best director, the best female star and so on and on and on. In all fairness there ought to be a prize for the best prize-giver of the year. Britain compounds this system by awarding honours, which have not only all the disadvantages of prizes, but the additional one of promoting snobbery.

As should be clear from the two imaginary examples, one must distinguish between the harm done to the prizewinner and the unhappiness produced in his rivals: both are the product of an irrational institution. The experimental evidence (reviewed in the next chapter) suggests that people who are trying to gain a prize will do less imaginative and less flexible work than those of equal talent who are not. In addition they may come to work less hard after winning the prize. There have been no studies of the effects of Nobel Prizes, but one has the impression that many Nobel Laureates deteriorate markedly, though in some cases allowance must be made for senility. Many develop considerable hubris, and turn to fields in which they are totally unqualified; others try to solve grand but meaningless problems like the nature of consciousness or devote themselves to promoting vitamin C as a cure for everything from cancer to the common cold (unfortunately these examples are not imaginary). Many feel that after the Nobel Prize there is nothing else to accomplish in their own discipline.

As to the effects on their rivals, these hardly need documenting. It is in the nature of things that for everyone who wins a prize there will be dozens who do not. The novelist David Lodge is in a good position to speak since he both won the Whitbread Prize for fiction and acted as a judge in the Booker Prize. He wrote, 'Prizes are inevitably unjust and divisive . . . A novelist of a certain kind cannot publish a novel today without his or her chances of the Booker being publicly discussed and is therefore apt to feel a factitious sense of failure if the book is not short listed. . . . This situation, I can personally attest, creates quite as much anxiety for the judges as for the candidates – indeed rather more.' So prizes cause the judges agony as well as the contestants. Doubtless Celia Blagworthy's headmistress spent many sleepless nights pondering the length of mufflers. And yet despite the anguish it causes, the system of prizes and honours continues unchecked. Is that rational? And given the thesis of this book, namely, that complex judgements are usually wrong, is it rational to make more judgements than are strictly necessary?

One should distinguish between giving prizes, which adds to the sum total of human unhappiness, and giving awards which enable someone to complete a useful piece of work that would not otherwise be undertaken. If it is thought desirable that there should be a definitive book on, say, the history of Portuguese navigation, it makes sense to give the prospective but needy author a grant to enable him to consult the relevant manuscripts that repose in Lisbon or Rhode Island. Similarly, scientific research is now so expensive that little would be undertaken if it were not for the existence in all developed countries of grant-giving agencies. As was demonstrated in Chapter 2, the decisions about the quality of a scientist's research made by his peers are often bad, but since it is necessary to decide who should have grants one has to live with that. But we do not have to live with prizes: they serve no useful function.

If rewarding an activity makes people devalue it, one can ask whether the threat of punishing someone for doing something will make them overvalue it. There is convincing evidence that children who are induced not to misbehave under mild threat are much less likely to do the naughty deed when the threat is removed than are children who are threatened with severe punishment. Several studies have examined children's responses to being forbidden to play with a particular toy: some were threatened with mild punishment some with more severe. In all cases the toy was liked more by those threatened with strong punishment. Moreover, when the threat of punishment was removed, they played with the toy more than did those who were only under mild threat.

It is hardly necessary to document the practice of punishing children, but here is an example of some unhelpful advice recently given to parents by a behavioural psychologist: 'With a little ingenuity, this basic procedure can be modified and used with most bedtime problems. While opening and closing a door will work, a light or a child's favourite blanket may be used. That is, a light in the child's room is either left on or turned off according to the behaviour he exhibits; or the child's favourite blanket – or toy or teddy bear – can be removed until he behaves properly.' In short,

> Speak roughly to your little boy,
> And beat him when he sneezes;
> He only does it to annoy,
> Because he knows it teases.

In fact, studies in the home have found that the less the child is punished, the more obedient it is both in the presence of the parents and when on its own. Moreover, children who are neglected when crying cry more than children whose mother comes whenever she hears them cry. It might be supposed that people, including children, are just cussed: the more something is forbidden, the more it is wanted. But it is more likely that cognitive factors similar to those that determine the reaction to external rewards are at work. The child who elects not to do something, possibly under the threat of a mild punishment, will continue not to do it when the threat is no longer present since it has made a voluntary choice. The child who refrains from misbehaving for fear of punishment sees its behaviour as controlled by an external threat: there is no reason for not being naughty once the threat is withdrawn.

What all this amounts to is that people, including quite young children, do not respond to external rewards and punishments in the simplistic way that behaviourists would have us believe. They develop their own internal values and in the long run these cannot be controlled by rewards or punishments, perhaps particularly ones that have no real connection with the activity they are intended to promote or prevent. Just how these values are developed is a complex and vexed question, though modelling one's behaviour on that of others whom one admires certainly plays a part. For our present purposes it is enough to note the folly and irrationality of attempting to control behaviour by rewards or punishments unless they can be permanently maintained.

The last two chapters have emphasised the effects of choice. People only minimise the unpleasantness of an act's consequences if they have freely chosen to do it and they only make the consequences of a decision more desirable than they really are if they have freely taken the decision themselves. What happens if something is thrust upon them and they have no choice?

In general people prefer something freely chosen to the same thing forced upon them. The effect is dramatically revealed in a study that did not directly involve reward or punishment. Lottery tickets costing $1 each were sold to the employees of two companies. Some of the employees were allowed to choose the number of their tickets, others had no choice but were merely handed a ticket. Just before the draw, the experimenter approached each subject offering to buy the ticket back. The subjects who had no choice were prepared to sell back for $1.96 on average, but those who had selected their own tickets held out for an average of $8.67. There could be no better demonstration that we irrationally overvalue what we freely choose.

In another experiment, children of about ten years old were told they would be given toys and would be allowed to choose which toy they would receive. Each was next asked to say which toy he preferred. In the event, the experimenter said, 'Here are the toys. Hmmm, well they both look the same to me, I guess I'm going to give you this one.' They were then given the toy they originally preferred. Simply because at the last moment their freedom of choice had been removed, the children liked the toy far less than they had before being given it, even though it had originally been their favourite one. Moreover, after receiving it, they liked it less than did another group of children who had genuinely been allowed to choose themselves. Although freedom of choice is rightly valued by people, it is irrational to lower one's opinion of an object just because it is not freely chosen. It is as though the annoyance at not being allowed to make one's own choice rubs off on the gift, a typical example of the sloppiness of people's thinking.

Similar experiments have been performed with university students, who were asked what piece of poetry they would like to recite.

Subsequently, they were all allowed to recite the piece they preferred, but half were told they must use that piece, the others were told they could change their minds and recite any piece they wanted. The students allowed to choose for themselves attended the classes more frequently, were better pleased with them, and performed better in their recitations.

This and many similar findings have important implications for medicine and other professions. In a study of women who had abortions in a Boston hospital, it was found that those who felt they had been coerced into the abortion had far more psychiatric illness after it than those who felt they had freely chosen to have it. In a British study of breast cancer some women, after discussion with the surgeon, were allowed to choose whether to have a lump removed or to have the whole breast excised, others had the decision made for them by the surgeon. The women who were allowed to choose were less anxious and less distressed post-operatively. Even more dramatically, of seventeen women who felt they had been compelled to enter a nursing home for the old, all but one died within ten weeks, while only one of thirty-eight women who felt they had themselves freely chosen to enter the home died within that time. There was no difference in their state of health when they first entered the home.

Normally, one is only compelled to do things one does not want to do. For consistency then, people come to believe that anything thrust upon them must be bad. Not only is this irrational, it is equally irrational to force compliance on others: it often has the opposite effect to the one intended.

It is likely that many readers will regard much of this chapter as too idealistic. Unfortunately, not all jobs can be restructured in such a way as to make them intrinsically interesting, the threat of punishment may be the only way to deter a child or an adult from misbehaviour, and when a patient's life hangs on a particular treatment it would be wrong to offer others. Nevertheless, it is important to remember that both rewards and punishments may be damaging and that the opportunity to choose freely where possible is beneficial.

moral

1. If you want someone to value a task and perform well, do not offer material rewards.
2. If you are a manager, adopt as participatory and egalitarian a style as possible.
3. If you want to stop children (and almost certainly adults as well)

from doing something, try to persuade rather than threatening them with punishment.

4. Give people as much freedom of choice as possible, particularly in medicine and education.

5. If you happen to be offered a Nobel Prize, turn it down.

9 drive and emotion

From the lover who grossly overestimates the charms of his beloved to the coward who dies because he remains rooted to the spot in paralytic fear, everyone under strong emotion can be driven to irrational thought and action. Emotions have proved difficult to define and have been recalcitrant to most efforts at investigation. Roughly speaking, emotion is a disposition to act and think in a particular way, combined with certain feelings. Strong emotions have physiological components, such as a rapid heartbeat or a dry mouth, which occur when the person is highly aroused: it is debatable how far these physiological changes vary from one emotion to another. This account is unsatisfactory since there are many marginal cases. Is feeling shy an emotion? Is curiosity one? Why don't we call hunger and thirst emotions? One way in which emotion causes irrationality is simply that many strong emotions, like sexual jealousy, depression or sadness, may cause people to brood or become obsessed. As a result, they lack the concentration needed for rational thought or rational decision making. Emotions may also make us see the world in a distorted way, as is notorious in the case of sexual jealousy, which is often not founded on fact: this applies just as much to depression in which the future is seen in gloomier terms than are warranted and even more so to elation which makes people too optimistic. Much emotion involves a vicious circle: gloomy thoughts, sometimes caused by external events, can give rise to a depressed mood and the depressed mood in turn produces further gloomy thoughts. All this is commonplace, but before we examine some counterintuitive effects of strong emotion, it is necessary to say something about drive. I shall use the word to mean the internal state that motivates us to pursue a particular goal: hunger, ambition and cupidity are all drives.

Drives vary in strength even within the same person: if we have just eaten ten cream buns, we are unlikely to want to consume a beef-steak, however delicious we might otherwise have found it.

Moreover, drives can be strengthened by the expectation of achieving the relevant goal, the incentive. The sight of food sharpens one's hunger and the presence of the right partner can provoke the sex drive, no matter how dormant it had previously been. Mainly for ethical reasons, it is difficult to rouse high emotions in an experiment, hence most of the work to be discussed has been on drives whose strength can be manipulated by varying the size of the incentive, usually a monetary reward. But as will be shown, high drive, strong emotion and stress all have the same drastic effects on rationality.

The last chapter demonstrated that the offer of a large reward for an activity could make one devalue it and cease to engage in it once the reward was withdrawn. I now consider the effects of expecting a reward on how well one performs a task. Naïve adherents of the behaviourist B. F. Skinner, of whom a few remain, believe that the stronger the reward, the better the performance should be. In one of the first experiments on this problem, eight-year-old children were shown a hundred pairs of drawings of people: a boy called 'Bill' appeared in different clothes and postures in every pair and the children were asked to say which member of each drawing was Bill. The subjects were always told whether their response was right or wrong. Some were offered $0.50 and others $0.01 for each correct identification; a third group was given no monetary incentive. This group performed better than either of the reward groups and the group with high reward did marginally worse than that with low reward. This kind of study has been repeated many times both with children and adults, using many different tasks from solving puzzles to writing essays: the same results were obtained. In general, the higher the incentive, the worse people perform. Intuitively one might think that the bigger the reward, the harder the person would try and therefore the better he would do. What is going on?

In fact, reward does facilitate performance on very easy tasks but impairs it on more difficult ones. It has been found that subjects rewarded for recognising easy words, like 'COMMON' or 'FALL', do better than non-rewarded subjects in terms of speed, whereas if difficult words, like 'VIGNETTE' or 'ELEGY', are presented, reward decreases accuracy and increases the time taken to respond.

Further light is thrown on the effects of reward in an experiment in which subjects were set problems of the type, 'If you had three empty water jars that hold 21, 127 and 3 quarts respectively, how would you measure out 100 quarts using only these jars?' The answer is fairly obvious: you fill the 127 quart jar and then pour some of its contents once into the 21 quart jar, and twice into the 3 quart jar: you are then left with 100 quarts in the biggest jar. The experimenter gave a whole series of problems that could be solved in just this way – fill the biggest jar and then pour some of its water once into one of the smaller ones and twice into the other. At this stage subjects offered a monetary reward performed at about the same level as those offered no reward. But now comes the crunch: the final problem had to be solved in a different way. Instead of requiring the use of three jars, it only needed two – for example, measure 52 quarts using a 26 quart jar, a 100 quart jar and a 5 quart jar. All one needs to do is to pour the 26 quart jar twice into the 100 quart one. On this problem the subjects who were rewarded did much worse than the others. The reason is that if you try too hard, you tend to keep on doing whatever is uppermost in your mind. In this case the subjects kept trying to solve the final problem by using the technique that they had found to work on all the previous ones: they found it difficult to switch to the new method required to solve the new type of problem.

Here is another ingenious but straightforward problem that many people find difficult. You are told to imagine that you have a candle, a cigarette lighter and a box of tacks and are asked how, using just these three objects, you would attach the candle to a wall. Pause to think of the answer. If you get it in less than three or four minutes you are unusual. The solution is to empty out the tacks, burn some wax off the candle with the lighter and use the molten wax to attach the empty box to the wall; finally the candle is placed upright in the box being held steady by wax burnt off its base. The difficulty with the problem is that most people see the box as a container: so long as they concentrate on its ordinary function they do not spot that it can have a different use, namely, to serve as a platform for the candle. Similarly, they see the candle as a source of light not as providing a substance, wax, that can be used as a glue. Subjects who were rewarded for solving this problem took on average three and a half minutes longer to do so than subjects given no reward. Once again, trying too hard prevents flexibility of thinking: one sticks with what is uppermost in one's mind (the 'availability' error again).

As an everyday example of trying too hard, think of the irrational behaviour of someone who has lost a wallet containing £100, all his credit cards, his driving licence and so on. He tends to look for it over and over again in the same places, namely, those in which he immediately feels he is most likely to have lost it. In his frenzy, he does not stop to think out carefully exactly when he last saw it and where he has been since. His frantic eagerness to find it makes it impossible for him to search the recesses of his memory – he sticks to the first few places that come to mind.

It has been found that any high level of emotion is inimical to the careful consideration of different alternatives. The stereotyped thought processes that result from rewards or from the threat of punishment prevent people from working out the general principles governing the task on which they are engaged. In one study, subjects were shown a display of twenty-five squares, arranged in a five-by-five array. There was a light present in the top left-hand square. They could press two buttons marked L and R: the L button moved the light down one square and the R moved it one square to the right. One group of subjects were told that certain patterns of button presses would result in a monetary reward. A second group were told that they had to discover the correct rule governing the sequence of button presses. The rule was any sequence of four Ls and four Rs (e.g. LRLRLRLR or LLLLRRRR): any such sequence takes the light to the bottom right-hand corner without going off the edge of the array. After the rewarded group had learned how to obtain the reward, they were asked what the rule was. They gave a fixed pattern such as LLLLRRRR, whereas the other group had discovered the more general rule which was correct. You may think this is hardly surprising, since one group was asked to discover a rule, while the other was not. But there was a second stage to the experiment, in which the group that had been rewarded was asked to discover the rule without reward. At this stage they were much less successful than the non-reward group when faced with precisely the same task at the first stage. This experiment shows that the inflexible behaviour caused by rewards may continue even after the reward has been withdrawn.

It is not merely strong motivation that causes inflexible thinking: any form of stress produces it. In one study subjects were asked to solve anagrams: they were presented with a word, and had to decide which of six further words was its anagram. Some subjects were under stress induced by the fear of electric shocks, others were not. As compared with the latter group, the stressed subjects failed to examine the six alternatives four times as often before making their minds up; they scanned the alternatives in a much less systematic fashion; and they made incorrect choices twice as often. It may be that the inflexible thinking of many military commanders, some examples of which are given in the next two chapters, is in part caused by stress.

Stress also affects memory, which is closely tied to our ability to reason. In a real-life experiment, servicemen aboard a plane were given instructions on how to escape in an emergency. They were subsequently asked to recall the instructions while still in flight. For one group the intercom was left on and they heard a rehearsed discussion between the crew, the upshot of which was that because of a mechanical failure they were about to ditch. This group recalled their instructions very badly, as compared with a second group who went through exactly the same procedure, except that they did not overhear the alarming conversation on the flight deck.

Stress, rewards, punishments and strong emotions, then, reduce flexibility in thinking and lead to irrational behaviour. They have deleterious effects in everyday life. For example, if workers are rewarded for the number of items produced, they are likely to concentrate on quantity at the expense of quality. Although partly for this reason, there is much less piecework now than in the past, some British firms continue the practice. Similar arguments apply to the use of reward in education. It will have the effect of making children pick easy problems, in addition to preventing them from reflecting on the general principles involved rather than merely providing routine solutions. This may apply even if the reward is merely in the form of praise from the teacher. Praise should be given not just for solving problems, but for developing an understanding of general principles. Encouraging such creativity may be too little regarded today, perhaps as a result of the mistaken identification of creativity with the ability to produce unusual but meaningless material, as fostered by writers like Edward de Bono. True creativity is not thinking of a hundred uses for a brick: it is the ability to solve new problems, to induce general principles and to construct sound explanatory theories. Nor is creativity randomly throwing patches of paint at a canvas: it is the ability to paint a picture that in some way or other moves the beholder.

Like other emotions, fear inhibits rational thought, but it has further adverse consequences. Many people who think they might have a serious illness put off consulting their doctor for as long as possible because they do not want to hear the worst. Unless you hold the not entirely irrational belief that most doctors are likely to do you more harm than good, this is a foolish thing to do. Seeing a doctor will not in itself create the illness you fear: it is either there or it is not. The tendency to postpone a visit to the surgery is not caused by ignorance of what the symptoms might mean. In one American study, it was found that one third of patients with cancer had failed to see a doctor for three months after they first noticed the symptoms. Moreover, the patients who delayed taking medical advice had *more* knowledge of the possible significance of the symptoms than did those who went more promptly.

People may put off the time when they might hear the worst, but equally they cannot wait to grab what they want. They act under impulse even when in the long run they would do better by delaying or by acting in a way that would bring a large long-term benefit rather than a small short-term gain. Smoking, heavy drinking, overeating, taking addictive drugs, and, with the spread of AIDS, casual sex are examples.

These cases all concern physiological appetites; the more often we indulge them, the harder it is not to indulge next time. But practising self-control can almost certainly reduce impetuosity in all aspects of life. If you are a man who explodes with anger because your wife is late cooking the dinner or, more likely these days, because she is late coming home for the dinner you have cooked, you will find it more difficult not to become angry next time. It is almost certainly true that self-control (and also the lack of it) can become a habit, a theme to which I shall return in the final chapter.

We are descended from animals that lived from day to day. They strove to find sufficient food and water to stay alive, to find mates with whom to procreate, to keep their offspring alive and to avoid the onslaught of predators. Animals solved these problems not by thought but by immediate and instinctive action, for example, by flee-ing or fighting. Some animals of course do make provision for the future. They build nests or dig burrows or travel huge distances in autumn and spring to seek a better clime. But these activities are instinctive: they are inborn and not the result of conscious planning. Only man has the capacity for long-range planning, but the lust for immediate gratification, inherited from our animal ancestors, too often prevents him from using it.

In the puritanical age in which we live, it is perhaps unnecessary to labour the point that one should not always give way to immediate gratification. Paradoxically, it may be more important to stress the folly of avoiding such gratification without checking that the long-term benefits are really worth it. America has become a nation of masochists who spend hours aimlessly jogging and deprive them-selves of all but the nastiest foodstuffs. No rational hedonistic calcu-lations are made. Even cigarette smoking, which of all bad habits is the one that is best established as a cause of death, only knocks an average of about two years off the smoker's life and those years are unlikely to be his happiest. As to blood cholesterol, there is no good evidence that its level is affected by what we eat, while there is evi-dence to be discussed later that reducing cholesterol levels does not increase longevity: you simply die of cancer rather than heart disease. The death rate among joggers whether from motor accidents, heart attacks or muggers appears to be high and it is almost certainly safer and less uncomfortable to go for a brisk walk. These self-punitive tendencies are just as irrational as always clutching the nearest pleasure.

It is tempting to believe that doctors do make joggers of us all, but the medical literature on diet and extreme forms of exercise is for the most part quite cautious. Experimental results are distorted and sensationalised both by the press and by the companies exploiting the public with their so-called 'health foods'. But there is more to it than this: the desire to live for ever and the self-punitive activities that accompany it are surely as much caused by fashion as the crinoline and the mini-skirt. And behind it all lies the most widespread, irrational and powerful fear of all, the fear of death.

One's motives can affect how one sees the world and thus introduce bias. In an experiment demonstrating this, subjects submerged their forearms in icy cold water until they could bear the pain no longer. They were then asked to pedal an exercise bicycle. Next, they were given a lecture in which half were told that people with healthy hearts increased their tolerance of extreme cold after exercise, while the rest were told that if they had healthy hearts exercise would decrease tolerance. Finally, they were subjected to the cold test again. The subjects changed the length of time they endured this test in a direction consonant with having a healthy heart. That is to say, those who had learned that exercise increases tolerance for people with good hearts kept their forearm in the icy water for longer than before, those told that tolerance decreases if the heart is good took their arm out sooner. When questioned, only a few said that they had deliberately changed the length of time: most had done so unknowingly. The desire to have a healthy heart can therefore affect a person's perception of pain without his being aware of it.

This result is a form of wishful thinking. There is of course plenty of evidence that wishful thinking is a reality, not just an empty phrase. Smokers attach less credence to the evidence that smoking is harmful than do non-smokers. In one study subjects were given a lecture on the illnesses that coffee can cause: coffee drinkers thought it much less plausible than did people who did not drink coffee. It has been shown that people overestimate their chances of winning lotteries and underestimate their chances of being a victim of a robbery or road accident. There are also many experiments reporting 'self-serving' biases, in which a person takes credit for being successful, but blames the situation for failing: 'It was a difficult examination,' 'I didn't like my new racquet,' and so on. It has been argued that this bias may be nothing to do with motivation but is simply a mistake in thinking. The person has planned for success: if he achieves it, he puts it down to his planning and skill because these are connected in his mind with success. If he fails, he has to think again: because his plans were not connected to failure, he puts it down to the situation. This issue is unresolved: probably both 'self-esteem' and faulty thinking are at work.

Emotions are neither rational nor irrational: we just have them and they are hard to suppress. But they can lead to irrational acts in many further ways. Consider the power of envy, as exemplified by an experiment run by one cunning psychologist on his two young sons. He put two dishes of peanuts before them. One contained three peanuts and had four peanuts beside it, the other contained two peanuts and had a single peanut beside it. The boys, who were tested separately, were told that whichever dish one chose, the other would be allowed to eat the peanuts lying by its side. The younger son picked the dish with the two peanuts, since he could not bear to think of his brother getting more than him, while the older son chose the dish containing three. It turned out that he was no saint either, since he intended to bash his younger brother over the head until he relinquished the extra peanut. Whether you believe that the behaviour of the younger son was rational depends on whether you think it rational to sacrifice a peanut in order to gratify an ignoble emotion.

One might think that boredom was an unpleasant but harmless feeling. In fact, it has almost certainly been largely responsible for the pointless multiple shootings that occur from time to time in America and is part of the cause of football hooliganism and other wanton acts performed to relieve boredom by the excitement of danger and mayhem. In 1973 a DC10 was flying on autothrottle over New Mexico. The captain and flight engineer had nothing to do. According to the cockpit flight recorder, which was subsequently replayed, the flight engineer said to the captain that he wondered whether the autothrottle would respond if he pulled the number one manual throttle. The captain did not know, but he warned the engineer that the engines were on full speed. Nevertheless, they agreed to try the experiment. This relieved their boredom in short order, for the starboard engine increased speed to such a point that it broke up. It smashed a window and the resulting decompression sucked the passenger sitting next to it out of the plane to fall 39,000 feet. The Chernobyl disaster may also have been caused by boredom. Although its origins cannot be reconstructed with certainty from the ravaged remains of the plant, one hypothesis is that the cause was an operator's unauthorised manipulation of the controls, possibly undertaken out of boredom.

People find it difficult to do nothing, as any actor who has had to remain still on stage for any length of time will testify.

There is a final respect in which drives and emotions can lead to irrational behaviour: motives can conflict. Someone may wish to dominate others and at the same time want to be liked: the two aims are usually incompatible. The same applies to someone who is vain: being inordinately proud of one's appearance (or indeed any other personal attribute) is unlikely to win friends. Rational behaviour is acting, given one's knowledge, in the way most likely to achieve one's ends. In order to act rationally, therefore, one must establish priorities among them. One must also try to look at all the possible consequences of the action in order to assess which ends (apart from those most immediately in view) it will serve and to discover whether it might have any consequences that one wishes to avoid. Few people think hard about their goals and even fewer think hard about the many possible consequences of their actions.

The term 'love' was defined in an authoritative dictionary of psychology as 'a form of mental illness not yet recognised in the standard diagnostic manuals'. However that may be, falling in love is not in itself irrational but it can lead to irrational acts: the lover in pursuit of his beloved does not stop to calculate whether her vices outweigh her sometimes superficial virtues, let alone to consider his long-term priorities. Love, like other strong emotions or drives, makes people unable to think about anything except the dominant idea in their mind. they 'reject the lore of nicely calculated less or more'. Many may applaud the lover's behaviour as romantic and even admirable, but that does not concern us: it can rarely be called rational.

A psychologist who works on the emotions recently boasted that 'there are now dozens of distinguishable theories of emotionality, hundreds of volumes devoted to that topic, and tens of thousands of articles dealing with various aspects of human affect.' This is depressing news since psychologists know little more about emotion than does the layman. For this reason the second half of this chapter has conveyed little that the reader is likely to regard as new or surprising.

moral

1. Don't take important decisions when under stress or strong emotion.
2. If you are a teacher, don't set multiple choice questions; encourage the formation of general principles in your pupils.
3. Remember that every time you subdue an impulse it becomes eas-

ier to do so again.
4. If bored, restrain your impulse for excitement, particularly if you are piloting an aircraft.
5. Ask yourself whether the benefits of jogging and low-fat yogurt are really worth the misery.

10 ignoring the evidence

Anyone who has made a decision is usually extremely reluctant to change it, even in the face of overwhelming evidence that it is wrong. This can be illustrated by a well-known naval disaster that was at least in part caused by a refusal to change attitudes and to take contrary evidence into account. The following description of the events leading up to the battle of Pearl Harbor is largely derived from Janis and Mann. In the summer of 1941 Admiral Kimmel, Commander in Chief of the American Pacific Fleet, received many warnings from Washington about the possibility of war with Japan. Since his men were not fully prepared, he embarked on a course of training, but he thought that the danger was not sufficiently imminent to stop peace-time shore leave. In consequence, at weekends there were sixty American warships anchored in Pearl Harbor and the airports on Hawaii contained lines of planes wing-tip to wing-tip.

He seems to have been determined to stick to his long-term strategy of training, with which putting his sailors on full alert would interfere. On 24 November he was warned by naval headquarters that 'a surprise aggressive movement in any direction including attack on Philippines or Guam is possibility.' He held a meeting with his staff, who reassured him, presumably out of a combination of obedience, conformity and a desire to please the boss. One of them pointed out that Pearl Harbor had not been named in the message from Washington and was therefore not at risk. Although this was clearly not implied by the message, which referred to an 'attack in any direction', the meeting came to the conclusion that there was no need for further action. Kimmel was clearly defending his existing beliefs against the evidence. If he thought the message ambiguous, he should have asked Washington to clarify it. Moreover he assumed, wrongly, that the army, which manned the anti-aircraft guns, was on full alert. He had only to pick up the telephone to check his assumption, but he failed to do so, an omission which Janis interprets as caused by his reluctance to admit that he was wrong and that an attack on Pearl Harbor might occur.

Further warnings of war were received on 27 November and 3 December. The latter reported that American cryptographers had decoded a message from Japan ordering their embassies throughout the world to destroy 'most of their secret codes'. With the cleverness that enables people to interpret a message in the way that best suits their beliefs, Kimmel and his staff seized on the word 'most': surely if Japan were going to war with America they would have instructed their embassies to destroy all the secret codes.

On 6 December, the day before the battle of Pearl Harbor, there was more evidence of an impending attack. Kimmel was given emergency orders to burn all confidential documents on outlying Pacific islands. Moreover, his chief intelligence officer reported that the location of Japan's aircraft carriers was unknown, since for several days it had been impossible to intercept their radio signals. This information convinced him that the Japanese were about to attack: the question was where. Once again, his staff officers reassured him, arguing that the Japanese had not sufficient strength left over from their operations in the Asiatic area to attack Pearl Harbor.

Five hours before the Japanese attack, two American mine-sweepers saw a submarine which they assumed to be Japanese just outside Pearl Harbor. Because there was no full alert, this was not reported, but one hour before the attack, a Japanese submarine was sunk near the harbour entrance. The officer of the watch reported it to all the relevant naval officers he could contact and the message reached Admiral Kimmel. Instead of taking immediate action, he decided to wait for confirmation that the submarine really had been Japanese. The destruction of the American fleet followed. As for Admiral Kimmel, he was court-martialled and demoted.

Had Kimmel gone on full alert, he would almost certainly have saved most of his fleet. Full radar surveillance would have revealed the Japanese planes in time to take some action, and the incidents with the submarines would have been reported faster. Moreover, there would have been a proper anti-aircraft defence and the fleet would not have been sitting in Pearl Harbor over the weekend. It should be said that Kimmel had reasons for not going on full alert. The maintenance of aerial reconnaissance would have used up his short supplies of fuel, and his training programme would have been disrupted. Nevertheless, he could have adopted half-way measures, such as full anti-aircraft and radar alert, some dispersal of his ships, the cancellation of weekend leave, and the insistence that any sign of Japanese activity must be immediately reported to his headquarters. Janis and

Mann argue that in his anxiety to deny the presence of a threat, Kimmel became fixated on the two extreme alternatives of doing nothing about it and going on full alert. As we have already seen, such fixed ways of thinking tend to occur under stress.

The reluctance to relinquish one's own views permeates all walks of life. It makes doctors fail to change their diagnoses even when they are clearly wrong; it results in gross injustice, as when Home Secretaries refuse for many years to review the cases of innocent people who have been convicted; it makes scientists stick to theories that have been demonstrably falsified – even Linus Pauling, a Nobel prize-winner, persisted in his belief that massive doses of vitamin C were a cure-all for everything from the common cold to cancer long after the contradictory evidence had been obtained; and it is partially responsible for the inefficiency of most business managers, who as we have seen often pay more attention to tradition than to making the right decision.

Managers' reluctance to change their views can be illustrated from a personal experience of my own. When I was quite young, I conducted a routine piece of motivation research on a well-known brand of gin. I interviewed people throughout Britain to obtain their reactions to the bottle and label, and to ascertain the product's 'brand image'. I gave an oral presentation of my results to a party from the distiller's company, which was headed by the managing director, a large bluff Scotsman. When I said anything with which he agreed, he would turn to his colleagues and announce with much rolling of r's, 'Dr Sutherland's a very smart man. He's absolutely right.' When, however, my findings disagreed with his own views, he said, 'Rubbish, absolute rubbish.' I need never have undertaken the study for all the notice he took of it. He seemed unable to understand that his own opinions about his gin might not be shared by the gin-buying public to whom he was presumably trying to sell it. In short, he was determined to stick to his beliefs regardless of the evidence.

In what follows, I shall set out the reasons why people cling so tenaciously to their own beliefs, even when they are demonstrably false. This tendency is so pervasive that it can affect the way we see or hear. For example, look at the words in the three lines below.

PARIS

IN THE

THE SPRING

Many readers will not at first notice the mistake. Because people do not expect to find two the's in a row, they tend to read it incorrectly as, 'Paris in the spring'.

Here we are clinging unconsciously to our previous knowledge, but the example need not concern us further, for irrationality occurs not in perception but only in conscious thinking or voluntary action. It might be thought that the reason why people are so reluctant to change their beliefs is that they simply don't like to admit they are wrong. Apologies are hard to make and even to admit to oneself that one has been committed to a false belief may lower one's self-esteem. In the eyes of many, particularly of politicians, it is far better to brazen it out and find any supporting arguments no matter how bad, rather than admit to having been wrong. Although such factors undoubtedly operate, there are many more insidious reasons for not changing one's opinions, of which I deal with two in this chapter. The first is that people who have a belief often go to extreme lengths to avoid evidence that might refute it, even in situations where their prestige or self-esteem is not involved. The second is that when people do find evidence contrary to their own attitudes, they refuse to believe it.

Examine this series of numbers: 2, 4, 6. They obey a certain rule and you have to work out what the rule is. You are allowed to choose further sequences of three numbers and you are told for each whether or not it obeys the rule. You are also asked to announce the rule as soon as you are sure of it, and you will then be told whether you have got it right. If it is wrong, you go on picking more triplets until you again think you have discovered the right rule.

On being confronted with this task, most people pick as their first sequence something like 14, 16, 18; they are told it is right and pick several more sequences like 100, 102, 104. Presumably they start by thinking that the rule is, 'Even numbers ascending by two'. Since all the examples they have chosen conform to it, they eventually announce this rule, only to be told it is wrong. After some hard thinking they may decide to test a different rule like 'Any three numbers ascending in twos'. They then select 15, 17, 19 and are told that this sequence also obeys the rule. After picking some similar sequences they feel their second rule must be right and announce it, but to their dismay they are told yet again that it is wrong. They may try out many different rules, for example, any sequence whose numbers differ by plus or minus two. They test this with 11, 9, 7 and are now told this does not obey the rule. A few people do eventually find the correct rule, many do not. The rule is 'Any three numbers in ascending order' – 2, 90, 100; 1, 2, 3; or 1, 4, 1000 are all examples.

Why is it so difficult to find this simple rule? The main reason is that people try to prove that their current hypothesis is correct – they test it by picking only examples that will confirm it and do not look for ones that would disconfirm it. As the philosopher, Karl Popper, has pointed out, no general hypothesis can ever be completely confirmed – one may always come across something that is an exception to it. One of the most famous cases has already been mentioned: it is the generalisation 'All swans are white', which was only found to be false when black swans were discovered in Australia.

To establish that a rule is likely to be true, then, one must try to prove it false, but this is just what people don't do. This is a very important point and one that is poorly understood by many scientists. Because, no matter how many cases we examine, we may at some point always come across one that is an exception to the rule, no hypothesis is susceptible of logical proof, except in the trivial case where there is a limited number of items all of which can be inspected, for example, 'All the chairs in my office are black.' Although a general hypothesis can never be proven, we may yet have some faith in its validity, but the amount of faith should depend on how hard we have tried to disprove it. In our example, to disprove the rule 'Three numbers ascending in twos', it is no good just picking such sequences: we must pick triplets like 8, 11, 17 that, if found to obey the experimenter's rule, would show our hypothesis to be incorrect.

The difficulty of eliminating an incorrect hypothesis can be illustrated by the fact that many subjects simply give the same rule in a different form on being told that their current rule is wrong. I once put the problem to one of the most distinguished biologists in Britain, who proposed the rule 'Any three numbers increasing by the same amount'. After being told he was wrong, he said, 'Well, it must be any three numbers in which, starting from the last number, each of the other two decreases by the same amount.' This is of course an identical rule. Some of the subjects proposed the same incorrect rule as many as four times before abandoning it, even after they had picked several triplets that disproved the rule. They were committing the second fault dealt with here – denying the existence or relevance of contradictory evidence.

The initial study was performed in London by Peter Wason. He produced a further experiment on the same theme that has been equally seminal. He presented subjects with four cards lying on a table, two showing letters and two numbers. The cards might have on their front face:

A D 3 7

The subjects were told that every card has a number on one side and a letter on the other, and they were asked which cards they would have to turn over to establish the truth of the following rule: 'ANY CARD WITH AN A ON ONE SIDE HAS A 3 ON THE OTHER.' Before reading on, think which cards you would pick. In fact, most people pick the A and the 3. Now let us consider which cards it is rational to pick in order to establish the truth of the rule: I will call each card by the letter or number on its front.

Card A. Clearly people are right to pick this card. If it does not have a 3 on the back, the rule is disconfirmed. If it does have a 3 on the back some confirmation for the rule is provided, but bear in mind that no rule can ever be fully confirmed.
Card D. People are right not to pick this card. As far as the rule is concerned it is irrelevant what number it has on the other side.
Card 3. This is more interesting: most people pick it but they are wrong. Regardless of what letter is on the back – whether it is an A, B or Z – the rule could still be true. Remember that the rule is that all As have a 3 on the back *not* that all 3s have an A on the back. So whether or not there is an A on the back, the rule might still be correct. Since the letter on the back of this card has no bearing on the truth of the rule it is pointless to pick it.
Card 7. Few people pick this card, but it is crucial. If it turns out to have an A on the back, the rule would be disconfirmed, since it states that all As have a 3 on the other side.

Both of these ingenious experiments suggest that people tend to seek confirmation of their current hypothesis, whereas they should be trying to disconfirm it: although it is impossible ever to prove a rule with certainty, a single discrepant observation refutes it. In the first experiment, subjects picked triplets that were in line with their current hypothesis; in the second, they failed to pick a card (card 7) that might disprove their hypothesis, preferring to pick one (card 3) that might be in line with it but could not possibly disprove it. These experiments have been repeated many times, always with the same basic result. Many different tasks have been used, including one in which subjects had to discover the result of firing bullets at targets of different shapes and brightness in a game of space wars: again they made no attempt to disprove their current hypotheses about what determined the effects of the bullets.

One can ask whether it is possible to improve people's performance on such tasks. For example, in the task with the triplets of numbers, will instructing people to concentrate on disconfirming their rule improve performance? The results have been ambivalent. In some experiments performance improved slightly, in others it made little difference, since even when subjects obtained information proving their hypothesis wrong, they continued to cling to it.

Interestingly, subjects do much better on the '2, 4, 6' task if they are told the experimenter is entertaining two mutually exclusive hypotheses, called DAX and MED. DAX is the rule 'Any three numbers in ascending order' and MED is the rule 'Any three numbers that are not in ascending order'. Instead of being told when they pick a triplet that it is right or wrong, that is, it conforms or does not conform to a single rule, they are told it conforms either to the DAX rule or to the MED rule. Since the subjects were forced to develop two different rules, they were no longer fixated on one: they therefore chose a wider range of triplets each of which was bound to disconfirm one or other rule, and hence they solved the problem much more quickly. This illustrates the desirability of keeping more than one hypothesis in mind while attempting to disprove each of them, a theme to which I will return.

At this point, the reader should perhaps be warned that there is an alternative explanation of the results on the card-turning task, though it makes the outcome just as irrational. The rule states that all As have a 3 on the back. The A and the 3 are therefore before the person's mind when he has to select cards and perhaps he just selects these cards because of the availability error. There may be some truth in this explanation since Jonathan St Evans performed an experiment with four cards in which the rule was 'If there is an A on one side of the card, then there is not a 3 on the other side'. There was still a tendency to select the cards with the A and the 3 face up, but with this new rule these are in fact the right cards to choose. If there is a 3 on the other side of the A the rule is disconfirmed; if there is an A on the other side of the 3, it is also disconfirmed. Selecting the D or the 7 can yield no useful information since the rule could be true or false whatever is on their reverse faces. So here is another form of irrationality: people decide which cards to pick not on any logical basis but under the influence of which items have appeared in the rule to be tested. This is yet another example of the availability error. It is likely that the failure to pick the right cards in the original experiment was caused both by this error and by failure to seek disconfirming evidence.

* * *

There are many other experiments showing that people do not try to disprove a hypothesis they are entertaining. In one, some subjects were asked to interview a stooge to discover whether he was an extrovert, while others had to discover whether he was introverted. Both groups tended to ask the stooge questions that were in line with the suggested hypothesis. For example, those given the extrovert hypothesis might ask, 'Do you like going to parties?'; the other group might ask, 'Do you dislike noisy parties?' In both cases an affirmative answer would confirm their hypothesis.

Refusal to seek evidence that might disconfirm one's beliefs is known to operate as strongly in everyday life as in the '2, 4, 6' experiment. It has been found that people tend to associate with others who see them in the same way they see themselves. If you think well of yourself, it is hardly surprising that you will want to interact with others who share this opinion. But one study showed that American college students who thought poorly of themselves actually preferred to share rooms with other students who viewed them unfavourably than with students who held them in high regard. We seek confirmation of our own opinions of ourselves, even when they are derogatory.

There are many other examples of this tendency in real life. The supporters of a particular political party only attend meetings of their own party: they do not expose themselves to the arguments of the other side. People tend to buy newspapers that provide arguments in favour of their own political party not of the parties they oppose. Through market research it is known that someone who owns a particular make of car reads advertisements and anything else he comes across about that make, while largely ignoring anything on other marques. As to the refusal to accept unwelcome news, a recent study showed that 20 per cent of people told they had cancer simply refused to believe it.

It is, of course, not true that people always fail to look for evidence against their own beliefs, but often the exceptions prove the rule: the evidence is sought for other reasons. One such case was documented in a realistic study of resistance to the draft for the Vietnamese war by American university students. They were divided into two groups according to whether they had or had not signed an anti-draft pledge, which among other things stated, 'We cannot in conscience participate in this war. We therefore declare our determination to refuse induction as long as the United States is fighting in Vietnam.' An assessment was made of how far students who had signed the pledge and those who had not yet signed wished to read material in favour of signing or against. Those who had signed elected to read almost as much anti-pledge material as pro-pledge. When they were interviewed, it turned out that there were two reasons for doing so. First, they wanted to know what objections would be made to their decision by parents and others so that they would be in a position to counter them. Second, some of them wanted to find out how best to go about avoiding the draft, for example by becoming a conscientious objector, taking a job like teaching that would exempt them from the draft, or emigrating from America. Notice that there were further decisions to be made even though the major decision, to avoid the draft, had been taken. The anti-draft literature was read in order to take actions that followed the major decision, not in order to decide whether or not that decision was correct. There are, however, some instances in which counter-evidence may be sought for its own sake. This can occur when an attitude is very weakly held and when it is possible without loss to reverse a marginal decision, but the evidence that normally people studiously cling to their beliefs by avoiding anything that might disconfirm them is overwhelming.

We have now established two ways unconsciously used to maintain beliefs – refusal to look for contradictory evidence and refusal to believe it or act on it if it is brought to one's attention. Admiral Kimmel was guilty of both faults. He failed to seek evidence from Washington to clarify an ambiguous message, and he refused to believe that the submarine sunk outside Pearl Harbor was Japanese.

moral

1. Search for evidence against your own beliefs.
2. Try to entertain hypotheses that are antagonistic to one another.
3. Be particularly careful to take into account anything that conflicts with your beliefs.
4. Remember nobody is always right, though some people are always wrong.

11 distorting the evidence

Ignoring or failing to seek contradictory evidence are only two of the irrational methods of maintaining one's beliefs. The same effect can be and often is achieved by distorting the evidence. One example is another military fiasco, the battle of Arnhem, one of the most unnecessary disasters to British troops in the Second World War. General Montgomery, like many other generals, appears to have been more in search of personal glory than of winning the war. Because his troops were blocked before the sodden countryside of southern Holland, he conceived the plan of a parachute drop near Arnhem, where the parachutists were to seize a bridge across the Rhine before the Germans could blow it up. They were to hold it until a column of XXX Corps relieved them. As Norman Dixon and others have pointed out, the plan was ill conceived from the outset for the following reasons. First, before executing it Montgomery should have taken Antwerp, a dull but important operation. His failure to do so, activated by his desire to be first across the Rhine, allowed the German 23rd Army to escape from northern Holland and to take part in the defence of Arnhem. Second, to reach Arnhem, XXX Corps had to proceed on an exposed road flanked by a boggy landscape with waterways across which tanks could not operate. Moreover, the road was so narrow that there was only room for one tank at a time and had it become blocked at any point, for example, by a blown bridge or by an enemy attack, XXX Corps would have been severely delayed. In fact, they never reached Arnhem even after nine days, let alone the two days allocated in Montgomery's plan. Third, and most important, the whole operation depended on there being no strong German forces near Arnhem so that the parachute troops would have time to assemble before coming under attack. Added to these problems were the inadequacy of the radios used by the British and the fact that mists in England, which are to be expected in September, delayed the dropping of reinforcements for the initial parachutists.

Having decided on a plan, which was at best risky and at worst stupid, Montgomery failed to take into account further information that showed the plan was bound to fail. He was informed by SHAEF that two Panzer divisions, whose location had previously been uncertain, were encamped next to the dropping zone. He described this report as 'ridiculous'. What he meant of course was that it did not fit in with his plans and therefore he refused to believe it. His staff supported him in his folly, as staffs usually do. When an intelligence officer showed General Browning, a staff officer, pictures of German tanks in the area, he said, 'I wouldn't trouble myself about those . . . they're probably not serviceable,' a typical example of twisting the evidence to suit one's beliefs. Browning even tried to dispose of the inconvenient news by having a doctor suggest to the intelligence officer that he take some leave because he was overtired.

Both the British and the German soldiers fought with great courage, but as we have seen XXX Corps never reached Arnhem, while the British Airborne Division only gave up after losing three-quarters of those dropped. It is, of course, easy to be wise after the event, but in the case of Arnhem no great prescience was needed to be wise in advance.

The behaviour of Montgomery and his staff is reminiscent of that of Kimmel and his. The tenacity in sticking to a decision, the rejection or ingenious distortion of messages that conflict with it and the tendency of subordinates either to bolster the position of their leader or to conform to the majority view all occur in both cases.

This chapter is concerned with the tendency to distort evidence that is inconsistent with one's own beliefs, a phenomenon recognised long ago by Sir Francis Bacon, who wrote:

> The human understanding when it has once adopted an opinion draws all things else to support and agree with it. And though there be a greater number and weight of instances to be found on the other side, yet these it either neglects and despises, or else by some distinction sets aside and rejects, in order that by this great and pernicious predetermination the authority of its former conclusion may remain inviolate.

One ingenious study, which would doubtless have delighted Bacon, showed that the evaluation of evidence is highly biased by existing beliefs. The experimenters fabricated four pieces of plausible evidence on the effects of capital punishment. Subjects were told that these were the results of genuine studies on murder rates and were asked to read them. Two of the purported studies each showed the number of murders before and after the introduction of capital punishment within various states of the US. One member of this pair provided figures that suggested capital punishment was a deterrent, the other that it was not: the first showed that the murder rate had decreased in a particular state after the introduction of capital punishment, the second that it had increased. The other two studies compared murder rates at the same time between states that had introduced capital punishment and those that had not. Once again the figures were manipulated so that one of this pair of statements suggested a deterrent effect, the other did not. Since half the statements compare murder rates at different times and the rest compare rates at the same time between states, I will call them respectively *successive* and *concurrent* statements. Now clearly the evidence given in both the successive and the concurrent studies is open to objection. Over time, murder rates within the same state might vary for reasons quite other than the introduction of the death penalty, for example, an increase in the use of narcotic drugs. Equally clearly, many factors affect the murder rates current in different states other than whether a given state has the death penalty: indeed the death penalty might have been introduced in a state just because it already had a high murder rate. In short, all four studies have serious flaws.

All the subjects chosen for the experiment either strongly believed in the death penalty or were strongly against it; potential subjects who had no firm views were rejected. Each subject was first asked to read two of the four prepared statements, one of which was successive and one concurrent; one of these two statements gave evidence suggesting that the death penalty was effective, the other that it was not. Everything was neatly balanced so that some subjects had a concurrent statement favouring the death penalty and a successive statement against it, while others had a concurrent statement against it and a successive statement supporting it.

While reading the results, then, bear in mind that exactly the same studies were read by subjects in favour of the death penalty and by those against it. There were three main findings. First, all subjects thought that of the two studies presented the one that favoured their own views was 'more convincing' and 'better conducted' than the one that ran counter to their beliefs, regardless of whether they were themselves for or against the death penalty. Moreover, they noticed the obvious flaws in the studies that were against their beliefs, but they did not notice the flaws in those that were in line with their beliefs.

Second, the strength of their attitude towards capital punishment (pro or con) was measured after they had read the first of the two studies. If it was in line with their belief, their attitude was intensified; if it was against, the strength of their beliefs remained unchanged. People only accept evidence that agrees with their own views.

Third, after reading *both* studies, the subjects' original beliefs were not merely intact, they were strengthened. Those in favour of the death penalty became more in favour of it, those against became even more strongly against. The results show that when two equally strong (or weak) pieces of evidence pointing in opposite directions are encountered, completely different standards are used to evaluate the evidence that favours one's own attitudes from those used to assess the evidence against them. Moreover, evidence favouring a belief strengthens it, while when the same evidence disconfirms a belief, it is ignored: the belief remains intact.

Even attitudes that at least on the face of it are not strongly held and have no connection with a person's other beliefs are remarkably persistent: they may resist overwhelming contradictory evidence. In another experiment undertaken in the US, subjects were handed twenty-five suicide notes: they were told that some were genuinely written by people who had subsequently committed suicide while the rest were faked. Their task was to decide which were authentic. After reading each note and making their decision they were told whether they were right. In fact all the notes had been made up by the experimenter, who informed half the subjects that they were doing extremely well and the other half that their judgements were very poor. Afterwards, the subjects were thoroughly debriefed. Not only was the origin of the notes explained to them, they were told that the information about their success or failure was meaningless. They were even shown the table used by the experimenter to assign them randomly to the success or failure groups. Finally, they were asked to fill in a questionnaire on which they estimated how well they would be likely to do in the future at the same task, but this time with some genuine suicide notes. The estimates of future performance made by the subjects in the success group were very much higher than those in the failure group.

In a variant of the experiment just described, it was shown that the results were not caused by subjects being emotionally involved with their *own* degree of success or failure. A new batch of subjects watched stooges performing the same task. Again, some stooges were told they were being highly successful, others that they were failing miserably: the genuine subjects observed all this going on. When the stooges had completed the task, they were told, with the subjects still watching, that it was all a trick and the information they had received was meaningless. Amazingly, the observers still clung to their beliefs about which stooges were good and which were poor even after listening to the debriefing. Before rating the stooges on their ability at the task, a second group of subjects took part in a lengthy discussion of the way in which beliefs tend to persist despite contradictory evidence. This discussion did lessen the effect considerably, though there was still a slight tendency to think that the stooges who had been told they were successful had in reality performed better than those who had been told they were failures. This experiment shows, then, that people's opinions about others, as well as their opinions about themselves, are extremely resistant to change.

The findings are supported by many similar experiments. For example, subjects were told there were two baskets, one containing 60 per cent red balls and 40 per cent black, the other 40 per cent red and 60 per cent black. They were presented with one of the baskets and asked to discover which it was by drawing balls from it: each ball was replaced after it had been drawn. After a few draws they formed a hypothesis that it was one basket or the other. When they next drew a red ball and a black ball in succession, their hypothesis was strengthened. If they thought it was the basket with 60 per cent red balls, drawing a red and a black ball strengthened this belief. Equally, drawing the same two balls confirmed the hypothesis that there were 60 per cent black balls for those who already believed it. Now, clearly, drawing a red and a black ball has no bearing on which basket it is: these two draws are equally likely from either basket. This is a further instance of people interpreting evidence that is completely neutral as supporting their beliefs.

These experiments demonstrate convincingly that one cannot account for the persistence of belief merely in terms of people's desire to prop up their self-esteem. What emotional investment can subjects have in maintaining their beliefs in how good others are at spotting genuine or false suicide notes after being told that all the notes were faked? The persistence of false beliefs is, therefore, caused at least in part by a failure to think correctly not by emotional factors.

If, in the face of overwhelming counter-evidence, people are so reluctant to change their views about something as trivial as their own or others' ability to judge whether a suicide note is genuine, how much more resistant must they be to changing deeply held attitudes towards important matters that fit with a whole set of their beliefs. For example, a belief in Conservatism or an adherence to the Republican party includes favouring a host of different but overlapping policies, such as free enterprise; a minimum role played by the state; the promotion of self-sufficiency in individuals; minimal support for the poor, the sick and the old; low taxation and so on. These beliefs form a coherent pattern, and they have usually been developed and refined by the individual over a long period of time. I write 'developed' not 'thought out' because in most cases the beliefs will have evolved as a result of entirely irrational factors such as a person's position in life and the beliefs of his immediate associates.

The desire to confirm a current hypothesis even affects people's memories. In one experiment subjects read a detailed description of a woman. Two days later some were asked to assess whether she was a suitable candidate for a job selling houses in an estate agency. In most people's eyes this is an extrovert occupation. Others were asked whether she would make a good research librarian, a post normally thought to be suitable for someone fairly introverted. The subjects had to give reasons for their opinions. Those asked whether she would make a good estate agent recalled from the original description many more of her extroverted aspects, while those judging whether she would make a good research librarian recalled mainly her introverted traits. That is to say, subjects remembered just those aspects of the woman that favoured the hypothesis they were asked to entertain. Of course, since one is the opposite of the other both extroversion and introversion affect her suitability for each position.

In this and the previous chapter, I have demonstrated that beliefs – and even current hypotheses that there is no reason to hold strongly – are remarkably resistant to change. I have also outlined four reasons, all of which have received experimental support. First, people consistently avoid exposing themselves to evidence that might disprove their beliefs. Second, on receiving evidence against their beliefs, they often refuse to believe it. Third, the existence of a belief distorts people's interpretation of new evidence in such a way as to make it consistent with the belief. Fourth, people selectively remember items that are in line with their beliefs. To these four reasons one might add a fifth, the desire to protect one's self-esteem. These factors even when combined do not seem sufficient to explain the tenacity of the beliefs held in the experiment on suicide notes. The contrary evidence (that the information given to the subjects about their successes and failures was completely meaningless) was emphasised as strongly as possible; it would be hard to refuse to believe the evidence that all the suicide notes had been rigged; this new evidence could not be interpreted as supporting the subjects' beliefs; lapses of memory could have played no part; and it seems unlikely that a person's self-esteem would be much affected by altering his opinion of the capacity of stooges to judge suicide notes.

A sixth and highly ingenious mechanism to account for the persistence of this and all other irrational beliefs has been proposed. People excel at inventing explanations for events or phenomena. For example, if a woman making judgements on suicide notes is told she is doing very well, she is likely to look for reasons why she is so good.

Her familiarity with the writings of a famous novelist who recently committed suicide, her part-time job as a paramedical assistant, and her generally 'open' relationship with her parents and friends all might serve to explain her high level of ability at a task requiring social sensitivity.

A woman who has failed at the task may on the other hand explain her failure by thinking to herself that she has never met a suicide and has never read a suicide note. How could she possibly expect to distinguish genuine from false notes? Despite the debriefing, subjects may cling to the explanations they have invented, and hence think they are especially good or bad at the task.

It has been demonstrated that in ordinary conversation giving explanations for phenomena is extremely common: in one study about 15 per cent of all remarks were attempts to provide an explanation. Of more importance, it has been shown that people are so facile at making up explanations that they can use almost any event in a person's past life to explain why he did something later on. Subjects were given a genuine potted biography of a man and were then asked to explain something he did subsequently in terms of his previous history; for example they might be asked to account for his committing suicide, having a hit-and-run accident, joining the Peace Corps or becoming a politician. One of the events recorded in one of the biographies was that the man had joined the navy as a youth. Subjects who were asked to explain why he later became a politician thought that joining the navy was a mark of gregariousness and the desire to serve his country. On the other hand, the subjects who were asked to explain why he committed suicide also mentioned that he had joined the navy, but they thought that was a sign of running away from his family and friends and of wanting to punish them: suicide can be regarded as running away from life and as a punitive act against close friends and relatives. After the subjects had given their explanations, they were all told that the event they had to explain had not really happened and were asked what was the likelihood of it and of a number of other events occurring to the man in the future.

Needless to say, each subject thought on the basis of the biography that the event he had been asked to explain was the most likely.

There is a further decisive experiment demonstrating that the irrational persistence of a belief can be caused by the refusal to abandon a good story concocted to explain something a person believes to be true. Subjects were told about two firemen, one of whom had been very successful and the other very unsuccessful at his job. Half the subjects were told that the first was prepared to take a lot of risks, while the second was not. The other half were told just the opposite. Later they were all informed that the two firemen did not exist and that the experimenter had simply made everything up. Nevertheless, when asked, they still drew inferences based on the phoney information they had been given. If they had been told that the risk-taking fireman was successful, they thought firemen should be picked for their willingness to take risks. The crucial part of the experiment was that some subjects were asked to explain to the experimenter the connection between risk-taking and being a good (or bad) fireman. The beliefs of these subjects after debriefing were even more strongly influenced by what they had been told. They had been forced to articulate their explanations in more detail than the others and hence they clung to their original false belief even more strongly.

So people first concoct an arbitrary but plausible explanation for something they are told is true and then they continue to believe it even when they are told the original information was false. In providing explanations people are too clever by half, certainly too clever to be rational. One only has to listen to the specious arguments of politicians to realise how cunning people are at twisting the evidence to suit their own beliefs. But the very coherence of the explanations people fabricate makes them reluctant to part with them. Doubtless Montgomery had concocted elaborate reasons for believing that his plan of campaign would be successful: hence he could not readily abandon it.

moral

1. Don't distort new evidence: consider carefully whether it could be interpreted as disconfirming your beliefs rather than supporting them.
2. Be wary of your memory: you are likely to recall whatever fits with your current views.
3. Remember that changing your mind in the light of new evidence is a sign of strength not weakness.

4. Beware of being influenced by any explanations you may have concocted in support of your own beliefs.
5. Don't adopt the Greek system of ignoring bad tidings by killing the messenger – or sending him on sick leave.

12   making the wrong connections

Why in the present era when science flourishes as never before, are there so many thriving quack nostrums, such as homeopathy, naturopathy, biodynamics, herbalism, radionics and dietetics? Even psychoanalysis is still with us despite all the evidence that its techniques are worthless. How is it that psychoanalysts, most of whom are presumably honest men, continue to believe that their treatment is helpful? There are many reasons. First, they have themselves been through a lengthy, expensive and usually painful training analysis: to justify undergoing this experience, they must, as we have seen, believe that some good has come of it. Second, patients often get better of their own accord and the analyst will of course believe that he has wrought the improvement. Third, many of the patients who are being made worse by their treatment simply drop out, whereupon the analyst convinces himself that the patient would eventually (some analyses last five years or more) have improved. Fourth, the analyst may fail either to keep or to consult careful records of his patients. Fifth, he has no access to the records of patients who had other forms of treatment or even no treatment at all, so he cannot tell whether they fared better or worse than his own. Finally, in the case of patients who show no sign of improving, the analyst can – and to my certain knowledge often does – believe that it is the patient's own fault for failure to co-operate.

This is an extreme case of faulty reasoning about causes and connections. Analysis *per se* is rarely if ever the cause of an improvement in mental health, though an empathetic analyst may sometimes do some good, despite the futility of psychoanalytic techniques. There is of course a good deal of unconscious rationalisation going on in the analyst's mind, but for present purposes, I want to concentrate on the fact that he fails to seek out information about patients similar to his own who do not have psychoanalysis. Most neuroses, and particularly the commonest form, depression, are self-limiting: the patient recovers regardless of his treatment. When controlled studies are run comparing the effects of analysis with what is called a placebo treatment (in which someone sees the patient, listens to his problems and makes supportive noises without attempting any real therapy), it turns out that the placebo treatment does as well as or better than psychoanalysis.

This chapter will consider the mistakes people make in determining the correct associations between events; mistakes about causal connections will be dealt with in the following chapter. The analyst erroneously connects his treatment with improvement in the patient's condition. Making the wrong connection between events in this way is a widespread fault: it is known as 'illusory correlation'.

Consider a physician who is investigating a particular disease. It presents certain symptoms, all of which occur with other diseases: none of them can be used to diagnose it with certainty in the early stages, but there is one that he thinks is more diagnostic than any of the others. To establish that this particular symptom really is specifically associated with the disease, he keeps records of all the patients whom he suspects might develop the illness. When he has collected enough cases, it turns out that eighty of those with the symptom subsequently turn out to have the disease and twenty do not. Because four times as many people with the symptom contract the illness as do those without it, he concludes that the symptom is a good though not a perfect indicator of the presence of the disease. Is he justified? The answer is no. As it happens he meets a friend who is a statistician: he tells the friend of his discovery, but the statistician is unimpressed. He points out that the doctor cannot conclude anything by looking only at patients who have the symptom: he must compare the frequency of the disease when the symptom is present with its frequency when the symptom is absent. The doctor goes back to his files cursing himself for being so foolish and finds that forty of the patients without the symptom developed the illness, while ten did not. He believes that this supports his case. After all twice as many patients (eighty) with the symptom subsequently exhibited the disease as did those without it (forty). But the doctor's reasoning is again wrong. Examination of Table I will show why. It is clear that the same proportion (four-fifths) of patients develop the illness whether they have the symptom (eighty out of a hundred) or whether they do not (forty out of fifty). The symptom is therefore totally unconnected with the disease.

To put this more generally, nothing can be concluded about the association between two events (Event A and Event B) unless we take into account all of the four figures that represent the frequencies with which Event A and Event B are present and absent. These are:

Event A and Event B
Event A but not Event B
Event B but not Event A
Neither Event A nor Event B

The quickest way to assimilate how frequently each of the four cases occurs is to set out their frequencies in a 'two-by-two table', of the sort shown here. The reason for the doctor's mistakes is that he ignored the negative cases. His first mistake arose from not considering what happened to patients without the symptom: he ignored the second line in the table. His second mistake arose from ignoring the ten patients who had neither the symptom nor the disease (the bottom right-hand figure in the table).

Table 1

	Illness	No illness	Total
Symptom present	80	20	100
Symptom absent	40	10	50

As I shall demonstrate, this failure to notice negative evidence is common even among knowledgeable people. It is presumably caused by the availability error. The occurrence of an event is more striking (available) than the non-occurrence: patients who have neither the symptom nor the disease are less striking than those who have one or other or both.

There are many experiments demonstrating the failure to make correct decisions about whether two things are associated. In one, nurses were asked to look through a hundred cards each of which reported a single case history. The patients fell into the same four groups just discussed – they had either a particular symptom and a disease, the symptom but not the disease, the disease but not the symptom, or neither the symptom nor the disease. The number of patients in each category is shown in Table 2.

Table 2: Incidence of symptom and disease for 100 patients

		Disease	
		Present	Absent
	Present	37	33
Symptom			
	Absent	17	13

When this table is examined carefully, it is clear there is no association between the symptom and the disease: the percentage of patients who developed the disease was roughly the same whether the symptom was present or absent. Yet 85 per cent of the nurses who examined the cards summarising all the individual cases thought they showed that the symptom was diagnostic of the disease. Once again, in this sort of task people tend to concentrate on the positive information: the nurses were more impressed by the thirty-seven cases that had both the symptom and the disease than by the other cases shown on the cards.

Journalists are particularly remiss in their failure to use all four figures. An article in the American magazine *The Week* argued that motorists were four times more likely to be killed if they drove at 7 p.m. than if they drove at 7 a.m., because there were four times as many deaths on the road in the evening as in the morning. The argument is fallacious: it ignores the number of motorists not killed in the morning and in the evening (the negative cases). In fact, there were four times as many cars on the roads in the evening as in the morning: once this is taken into account, it is clear that the risk for the individual motorist is the same at each time of day. *Which?*, the British consumer magazine, argues that drunk drivers cause deaths because 'one in six road deaths in Britain happened in an accident in which drunk driving was involved': this statement cannot be interpreted unless one knows what proportion of all drivers were drunk. Again, a leader in *The Independent* argues that 'Rail travel is safer than road. More people are killed on the roads in the course of a week than die in railway accidents in the course of a year.' The conclusion may be true, but it does not follow from the premises: the only meaningful comparison is in terms of deaths per passenger mile. Once again, the negative cases are omitted the train passengers and car drivers who were not killed. One could give innumerable other instances. Suffice it to say that by propagating such sloppy arguments about connections, newspapers set a poor example to the public.

So far I have argued that people make mistakes in interpreting data on the co-occurrence of two events mainly because they tend to ignore the negative instances. In real life, however, we are rarely presented with a tidy set of figures. Rather we are exposed at irregular and often lengthy intervals to instances of each of the four cases needed to form a rational judgement on the association between two events. Consider for example the difficulty of determining whether people with blue eyes are more innocent than those with brown eyes.

Since nobody can retain figures in the head for any length of time, this connection could only be established by keeping careful records of all four cases as they are encountered: blue eyes – innocent; blue eyes – not innocent; brown eyes innocent; brown eyes – not innocent.

The irrationality of human judgement when such figures are not systematically assembled is demonstrated by a set of remarkable studies performed in Wisconsin by Loren and Jean Chapman. Part of the problem is that when trying to decide what goes with what, people almost invariably bring to the task prior expectations that distort their interpretation of their observations.

The experiments were on the use of projective tests. These tests purportedly reveal characteristics of a person (usually someone mentally disordered) that he would not openly disclose either because he feels ashamed of them or because (on Freudian theory) they have been repressed and hence he has no conscious access to them. One of the best-known projective tests is the Rorschach. Patients are asked to say what they see in a series of complex ink blots, one example of which is shown here.

They may see this blot as a monster or as a woman who looks like a bat, or their response may be made only to parts of it, for example, they may see the central part as a man upside down with a large bottom and the outside part as a woman with prominent breasts who has been beheaded.

Psychologists and psychiatrists who use the Rorschach claim to be able to tell from the nature of the responses to the different ink blots whether a person is a homosexual, whether he has paranoia, whether he is a potential suicide and so on. Responses that refer to the rectum or buttocks, to feminine clothing, to the sexual organs, or ones that involve seeing a person of indeterminate sex (for example, 'I guess this is a man or maybe it's a woman') or of confused sex ('Looks like a man below the waist, but a woman above') are all supposed to be diagnostic of homosexuality. Any response of a certain type (e.g. one referring to the anus) is categorised as a 'sign'. Careful research has shown that in fact the five signs listed above are given just as frequently by heterosexuals as by homosexuals: there is no difference whatsoever. Indeed as a diagnostic tool the Rorschach along with other projective tests is virtually worthless and yet it has been very extensively used and indeed still is (one estimate is that six million Rorschach tests are given a year) – a glaring example of irrationality among psychologists.

The Chapmans set out to find out why clinicians should continue to believe that the responses made in this test are diagnostic of particular traits, despite the carefully collected evidence that they are not. They concentrated on the diagnosis of homosexuality. They began by circulating a questionnaire to clinical psychologists to discover which signs they thought were most strongly associated with homosexuality. Those most frequently reported corresponded to the conventional five signs already given: they were references to the anus, to feminine clothing, to male or female sexual organs, to people of uncertain sex, and to people having attributes of both sexes. Although none of these responses is made more often by homosexuals than by heterosexuals, the clinicians were convinced that they had discovered an association with homosexuality in the course of their own clinical experience.

Now it is obvious that these responses to the Rorschach ink blots are just the sort that one might naïvely expect a homosexual to give – each of them is associated in our own minds with homosexuality. To check this, the Chapmans constructed a list made up of the same five responses and eighty others that were thought by the clinicians *not* to be diagnostic of homosexuality. They showed the list to over thirty undergraduates, asking them to rate how far each of the eighty-five responses was connected in their minds with homosexuality. The undergraduates, who of course had had no clinical experience, picked exactly the same five responses as the clinicians as diagnostic of homosexuality. This demonstrates that the clinicians had learned nothing from their clinical experience: they had been influenced only by their false preconceptions.

As a matter of fact, there are two responses which rather unexpectedly are genuinely given slightly more frequently by homosexuals than by heterosexuals: they are seeing a blot as a monster or as something that is part animal, part human. The Chapmans called these two types of response 'valid signs' of homosexuality, and used the terms 'invalid signs' for the five responses mistakenly thought to indicate homosexuality.

In a further experiment, a different set of undergraduates was given thirty cards to examine. Each card contained a Rorschach ink blot, the sign allegedly made to it by an imaginary patient and two emotional disorders from which he suffered: the subjects were told the cards described genuine cases. Each subject was presented with a total of four different emotional problems, including homosexuality, and five different signs – one invalid sign, the two valid signs and two neutral signs (for example, food or plants). Each of the five invalid signs was presented to different subjects. The pairing of the signs and the disorders was random so that there was no connection in the cards between any sign and any personality trait. The following written instructions were given.

> I am going to show you a series of ink blots, one at a time. On each ink blot you will find a typed statement of what one patient saw on this blot and also what his two chief emotional problems are. Each of these thirty cards represents a different patient. You will see what thirty different patients said they saw on a card. Now let me tell you what I want you to do. Please carefully study each ink blot and the statement of what the patient said he saw in it. Also study the statement of the patient's two severe emotional problems. When everyone has looked at all of the cards, I am going to give you a questionnaire in which I will ask you about the kinds of things seen by patients with each kind of problem.

After they had examined the cards, the subjects were asked to say whether they had noticed any kind of response that was most often made by homosexuals. The undergraduates mistakenly thought that each of the five invalid signs (those having to do with the anus, feminine clothing, confusion between the sexes, and so on) were more often paired with the trait of homosexuality than the other signs, thus demonstrating 'illusory correlation'.

The Chapmans' next experiment produced an even more sensational and upsetting result. They again showed undergraduates thirty cards, but this time the two *valid* signs (that is those having a genuine association with homosexuality – 'monster' and 'part animal, part human') were present and were *always* paired with the trait of homosexuality. Despite the complete correlation between these signs and homosexuality the students completely failed to notice the association. Whereas 17 per cent of them thought these two signs occurred most frequently with homosexuality, 50 per cent picked the invalid signs, that is those associated in their mind (but not in reality) with homosexuality, although these signs had not been selectively paired with homosexuality on the cards.

Before dealing further with the implications of these findings, it should be noted that the Chapmans performed a second series of similar experiments that had identical results. In these, they used a different projective test, known as the 'Draw-a-Person Test'. The patient is required to draw a picture of a person and the picture is then interpreted by the therapist. Therapists – and also laymen when questioned – believe that the drawing can reveal something about the character of the person who drew it: for example, they may think that distortion of the eyes indicates paranoia; that dependent patients emphasise the mouth or draw women or children; that impotent patients draw powerful-looking men and so on. In fact it has been repeatedly shown that none of these associations exist; indeed, as far as we know, it is impossible to learn anything about someone's personality from the way he draws a person. Yet as in the case of the Rorschach test, psychologists have used the Draw-a-Person Test for forty years and many irrationally continue to do so.

The Chapmans have provided a striking demonstration of the difficulty people have in spotting that two events occur together. It might be thought that it was simply the subjects' prior expectations about the five invalid signs that caused them to ignore the perfect correlation between homosexuality and the valid signs. But when the Chapmans ran further experiments without the misleading invalid signs appearing at all, the subjects still failed to detect that the valid signs were associated with homosexuality, even though they were again always paired with it on the cards.

These startling results suggest that we have little or no ability to determine what goes with what unless we convert our observations to figures. When we bring preconceptions to the judgement, we are heavily influenced by them. But even when we have no preconceptions, we fail to see associations that if represented in numbers should be completely obvious. Moreover, in the experiments described, the conditions were almost ideal. Since each subject viewed each card for a minute, there was no time pressure. Since the experiment only lasted half an hour, there was no strain on memory. Since for any one subject, there were only five signs and four emotional problems, it should have been fairly easy to see the connections between the valid signs and homosexuality. Compare this with the task of a psychiatrist or psychologist trying to determine which responses go with which traits. He may be under time pressure; it may be weeks between the Rorschach testing and discovering whether the predicted emotional problem is present; and finally, there are many more than five Rorschach signs, and a vast number of possible emotional problems.

The Chapmans' results obviously have implications for our everyday life judgements. Is there really a connection between blue eyes and innocence, or is it that they call to mind the eyes of a newborn baby and are associated with blue skies and gentle seas? Are red-haired people really prone to anger, or is it just that red is the colour of fire, which reminds us of anger? Of more importance, one would have to make very careful observations and keep detailed records if one wanted to support or disprove stereotypes, such as the Jews being mean or the blacks lazy, and these observations and records would have to include a random sample of people who were not Jews or blacks.

The errors made by the Chapmans' subjects seem so crude that you may well feel you could never make them yourself. If this is so, you are exceptional. It has recently been found that 85 per cent of the largest companies in continental Europe make the same mistake at considerable cost to themselves: they employ graphologists in personnel selection. In the USA 3,000 companies, including most banks, employ graphologists. What could be more natural than to believe that a person's handwriting reflects his character? The belief may be natural, but it is wrong. A recent review of studies on graphology concluded that the validity of graphologists' assessments of personality was 'virtually zero'. In one study an 'expert' graphologist was given a large number of samples of handwriting in which the same writing was presented more than once. She gave different and completely unrelated responses to different samples of the same handwriting. Graphology does little if any better than chance, but because it sounds plausible and perhaps because it is a little *outré* it has fooled the majority of Europe's major companies. There is no record of the number of businessmen who take major decisions by reading tea-leaves, but it would be just as rational to do so as to use graphology.

Even when we are not influenced by preconceptions, it is virtually impossible to spot an association between two events unless careful records are kept. Consider, for example, how many years it took the medical profession to uncover the association between smoking and lung cancer: this is a particularly telling case since it is natural to suppose that if smoking damages any part of the body, it will be the lungs. And yet the connection went unsuspected for centuries until Doll and Peto collected careful figures.

I have now covered three reasons for the errors made in spotting connections – failure to attend to the negative cases when all four possibilities are set out in figures; being misled by expectations; and the inability to spot a genuine correlation (even when not misled by expectations) caused by our being unable to maintain several numbers in the head at once. There are two further causes of error, the first of which mainly concerns judgements of a person's characteristics.

When observing a group of people, we pay particular attention to any member of the group who is different from the rest, for example a woman in a group of men or a black in a group of whites or – in both cases – vice versa. There is nothing irrational about that. However, when subjects were shown a videotape or slides of interactions within such groups, they subsequently evaluated the person who differed from the rest and what he or she had done or said in much more extreme terms than they did the others. In such experiments the subjects see the odd person out more positively or negatively than they see the other members of the group. If the very same person is shown in a group of people similar to himself, there is no tendency for this exaggeration to occur even though he behaves in exactly the same way as he did when he was the odd man out.

Finally, in making connections there is a similar but even more extreme form of irrationality. When each member of one set of items is paired with a member of another set and each set has an odd member, people often wrongly think that the unusual member of one set has been selectively paired with the unusual member of the other. This was first demonstrated by Loren Chapman who showed subjects pairs of words such as:

shy – coin
man – dark
trousers – book
clock – carpet

Notice that the words in each set are all monosyllabic, except for two disyllables. Subjects thought that the odd words out (the disyllables) had been paired together much more frequently than they in fact had.

David Hamilton followed up this finding. Subjects were told that they would receive information on slides about the members of two different groups of people, Group A and Group B. Each slide contained the name of a person, the group to which he belonged and a statement about him that was either favourable or derogatory. Two such statements were, 'John, a member of Group A, canvassed his neighbourhood soliciting for charity' and 'Bob, a member of Group B, lost his temper and hit a neighbour he was arguing with.' There were more favourable statements than unfavourable, though the same proportion of favourable and unfavourable statements was made about each group. The statements themselves therefore provided no reason for subjects to evaluate one group more highly than the other. When subjects were asked to say what they thought about the groups, they saw Group B as being worse than Group A and falsely assigned more of the unfavourable statements to Group B than to Group A. They had associated the unusual (derogatory) statements with the group that had fewer members: those statements and that group stood out in their minds. A similar result is obtained if there are fewer favourable statements than unfavourable: the smaller group is now viewed in a better light than the larger. Given the minimal difference in the groups (merely the difference between the labels Group A and Group B) this is a remarkable result. As mentioned in Chapter 5, it goes some way to explaining prejudicial stereotyping. Minority groups such as blacks and Jews are more conspicuous than majority ones: in addition, bad behaviour – erratic driving, meanness, laziness – is more conspicuous (rarer) than normal behaviour. There is likely, therefore, to be a tendency to associate bad behaviour with minorities, even though it is no more frequent in their members than in those of the majority group.

The two effects just described – exaggerating the qualities of a person who stands out from others and associating a rare quality with a rare type of person – are further reasons why we find it so difficult to form the right associations. They are of course also further examples of irrational thinking.

moral

1. If you want to determine whether one event is associated with another, never attempt to keep the co-occurrence of the events in your head. Maintain a written tally of the four possibilities set out on page 115.
2. Remember that A is only associated with B if B occurs a higher percentage of the time in the presence of A than in its absence.
3. Pay particular attention to negative cases.
4. Be careful not to associate things together because of your expectations or because they are unusual.
5. Flee any psychologist or psychiatrist who asks you to do a Rorschach test: he does not know his job.

13 mistaken connections in medicine

Misinterpreting the probabilities of events occurring together can be extremely damaging, as David Eddy demonstrates in his devastating account of the mistakes made by doctors in the detection of breast cancer. Before giving a résumé of his research it is necessary to introduce the concept of 'conditional probability'. All that this portentous expression means is the probability that one thing is true, given that we know some other thing to be true. As an example, consider a person who always carries an umbrella, either because he hates to get wet or because he is a City gent. Now it is clear that the probability of his carrying an umbrella if it rains is 1.0 (certainty): since he always carries an umbrella he will be carrying one whenever it rains. Consider now a different probability, namely, the probability that if he carries his umbrella it will rain, and let us assume it rains one fifth of the time. This probability (known as the inverse probability of the first one) is only .2 (that is, it will rain on one fifth of the occasions on which he is carrying his umbrella). It is important to be clear that except under special circumstances the inverse probability is not the same as the original probability. As we shall see, many workers in medicine believe that it is and as a result have caused much harm. Instead of using the phrase 'the probability of X (raining) if Y (carrying an umbrella)', the expression 'the probability of X given Y' is often employed, and for short it is written by mathematicians as 'pX/Y'. As will become clear, conditional probabilities can be derived from the figures in two-by-two tables, which were discussed in the previous chapter.

The technique that Eddy discusses is mammography, an X-ray of the breast designed to detect breast cancer. Such X-rays, like most others, cannot be interpreted with complete certainty. Medical research workers evaluate the accuracy of a given test and publish their results for the benefit of the doctors who will use it. One such result is that if a woman has breast cancer, there is a .92 probability of her test results being positive (that is, indicating that she has cancer); in other words on average ninety-two women out of every hundred with breast cancer will have a positive result on mammography. The same research worker found that women without breast cancer have a .88 probability of testing negative. (The figures vary slightly from one study to another: they depend among other things on the state of the X-ray apparatus and the skill of the radiologist.) You may wonder why the evaluation of diagnostic tests is given in this way: what the doctor confronted with the result of a mammography needs to know is not the probability that a woman with cancer will test positive, but the probability that a woman who tests positive has cancer (and also the probability that a woman who tests negative does not have cancer). As will be shown, the latter two probabilities vary with the population of women being tested: women who routinely take the test as a screening procedure have probabilities that are much lower than those of women who already have symptoms and are sent by their doctor to have the test. Medical textbooks and journals, therefore, quote the probability of a positive or negative outcome on the test for patients with and without cancer, since these figures are more stable.

Unfortunately, however, many doctors confuse the two sets of probabilities. In a recent survey undertaken in the US, it was found that 95 per cent of doctors think that because the probability of testing positive if a woman has breast cancer is .92, the probability of having breast cancer if the test is positive is also .92. This is completely erroneous: indeed the true probability of having breast cancer given a positive test may be as low as .01 (that is, one woman in a hundred instead of nine in ten). 95 per cent of the doctors tested made the elementary mistake of thinking that the inverse conditional probability is the same as the original, a mistake exposed in the first paragraph of this chapter.

The problem is illustrated in the two tables (based on David Eddy): Table 3 shows the results of mammography on 1,000 women who had the test because their doctor on the basis of physical symptoms thought they might have cancer. Table 4 presents results from women who had it as part of a routine medical check-up. The tables show the total numbers of women having positive and negative results who subsequently turned out to have cancer or not to have it. In both tables the proportion of women with cancer who tested positive is approximately the same (.92 in Table 3, that is 74 out of 80, and 1.0 in Table 4 – since in this table only one woman had cancer, an accurate estimate of probability cannot be obtained). In both tables women without cancer test negative with a probability of .88 (810 out of 920 in Table 3 and 879 out of 999 in Table 4). But the two tables yield dramatically different inverse probabilities. In Table 3 the probability that if the test is positive the woman has cancer is .4 (110 out of 184), while in Table 4 it is less than .01 (1 out of 121), which is under one in a hundred. Similar reasoning shows that the probability of a woman who tests negative having cancer is .01 in Table 3 and zero in Table 4.

Table 3: Presence of cancer and results of X-rays in 1,000 women who have abnormal physical examinations.

	Women with cancer	Women with no cancer	Total
Women with positive mammography	74	110	184
Women with negative mammography	6	810	816
Total	80	920	1000

The conditional probabilities are:
Positive mammography given cancer: 74 out of 80 = .92
Negative mammography given no cancer: 810 out of 920 = .88
Cancer given positive mammography: 74 out of 184 = .40
Cancer given negative mammography: 6 out of 816 = .01

Table 4: Presence of cancer and results of X-ray in 1,000 women who have no symptoms.

	Women with cancer	Women with no cancer	Total
Women with positive mammography	1	120	121
Women with negative mammography	0	879	879
Total	1	999	1000

The conditional probabilities are:
Positive mammography given cancer: 1 out of 1 = 1.00
Negative mammography given no cancer: 879 out of 999 = .88
Cancer given positive mammography: 1 out of 121 = 0.01
Cancer given negative mammography: 0 out of 879 = 0.0

The differences in the probabilities yielded by the two tables stem from the difference in the initial probability of a woman having cancer. Obviously if some symptoms are already present (Table 3) and therefore the chances of cancer are quite high, a higher proportion of women will be correctly diagnosed as having cancer than when the general population is screened: this accounts for the massive difference between .4 correct positive diagnoses in Table 3 and .01 in Table 4. But, as we have seen, many doctors simply apply the wrong probabilities – they assume that the probability of having cancer if the test is positive is .92 and the probability of not having it if the test is negative is .88.

Eddy gives a large number of quotations from medical books and journals in which doctors have in this fashion confused the probability of having a positive test given breast cancer with that of having breast cancer given a positive test. Here is a quotation from a reputable medical source, the *Journal of Gynaecology and Obstetrics*: '1. In women with proved carcinoma of the breast, in whom mammograms are performed, there is no X-ray evidence of malignant disease in approximately one out of five patients examined (that is, the probability of a negative test if the woman has cancer is .80). 2. If then on the basis of a negative mammogram, we are to defer biopsy of a solid lesion of the breast, then there is a one in five chance that we are deferring biopsy of a malignant lesion.' The author confuses the probability of a negative test given cancer, statement 1, with the probability of cancer given a negative test, statement 2: astonishingly – for he is not merely a doctor but a doctor conducting research – he thinks the two figures must be the same. Another author, dealing with mass screening of women for breast cancer, argues that since only 85 per cent of those with a negative test are actually free from cancer, the remaining 15 per cent 'will wind up with incorrect interpretations of the findings, or more likely, their mammograms will simply fail to demonstrate the disease. This means that 15 per cent of the women will be given a false sense of security if they are told their X-rays are normal. It is difficult to assess the harm done to this group . . .' Once again, he has confused the probability of the test being negative given no cancer with the probability of not having cancer given a negative test. If he were right, about 1,500 women out of every 10,000 taking the test would go away with a false sense of security: but he is not right – Eddy calculates that in mass screening as few as one woman in 10,000 who tests negative will in reality have cancer. This sort of faulty reasoning about incorrect diagnosis has led some physicians to argue that no screening should be carried out.

Whether doctors acknowledge it or not, most medical diagnosis relies on probabilities, though they may well not be expressed in figures. A doctor may think that a lump on the breast is almost certainly benign, probably benign, possibly malignant, probably malignant, or almost certainly malignant. He bases his judgement on how many cases similar to the present one have turned out to have cancer and on indications given in the medical textbooks and journals of how far each symptom is a good predictor of cancer. If he suspects breast cancer, he may order a mammography. The next step in diagnosis would be a breast biopsy: this is an unpleasant surgical procedure, necessitating a general anaesthetic that is fatal in about two cases out of 10,000 and that can have nasty consequences.

If doctors were rational, how would they decide whether to perform a breast biopsy? There is a risk in having one and there is a risk in allowing breast cancer to go untreated. If the risk of cancer were one in a million no woman would elect to have a breast biopsy and no doctor would recommend it; if the risk were thought to be one in two probably all women would have one. The cut-off probability below which women would choose not to have a biopsy must lie somewhere in between. In fact, Eddy produces evidence suggesting that over 30 per cent of women decline a biopsy if the chances of cancer are less than about one in six. The decision whether to have one should rest with the patient after being given the fullest information that the doctor can impart (something doctors are often loath to do, another curious piece of irrationality, since as we shall see the more information given to patients, the better they fare). The information should include the likelihood of cancer being present, and the likely consequences of having the breast biopsy and of not having it if it turns out that the patient actually has cancer. Now, if the doctor gets his estimate of the probability of a patient having breast cancer wildly wrong on the basis of a mammogram (as many of them do), a large number of patients will be submitted to unnecessary biopsies.

Doctors should put the result of the mammography together with other evidence including the presence or absence of physical symptoms, but the confused statements in medical journals suggest that many are quite unable to do this. Here is an extraordinary extract from the prestigious *Archives of Surgery*. 'The patients have symptoms referrable to the breast but no discrete mass or "dominant lesion" . . . In this category, the surgeon and clinician will find the greatest yield from mammography because here the modality is *confirmatory*. Here the mammogram will give confirmation and encouragement, if the clinical impression is benign. It should not, however, dissuade him from a prior opinion to biopsy.' In other words, if the mammogram is positive, do a biopsy, but if it is not, simply ignore it, and go ahead with the biopsy anyway. This reasoning, like so much of that in the other quotations from medical sources given by Eddy, is completely topsy-turvy: it fails to take account of the fact that a patient with a negative mammography may only have a very slight chance of having cancer. Eddy provides many other instances of such reasoning, for example, from the same journal, 'To defer biopsy of a clinically benign lesion of the breast which has been called benign on mammography is to take a step backward in the eradication of carcinoma of the breast.' Eddy points out that if we assume 'clinically benign' means that there is only a 5 per cent chance of cancer, a negative result on a mammography would reduce the risk to about one in a hundred. Rather than do a breast biopsy, the doctor should simply keep a further eye on the patient.

It should be emphasised that most medicine deals with uncertain situations and in particular diagnosis is usually uncertain: this leads to two final points. First, to obtain accurate diagnosis an attempt should be made to transform subjective feelings of uncertainty into mathematical probabilities: the probability of a disease given each of its possible symptoms can be calculated, though such variables as age, race and sex should also be taken into account when they affect the likelihood of the disease being present. Some doctors' ignorance of elementary probability theory makes them deny this. Here, for example, is yet another of Eddy's medical quotations: 'Younger women obviously have a fewer number of the malignancies which, however, should exert very little influence on the individual case.' I shall demonstrate subsequently that the formal manipulation of probabilities can result in much more accurate diagnoses than those made by doctors.

Second, despite the fact that intuitive reasoning is known to be very poor (see Chapter 20), many doctors have an allergy to statistics. They believe in treating the individual case, but fail to see that their treatment of that case can only depend on what has been found out about similar cases. Eddy quotes the following from yet another medical textbook: 'When a patient consults his physician with an undiagnosed disease, neither he nor the doctor knows whether it is rare until the diagnosis is finally made. Statistical methods can only be applied to a population of thousands. The individual either has a rare disease or doesn't have it; the relative incidence of two diseases is completely irrelevant to the problem of making his diagnosis.' The authors are apparently unable to see that if a disease is rare there must be less chance of the patient having it.

It should be added that to compound the mistakes already listed, it now appears that women under fifty who are routinely screened for breast cancer actually suffer more deaths from cancer than women who are not screened. This discovery was first made in a study of 50,000 Canadian women. The reasons are complex, but it is likely that the X-rays pick up small slow-growing tumours that would not otherwise be detected. The irradiation given after removal of the breast tumour impairs the immune system's ability to deal with secondaries. Hence, mass screening of women under fifty in Britain (under forty in the US) is no longer recommended. That does not mean that it was previously irrational: it was based on what was then known and was at the time rational in the light of that knowledge. The knowledge was inadequate: taking rational decisions does not always yield the best result.

Unfortunately it is not merely over conditional probabilities that doctors make the wrong connections. For example, objective evidence shows that large gastric ulcers are more likely to be malignant than small ones, but when nine radiologists were questioned, seven thought it was the small ones that were likely to be malignant.

Moreover, in diagnosing doctors have much more confidence that they are right than is justified. In one study it was shown that when they diagnosed pneumonia and were 88 per cent confident that they were right, only 20 per cent of the patients so diagnosed actually had pneumonia. The mistaken diagnosis is harmful to the patient but may be inevitable; the mistaken confidence is not inevitable but is equally harmful since it is likely to prevent the doctor looking for further evidence or revising his diagnosis if he encounters more evidence. Again, according to John Paulos, two doctors at the University of Washington have discovered that doctors' assessments of the risks of operations and medications are usually wildly wrong, often by a factor of ten or a hundred. The risks of any medical procedure in use for a period of time are usually well established, so there can be no excuse for such a degree of error.

Finally, there is massive evidence that it is beneficial to tell anyone undergoing a medical procedure what to expect. For example, in one study patients admitted to hospital for abdominal surgery were randomly assigned to two groups: before the operation took place, the patients in one group were given full information about how long it would last, the circumstances under which they would regain consciousness, the nature of the pain they were likely to experience and so on. This information was not supplied to the second group, who went through the standard hospital procedures. The patients who were thoroughly briefed about the operation subsequently complained less about pain, needed fewer sedatives and recovered more quickly: on average they were discharged from hospital three days earlier than the other group. The patient who is told in advance what to expect is prepared for it. He will be less upset by it, he will not regret his decision to have the treatment, he will not resent the hospi-

tal staff for misleading him, and he will not think that any unpleasant consequences are a sign of something having gone wrong. Yet
with few exceptions doctors completely ignore all the research done
on the topic over the last thirty years. A surgeon recently remarked
to me of one of his colleagues, 'Ah yes. We like him: he doesn't waste
time talking to patients.' Whether caused by arrogance, ignorance or
a misguided attempt to save time, this attitude must surely count as
irrational.

The knowledge that doctors make the same mistakes in their profession as do others in their everyday lives may make some readers
feel better about their own intellectual capacities, but it is hardly
encouraging for anyone who needs to consult a doctor. In fairness, it
should be added that doctors are probably no more inept than anyone else: their mistakes are, however, more available because of the
obvious damage caused to their patients.

moral

1. If you are a doctor, learn some elementary probability theory.
2. If you are a patient, set your doctor a simple test on elementary
   probability theory.
3. In order not to foul up medical research even further, nobody without a good knowledge of statistics, probability theory and experimental design should become the editor of a medical journal, even
   at the expense of a vast reduction in the number of journals.

14 mistaking the cause

The same five factors that produce errors in establishing the right connections between events also produce errors in inferring causes, for the first step in discovering a cause is to detect an association between two events. In making such associations, people often falsely connect like with like (as in the case of the invalid signs for homosexuality in the Rorschach). This fallacy is prominent in reasoning about causes. Until the end of the eighteenth century, doctors were taught 'the doctrine of signatures', that is that the medicine taken for any ailment must, in the words of one doctor, indicate 'by an obvious and well-marked external character the disease for which it is a remedy . . . The lungs of a fox must be a specific remedy for asthma, because that animal is remarkable for its strong powers of respiration. Turmeric has a brilliant yellow color, which indicates that it has the power of curing the jaundice . . . the polished surface and strong hardness which so eminently characterise the seeds of the *Lithospermum officinale* (common groundswell) were deemed a certain indication of their efficacy in calculous and gravelly disorders . . .' J. S. Mill was the first to nail this fallacy, writing of the 'prejudice that the conditions of a phenomenon must resemble the phenomenon'. The error is even more common in primitive cultures than in our own. As the anthropologist, Evans-Pritchard, pointed out, the Azande believe that fowl droppings cure ringworm because the two look alike and that the burnt skull of a monkey cures epilepsy because the movements of the monkey and the epileptic during an attack are not dissimilar.

These examples are derived from Nisbett and Ross, who go on to point out that the whole of psychoanalysis involves this primitive way of thinking. Fixation at the oral stage (the breast) will reveal itself in a preoccupation in adult life with the mouth – smoking, kissing and talking too much. Similarly meanness (hoarding money) is put down to the child's wish to hoard its faeces at the anal stage and so on. The error persists today in other ways. For example, homeopathy is based on the belief that illness can be cured by administering a tiny amount of a substance that if given to a healthy person in a larger amount would produce the same illness. The extraordinary success of modern science is largely due to careful recordkeeping which prevents the 'discovery' of false associations and to the fact that the connections established by these records have forced scientists away from the belief that like causes like, even though many people continue to exhibit it in their everyday judgements.

But even scientists can be mistaken about causes. A recent case in medical research can be used as a further illustration of the fallacy of like causes like. It is known that people with high cholesterol levels in the blood are prone to heart disease through the hardening of the arteries. What more natural than to assume that the more cholesterol people eat, the more likely they are to have heart attacks? One study found that the amount of saturated fat eaten in different countries was indeed correlated with the incidence of heart disease, but further research has shown a much less close association. Moreover, it is difficult to separate saturated fat intake from other factors that vary from country to country and that are known to affect proneness to heart disease, for example exercise which is beneficial and stress which is damaging. Nevertheless many people, particularly in that health-conscious nation, the USA, have reduced their consumption of dairy products and of animal fat. Studies on individuals have attempted to determine whether raising the consumption of cholesterol affects the level of blood cholesterol. For example, volunteers drank four pints of milk a day for a period: their blood cholesterol levels were unaffected. Even more damaging to the hypothesis that ingested cholesterol can damage the heart are the results of two recent and independent studies funded by the British Medical Research Council. One found that men who drink no milk have ten times as many heart attacks as men who drink more than a pint a day. The other discovered that men who eat margarine have twice as many heart attacks as those who eat butter. There are in fact good reasons why one would not expect blood cholesterol to vary with diet. First, the liver manufactures three or four times as much cholesterol as is normally ingested. Second, the body itself regulates the amount of cholesterol in the blood: its level is normally kept constant regardless of what is eaten, though some unfortunate people have too high a setting and are likely to die young through heart attacks. The true causes of high blood cholesterol are not known. What is known is that although decreasing cholesterol levels by drugs reduces heart disease, it does not increase longevity: people die of cancer instead. There is no solid evidence that cholesterol intake affects blood levels, yet jumping to conclusions on the basis of insufficient evidence has caused a considerable scare. The topic is much more complex than my description of it, but it provides a clear example of the like-causes-like fallacy.

You may wonder why so many false theories flourish in medicine. The reason is interesting. It can be illustrated by the history of a theory that people with a certain personality type are particularly susceptible to heart attacks. They are known as Type A and are characterised by driving ambition, a sense of time urgency, aggression and so on. The first reports indicating that people with this personality were on risk for heart attacks occurred about 1955. If one examines the number of published papers supporting this correlation divided by the number claiming that there is no correlation between Type A personality and heart disease, there was initially a very high proportion of papers with positive findings. This proportion has steadily decreased over recent years until at present there are about an equal number of papers being published on either side. How can this be? Originally the finding was new and interesting, so papers reporting it were published. Investigators obtaining negative results either did not submit their findings or had their papers rejected as being of little interest – as we saw in the last chapter, everyone tends to ignore negative cases. But once the hypothesis that Type A personalities were prone to heart disease was widely believed, papers refuting it became of interest and began to be published. The real truth is not known to this day. The policy of not publishing negative results is not necessarily irrational: the publishers of learned journals are after all interested in making money out of scientists (whose contributions are almost invariably unpaid) not in forwarding the progress of science. It can, however, lead only too readily to the drawing of false conclusions.

Another common error in assigning causes is to pick out as the cause the most salient (available) factor of a number of linked factors each of which might be the cause. This problem bedevils epidemiology, as the following example shows. In the 'thirties, an American medical journal published an alarmist article pointing out that cancer was much more frequent in New England, Minnesota, and Wisconsin than in the southern American states. It was also common in England and Switzerland, but rare in Japan. Since much more milk was drunk in the places where it was common than in those where it was not, the article concluded that milk was a cause of cancer. Although the conclusion sounds plausible, it was wrong. In the milk-drinking regions, people were comparatively well off: hence they lived far longer than those in the poorer areas where little milk was consumed. At that time the expectation of life of a Japanese woman was twelve years less than that of an English woman. Since cancer is mainly a disease of old age, it is hardly surprising that it should have been more prevalent in places where people lived longer. Old age, not milk, was the culprit.

Whether knowingly or not, politicians make the same kind of mistake as epidemiologists. For example, the Thatcher government, anxious to reduce subsidies to students, repeatedly claimed that going to university increases earning power. It cannot be denied that graduates do on average earn more than others, but there is no good reason for regarding this as cause and effect. After all, university students have higher than average IQs, and they may be more determined than others; moreover, their parents tend to have good positions and to be middle or upper class so that they can often help their children to obtain good jobs. These factors are surely enough to account for higher earnings. The causal connection between a university education and higher pay later in life is therefore not proven and the repeated assertions of this connection by British Ministers of Education demonstrate only that the British educational system has not succeeded in teaching them to think.

I have dealt so far with cases where there are two associated events neither of which causes the other, but where people's preconceptions make them infer a false causal relationship. A further error occurs when there is likely to be a genuine causal relationship, but people mistake the effect for the cause, again usually because of the biases they bring to their judgement. Here are two examples.

The first is taken from a book written by Christopher Bollas, a psychoanalyst. He writes, 'In all those [drug] addicts I have seen or whose treatment I have supervised, the mother and father appear psychically removed from their children', from which he concludes that the drug user is 'a person who when a child was deeply lonely and isolated'. Now it is surely obvious to anyone who is not a psychoanalyst that any parent with a child who is a drug addict is likely to be extremely upset, feel he does not understand the child and become distant from him. In other words, the child's addiction probably causes the parents to distance themselves, not – as Bollas would have it – the other way round. As is evident from the rest of his book, Bollas has a fervid faith in psychoanalysis: such partiality blinds him to the rational consideration of alternative explanations.

The second example is from clinical psychology. It has been discovered that mentally disordered patients who like their psychotherapist tend to recover rather faster than those who do not. It was concluded that a patient's liking for his therapist is an important factor in therapy. But it could equally well have been concluded that patients who are making progress like the therapist who is helping them and those who are not making progress or who are recovering slowly do not.

The examples given show that to demonstrate cause and effect it is not enough merely to establish that the two events tend to occur together. To prevent the kinds of mistakes outlined, it is usually necessary to have a more general theory that explains the causal connection. To revert to lung cancer and smoking, there is no question that there is a strong association between them in the sense that the frequency of cancer in smokers is much greater than in non-smokers. But R. A. Fisher, one of the greatest statisticians of this century, suggested that this correlation is the result of a hereditary mechanism: the same gene or genes cause both smoking and lung cancer. Fisher's suggestion is only unacceptable in the light of other evidence. It has been found that tobacco smoke reduces the beating of the cilia in the lungs; it contains a known carcinogen, tar; and the incidence of lung cancer is reduced in segments of the population that give up smoking, for example, in doctors. The last argument is subtle, for if it simply turned out that there was less lung cancer among doctors who gave up than among those who did not, Fisher could retort that it was the presence of the inherited disposition in a mild form that enabled some people to give up; if the genetic effects on smoking are not strong, equally they may not strongly predispose towards lung cancer. But it is hard to believe that there is a gene that makes doctors, so the fact that more doctors give up than other people and that those who do reduce their risk of lung cancer is strong evidence that the association between smoking and lung cancer is causal. It might be added that even after all the evidence had been obtained Fisher and subsequently Hans Eysenck persisted in their claim that smoking does not cause lung cancer. Their persistence was less irrational than might at first appear, for they were being supported by the Tobacco Manufacturers' Standing Committee.

The tendency to seize on non-existent associations between events and to infer causation in the absence of any underlying theory can be illustrated by the persistent mistakes made in medicine about the effectiveness of different treatments. As P. E. Meehl points out, patients with 'multiple sclerosis were treated by the use of vitamins, diathermy, oral administration of spinal cords, high dairy diets, potassium iodide, quinine bisulphate, and now we have histamine'.

At one time, psychotic and depressed patients were treated wholly ineffectively with metrazol and insulin, both of which provoke convulsions; they also had chunks removed from their brain (lobectomy), which turned them into cabbages; and young children were for years given calomel as a teething powder, a substance containing mercury which permanently damages the nervous system. Medical treatment is almost as much the slave of fashion as women's clothes. For example, until the mid-'fifties children's tonsils were removed indiscriminately. In one study undertaken in New York, 1000 eleven-year-old children were examined: it was found that 61 per cent had already had their tonsils removed. When the remaining 39 per cent were referred to physicians, it was recommended that 4 per cent of them should have their tonsils out. The remainder who had been passed as not requiring tonsillectomy by the first set of doctors were sent to other doctors who duly recommended that 46 per cent of them should have their tonsils removed. In other words, doctors had convinced themselves they could help the child by removing unhealthy tonsils, but they had no idea how to recognise such tonsils in the first place.

Doctors are of course no more irrational than anyone else, but they deal with the most complex known entity, the human body, and the equally complex ills to which it is prone. Moreover, as I have demonstrated, many psychologists hold equally groundless and false beliefs both about diagnosis and about the merits of discredited forms of psychotherapy. Nowadays, medicine is beginning to take a more rational approach. Possible cures are no longer widely accepted on a hunch: they are systematically investigated in controlled trials before being launched on the general public.

Three further oddities about causal reasoning should be mentioned. The first is that people display more confidence in reasoning from cause to effect than from effect to cause. When asked which is more probable – that a girl with blue eyes has a mother with blue eyes or a mother with blue eyes has a daughter with blue eyes more than three subjects in four thought it was more probable for the mother to have a daughter with blue eyes. Because the cause produces the effect and therefore may seem more powerful, people wrongly tend to think that it is more legitimate to reason from cause to effect than from effect to cause.

Second, inferences about causes are strongly influenced by the nature of the effect, at least when the causal agent is a person. The more dramatic the outcome of an event, the more likely we are to attribute the cause to the agent. In one study, one group of subjects were told that a man parked his car on a hill. After he had got out, the car rolled down the hill and hit a fire hydrant. Another group were given the same story except that they were told the car hit and injured a pedestrian. The second group – those told that the driver's action had serious consequences – held him more responsible than those told that the car simply hit a fire hydrant. This cannot be rational: the driver's actions were the same in both cases. This mistake is similar to one made by young children. They cannot distinguish between the blame attached to breaking a jar of marmalade by accident and smashing it on the ground in a fit of temper. They take into account only the seriousness of the consequences of an action, not the action itself.

Finally, it has been shown that we are more likely to believe that someone is responsible for an action that injures ourselves than one that injures a friend and we are more likely to blame someone for injuring a friend than for injuring someone we don't know. The more salient, that is available, the consequence of an action, the more we hold the agent responsible for it. The emotional importance of the consequence seems to strengthen in our minds the causal connection between act and outcome.

Before continuing, we must examine what it is that people regard as the cause of an event. If you turn on a light, it is natural to say that flicking the switch caused it to go on. But in reality there are several other conditions that have to be present, which could be – and sometimes are – regarded as the cause. For example, the wiring must be in order and the bulb must not be defunct. If the bulb is burnt out and we replace it with a new one, we might well regard this as the cause of the light going on when we flick the switch. Many events have multiple causes. A car may have overturned because it was going too fast, because the road was icy and because there was a steep camber at that point. Of the possible causes of an event we tend to pick the unusual one (or sometimes the one that interests us most) as *the* cause.

A person's actions can be caused either by his own disposition or by the situation he is in. For example, if someone behaves in an angry way, we can explain it by saying either that he is an unusually irritable person (his disposition) or that he was provoked beyond endurance (his situation). Although both his disposition and his situation play a role in causing his behaviour, just as in the case of the electric light, we should assign the cause to whichever is more unusual. If he is exceptionally choleric, we should fix on that; if he is normally calm, the cause of his anger is the situation. In practice, when it comes to inferring the causes of behaviour, people make gross but systematic errors. Consider the experiments in which Milgram induced his subjects to give potentially lethal shocks to strangers. If all you knew was that a person called Sam had gone to the highest level of shock, you might infer that the cause of his behaviour was that he was an unusually cruel and heartless person. Once you learn that most of Milgram's subjects go to the highest shock level, you should revise your judgement. There is nothing unusual about Sam if most people do the same thing: the cause of his behaviour was the unusual situation in which he found himself. But people do not think like this. In one experiment, subjects were told that 65 per cent of Milgram's subjects went to the highest shock level, but when confronted with Sam they still thought he was a particularly cruel and heartless person. This error – attributing an action to a person's disposition rather than to the situation – is extremely common. Many experiments, including the one just given, show that in making judgements about the causes of an action, people are influenced by information about whether the agent always or rarely does what he did in similar situations (is Sam always cruel?), but they disregard evidence about whether other people do the same thing in that situation, even though it is essential for making a correct judgement.

An extreme example of ignoring the situation was provided by the following study. Subjects watched two people, one of whom invented quiz-type questions while the other tried to answer them. Naturally, the questioner knew the answers to all the questions, while the other person did not. At the end of the mock quiz, almost all the subjects believed that the person setting the questions was more knowledgeable and intelligent than the person answering them. They had ignored the situation: anybody can choose questions to which he knows the answer, but which the person quizzed cannot answer.

This universal tendency to ascribe other people's behaviour to their character traits or dispositions rather than to their situation is known as the 'fundamental attribution error'. It arises for two reasons. First, what a person does in a given situation is highly conspicuous (available); what other people would do if they were in that situation is not as readily brought to mind. Second, the agent is normally seen to be more intimately connected with his action than is the situation. Proof of the influence of the second factor has come from several experiments. If it operates, then the agent should be less likely to commit the fundamental attribution error about himself than should people observing him: because he can see the situation but not himself, the situation should be more salient for him. In one study, subjects were arranged in pairs and the members of these pairs were asked to get to know one another. Other subjects (observers) could see only one member of a pair, though they could hear both of them. After the conversation, all the subjects who had been chatting were asked to rate themselves on how far they had shown nervousness, friendliness, talkativeness and dominance during the conversation. The observers were asked to rate the subject they had watched on the same qualities. They gave the subjects much higher ratings on almost all qualities than the subjects gave themselves. When, however, a videotape of the subject's own behaviour was played back to him he changed his evaluation of himself: he now gave self-ratings that were even higher than those originally given to him by the observer. This experiment strongly suggests that one reason why we are less likely to give dispositional explanations of our own behaviour than we are of others' is simply that we cannot see ourselves acting.

Although the tendency to ascribe others' behaviour to dispositional factors is universal, it is nonetheless irrational. It can result in allotting quite unjustifiable blame. Baron gives a hypothetical example. Suppose a candidate for an important position in a firm arrives early and is invited to lunch. He may be quite nervous and be unable not to show it. His potential employers may reject him on these grounds without stopping to consider how other applicants might have behaved when faced with the embarrassment of such a lunch.

There is another reason why personality traits are not as important as we think: they are less consistent than most people believe. The same person can be honest in one situation, dishonest in another; sometimes irritable, sometimes not; greedy on some occasions, but abstemious on others and so on. Moreover, it has been shown that many traits that people believe go together in fact do not. For instance, in children there is no connection between refusing to cheat and the ability to delay gratification, for example, by declining one chocolate on the spot in return for a promise of five a few hours later.

The fragility of character traits has been repeatedly demonstrated: here is one example. In the course of an interview some subjects were asked questions that were designed to produce an introverted response (for example, 'What things do you dislike about loud parties?'); others were asked questions designed to elicit an extroverted response (such as, 'What would you do if you wanted to liven things up at a party?'). In a subsequent conversation with a stooge, the latter subjects behaved in a much more extroverted way than did the former. For example, they started a conversation with the stooge sooner and they placed their chair nearer to him. If asking a few questions can cause a shift in what is thought to be one of the more stable character traits (extroversion-introversion), how much more will people be affected by really important changes in their situation?

The reader will doubtless think that the lack of consistent personality traits is disproved by his own experience, but for the nine reasons given at the end of Chapter 5, he is likely to form stereotypes of individuals and to think of their behaviour as more consistent than it is: building up a tidy picture of the dispositions and character traits of others can save a great deal of hard thinking. Once you have formed a judgement on someone, you are likely only to notice aspects of his behaviour that confirm it ('illusory correlation'). To be sure that a person is exceptionally irritable or exceptionally calm, it is necessary to keep records not only of his behaviour but of that of others, and also in both cases of the situation. But maybe it is more fun, and certainly less time-consuming, to form your own snap judgements.

Nor is the misattribution of causes for human behaviour a trivial matter. The Russian buildup of nuclear weapons was seen by most American politicians as a deliberate attempt to attain world dominance, but it may equally have been a reaction to the *situation* they found themselves in, namely, the proliferation of nuclear arms by another powerful country, the US. If a student is performing badly, one should decide whether it is because of a personality characteristic (such as laziness) or whether it is caused by his situation – the loss of his girlfriend or the death of his beloved grandmother. Not all actions are caused by the situation: I have known students with ten grandmothers, among whom the mortality rate was most distressing. Nevertheless, we tend to underestimate situational causes.

A further error made about people's dispositions is that we believe others are much more similar to ourselves than they are. This was demonstrated in an experiment in which subjects were asked to carry around the campus a large sign reading 'Repent'. Some agreed to do so, others did not. Of those who agreed, the majority thought other students would also agree, while most of those who refused to carry the sign thought other students would not agree. The reasons for seeing others as similar to ourselves are debated. It may be just another example of the availability error. Because our own behaviour (as opposed to our dispositions) is highly available to us, in judging what others would do the first thing that comes to mind is what we would do in their situation and that forms the basis of our judgement. The error of thinking others are like ourselves is reminiscent of the psychoanalytic defence mechanism called 'projection'. According to Freud, if someone has an undesirable trait, such as meanness, he tends to see it in others, possibly to disguise from himself that he has it to an unusual degree. This observation is probably valid, though as far as I know there is no proof. The phenomenon is just one more example of irrationality, whether it is caused by the dark workings of the libido or merely by the availability error.

Throughout the book I have given examples of people being mistaken about the reasons for their actions and beliefs. People conform, they exaggerate the value of anything in which they have a large investment, they are subject to the halo effect and they distort evidence to make it fit their own beliefs, all without realising the true causes of their actions and attitudes.

People can also be mistaken about the causes of their moods and emotions. In a famous experiment subjects were given epinephrine, a stimulant drug that creates high arousal. Some were told that it was a vitamin that would have no immediate effects, the rest that it was a stimulant which would arouse them. They subsequently sat in a room full of stooges, who were either extremely euphoric, among other things blowing up balloons and roaring with laughter, or extremely aggressive, repeatedly insulting the real subjects. Most subjects became to some degree cheerful or annoyed depending on how the stooges acted. But the important point is that those who had been misinformed about the drug showed considerably larger mood changes than those who had not. They had to account to themselves for the physical arousal produced unknown to them by the drug, so they assumed it was caused by the behaviour of the confederate and therefore they became more angry or more cheerful than the others. Many other experiments suggest that we are poor judges of the causes of our emotions. Male subjects were required to ride a stationary exercise bicycle for several minutes and were then shown pictures of female nudes. They rated them as more sexually stimulating than did subjects who had not been physiologically aroused by a spell on the bicycle.

These phenomena are related to our ability to find a plausible story to explain anything that people, including ourselves, do or feel. We are driven to explain to ourselves the causes of our own moods and emotions and in so doing we often go badly wrong. People make excuses to themselves for failure whether in an examination or in love. When people act maliciously out of jealousy, how many realise the true cause of their behaviour? In one of the depressions from which I once suffered, I became convinced that the reason for it was my fear that the trees in the adjoining land were pushing my house down. I had to find a cause for the depression, but when the depression disappeared the trees ceased to be sinister. Self-deceit exists on a massive scale: Freud was right about that. Where he went wrong was in attributing it all to the libido, the underlying sex drive.

One of the most convincing demonstrations of people's inability to determine the causes of their failings comes from a study of real life undertaken at Harvard University. Women were asked to keep a diary in which they were to record for two months how far they had been in a good or bad mood on each day. In addition they had to make a note of a number of preset items that might influence their moods, such as amount of sleep the previous night, the weather, their state of health, their sexual activity and the stage of the menstrual cycle. When the diaries were handed in, the investigators subjected them to a mathematical analysis that teased out how far each of these factors was in fact associated with different moods. For example, if a good night's sleep was always followed by a day in a good mood and poor sleep by a day in a bad mood, then there would be a complete association between quality of sleep and mood. If, on the other hand, the amount of sleep did not correlate at all with next day's mood, there would be no association and sleep could not be said to influence mood.

After their record-keeping was over, the women were asked to rate how far they thought each of the possible preset factors actually had determined their moods. Surprisingly, their ratings on these factors bore little or no relationship to those uncovered by the objective mathematical analysis. On this analysis, day of the week was found to be very important ('Sunday, Bloody Sunday'), while quality of sleep had very little influence. As a group, however, the women thought that sleep was the most important single factor, while day of the week had been comparatively unimportant. Moreover, there was no correlation between individual subjects' ratings of the factors and their importance as determined objectively. Indeed, the more a particular woman's moods had actually been determined by the day of the week or the weather, the less important she thought these influences had been. In short, people are poor judges of the causes of their moods and emotions.

moral

1. Suspect any explanation of an event in which the cause and the effect are similar to one another, even when it is made on the highest authority.
2. Suspect all epidemiological findings unless they are supported by more reliable evidence.

3. Consider whether an event could have causes other than the one you first think of.
4. In allocating cause and effect, consider the possibility that they may work in the opposite direction to that for which you first plump.
5. Be sceptical of any causal relationship unless there is an underlying theory that explains it.
6. Remember that in most circumstances it is as reasonable to reason from effect to cause as from cause to effect.
7. In apportioning responsibility for an action, do not be influenced by the magnitude of its effect.
8. Don't hold someone responsible for an action without first considering what others would have done in the same circumstances.
9. Don't assume that others are like yourself.
10. Eat what you fancy.

15 misinterpreting the evidence

We have already seen that people distort evidence to make it fit their beliefs. This chapter demonstrates that even when they have no preconceptions, they misinterpret evidence in highly systematic ways.

Here are two simple problems. First, think of a coin that is tossed six times and consider the following three possible results where H stands for head and T for tail:

    1. TTTTTT
    2. TTTHHH
    3. THHTTH

Ask yourself which of these three specific sequences is most likely to occur. Most people pick THHTTH, but in fact each sequence is equally likely. The mistake arises because there appears to be an element of order in the first two sequences: they seem not to be random because it is unusual to get runs of heads or tails from a series of tosses of a coin. People reason, perhaps unconsciously, that because there are many more unordered sequences than ordered, the unordered sequence is more probable than either of the other two. But the reasoning is fallacious. It fails to take into account that this is a *particular* unordered sequence and hence is no more likely to occur than any specific ordered sequence. Assuming the coin is not biased, the chance of a head (or a tail) turning up with each toss is one half and therefore any given sequence has the same chance of occurring as any other, to be precise one chance in sixty-four.

This is an example of what is called the 'representativeness' error. We cannot easily distinguish different scrambled sequences and since the sequence of heads and tails produced by tossing a coin is more often scrambled than not, we see the third sequence as representative of the usual outcome while the first two are not. We therefore think of it as being more probable than the others.

In the second problem, you are told, 'My next-door neighbour in London is a professor. He likes to write poetry, is rather shy, and is small in stature,' and you are then asked whether he is more likely to be a professor of Chinese studies or of psychology. Most people again give the wrong answer: they reply that the neighbour is more likely to be a professor of Chinese studies. The right answer is that the next-door neighbour is more likely to be a professor of psychology. Although his description fits that of a Chinese professor, there are many more professors of psychology in Britain than of sinology. Indeed there are so few professors of Chinese that there are likely to be many more professors of psychology who are shy, write poetry and are small than there are professors of Chinese with these attributes, but because the description is representative of a professor of Chinese people leap to the conclusion that he is one without considering how few professors there are in that subject.

Relying on the extent to which somebody is a typical example of a given group of people has been shown to lead to an even more extraordinary mistake. Subjects were given brief descriptions of individual people: for example, they might be told, 'Linda is thirty-one years old, single, outspoken and very bright. She majored in philosophy. As a student, she was deeply concerned with issues of discrimination and social justice, and also participated in anti-nuclear demonstrations.' They were then asked to rank the following statements about Linda in terms of how likely each was to be true. The order in which the statements were presented differed from one subject to another.

a. Linda is a teacher in an elementary school.
b. Linda works in a bookstore and takes yoga classes.
c. Linda is active in the feminist movement.
d. Linda is a psychiatric social worker.
e. Linda is a member of the League of Women Voters.
f. Linda is a bank teller.
g. Linda is an insurance salesperson.
h. Linda is a bank teller and is active in the feminist movement.

Needless to say, the subjects thought it much more likely that Linda was a feminist (statement c) than that she was a bank teller (statement f). But when asked to judge how likely it was that Linda was a *feminist bank teller* (statement h), they thought it much more likely than that she was simply a bank teller. This judgement cannot possibly be correct: obviously there must be more women bank tellers than bank tellers who are feminists for the simple reason that some bank tellers are not feminists. The mistake occurs because Linda's description is typical (representative) of a feminist so it fits half of the two categories whose combined likelihood the subjects are asked to judge. Irrationally the fact that she is probably a feminist increases in the subjects' eyes the probability that she belongs to both categories (feminist and bank teller). To put it more technically, the subjects seem to have averaged the two probabilities instead of multiplying them: if the probability of Linda being a feminist is .7 and that of her being a bank teller is .1, then the probability of her being a feminist bank teller is .07 not .4. When the question is put to them, even people who have a background in probability theory or statistics, such as graduate students in psychology or education, make the same mistake: so do doctors and business trainees.

This sort of error can produce the following effect. When someone is told something very implausible, he is more likely to believe it if at the same time he is told something highly plausible. But something implausible which is to say improbable – cannot become more probable just because some highly probable material is associated with it. Indeed the probability that all the material is true is reduced by adding extra material however plausible. This situation is exactly analogous to the experiment just described: the presence of the plausible material is likely to increase belief in the implausible statement. This is a trick used by all accomplished liars as well as by many lawyers. It should be added that a further mechanism is at work.

If we hear various plausible statements from someone, it may increase our belief in his veracity and so we come to believe his less plausible statements. This dodge is used extensively by advertising agencies. Indeed, they carry it one step further and try to find slogans that will be believed by the group of people who might buy their products but not by other groups. They may for example advertise a dog food called Yup-Yup with the slogan 'Dogs are just like people', which many dog lovers but few others are likely to believe. The dog owner's belief in the truth of this slogan lends credence to the advertiser's further claim that 'Yup-Yup keeps your dog's coat brighter, gives him added confidence', and so on. But the slogan alleging that dogs are like people has two further effects. First, the select group of dog lovers will think the advertiser is highly discerning and therefore trustworthy, for he is announcing a truth dear to them, but one which is not shared by the general public. Second, it identifies the advertiser with dog lovers as a group: in consequence in-group loyalty, already discussed, will make the decision to buy more likely. In short, the misled dog owner rushes forth to buy Yup-Yup because the advertiser has in one go shown that he is plausible and discerning, and that he belongs to the same in-group as the dog lover himself.

A related and perhaps more unexpected error has been demonstrated. The subjects were students taking a higher degree in social work. They were given information about an imaginary client that suggested he might have a particular emotional problem. When a client was described simply as 'having sado-masochistic sexual fantasies', the social workers thought it likely that he was a child abuser. But when other social work students were told that a client 'had sado-masochistic fantasies, fixes up old cars in his spare time and once ran away from school', they were much less likely to think he was a child abuser. Yet the additional information is completely irrelevant to his sexual proclivities. The social workers seem to have been misled by its normality into thinking that the person was not a sexual deviant, though as far as we know child abusers are just as likely to mend old cars as anyone else. The mistake could also have occurred through thinking, possibly unconsciously, that rather a small percentage of people who mend old cars are child abusers, but at the same time failing to take into account the fact that the percentage is the same for those who do not mend old cars: this is yet another instance of the failure to pay attention to the negative case as set out in Chapter 12. In summary, then, people's ability to infer one thing from another can be destroyed by the inclusion of irrelevant information.

I have now described three different errors, namely, the assumption that something must belong to a particular category because it is typical of that category, without taking into account the category's size; the tendency to believe that because part of a description is true, the whole description must be true; and the tendency to reduce the effect of unusual information about someone if he is described as normal in other (irrelevant) ways. These errors all occur because people are guided by whether an item seems to be representative of a particular group of items: if it is representative, they ignore the true likelihoods or probabilities. People's incapacity to deal with probabilities without special training can be illustrated by an example from real life. In Great Britain about 300,000 people die each year from heart disease, while about 55,000 die from lung cancer. Heavy smoking approximately doubles one's chance of dying from heart disease, and increases the chance of dying of lung cancer by a factor of about ten. Most people will conclude that smoking is more likely to cause lung cancer than heart disease and indeed both in Britain and elsewhere government campaigns against smoking have been largely based on this assumption. But it is false. If one takes into account the greater frequency of heart disease, then for every smoker who brings lung cancer on himself there will be more than two who die of self-induced coronary illness. The following simple calculation (which for simplicity assumes that half the adult population smokes) shows how this conclusion is reached. Since smoking doubles the risk of fatal heart disease, 200,000 smokers will die of it each year and 100,000 non-smokers. But 100,000 smokers would have died even had they not smoked, which means that 100,000 smokers die of heart disease each year as a result of smoking. Similarly, about 55,000 smokers die of lung cancer; since 5,000 of these would have died even had they not smoked, 50,000 die from smoking. Hence, about twice as many smokers kill themselves of heart disease as die from lung cancer caused by smoking.

It is less important to understand the manipulation of these figures than to grasp that when new information is received about the probability of an event that probability must be combined with the probability of the event in the absence of the new information, a probability known as the base rate (or the a priori probability). The formal theorem that determines how these probabilities should be manipulated was first put forward by Thomas Bayes, an English mathematician who lived in the first half of the eighteenth century. Despite the antiquity of the theorem, failure to use it is endemic. It occurs among doctors, lawyers, managers, generals and so on.

This failure has been repeatedly demonstrated in experimental studies, of which the best-known is as follows. Subjects were told that in a certain city there are two cab companies, the Blue Cabs, which own 85 per cent of the cabs, and the Green Cabs, which own 15 per cent. A cab is involved in a hit-and-run accident and a witness says she thought it was a green one. Tests were made and it was found she could correctly identify the colour of the cab 80 per cent of the time in the lighting conditions under which the accident took place; 20 per cent of the time she mistakenly thought a blue cab was green. The question is whether the cab in the accident is more likely to have been blue or green. When tested, the majority of subjects say 'green', but they are wrong. Although the woman's judgement is usually accurate, there are far more blue cabs than green. The probability of her having seen a blue cab (.85) and having thought it was green (.2) is .85 x .2 = .17, whereas the chance of her having seen a green cab (.15) and judging it green (.8) is .15 x .8 = .12 (these figures do not add to 1.0 because all her other possible judgements would be 'blue'). This means that the actual odds of the cab having been green are 17 to 12 against, or to put it a different way the probability that it was green is only .4. The subjects' error is to pay too much attention to new evidence about an event (the woman's judgement) at the expense of paying insufficient attention to the general frequency of that event (the frequency of green cabs).

An interesting example from real life of failure to take base rates into account comes from American business and involves the lie detector. As behoves a country whose Presidents, from Washington to Nixon, have shown a preoccupation with lying (or not lying), it is much more frequently used in the US than in Britain. It takes such measures as the electrical conductivity of the skin, breathing rate, and the pitch of the voice, all of which rise when a person is stressed or aroused. Various innocuous questions are asked, but they are interspersed with more or less subtle leading questions, such as 'Did you rob the Chase Manhattan Bank yesterday?', to which it is assumed there will be a rise in the lie detector measures if the person is guilty. For a variety of reasons including arousal caused by fear of being accused, the lie detector is imperfect: it is known to be fallible if only because people who have been wrongly convicted of theft by it have subsequently been exonerated when someone else has owned up. Nevertheless, it is widely used by American companies to detect employees who have stolen from them.

Now, suppose its success rate is 90 per cent (it is almost certainly lower), that is, one innocent person in ten gives a positive response to it and one guilty person in ten gives a negative response (in practice the two figures are unlikely to be the same). Any employee found guilty is discharged from the firm. On the face of it, it would appear that nine people are correctly found culpable for every one incorrectly found guilty: to the managers of the firm (though not to many other people) this might be acceptable. But the reasoning is false. There are likely to be many more employees who do not steal than ones who do. Consider a firm with 1,000 employees and let suppose that during a given year 1 per cent of them (ten) steal from the firm and 99 per cent (990) do not. All employees take the test and nine of the ten (90 per cent) who are guilty fail it; however, 990 employees are innocent and 99 (10 per cent) of these will also fail. Hence, for every guilty person caught by the test, nearly ten innocent people stand falsely accused. Once the 'base rate' is taken into account, it turns out that many more of the innocent suffer than of the guilty.

It should be added that there are cleverer ways of using the lie detector. For example, if a desk top computer is missing, people may be shown several different types of computer: only the person who knows the appearance of the missing one will respond selectively on the lie detector to this computer and not to others. In theory then, the innocent cannot be found guilty just because their nervousness shows up on the lie detector. However, such more subtle methods are rarely used and even when they are there is still the possibility of error: in consequence, because so many more people are innocent than guilty, the lie detector is likely to catch fewer culprits than innocent parties. Despite these problems the device continues to be used in many American states.

Failure to take into account the base rate can lead to serious mistakes in interpreting the results of medical tests. It underlies the failure of many doctors to use mammography appropriately, as described in Chapter 13. Here is a further example. Staff and students from the Harvard Medical School, possibly the most prestigious medical institution in the world, were asked what percentage of the patients testing positive on a test for a certain disease would actually have the disease if it was present in one person in 1,000 and if 5 per cent of people who had *not* got the disease tested positive. About half of the sixty medics to whom the question was put replied 95 per cent. Only eleven gave the correct answer, 2 per cent. Clearly high intelligence does not protect against making gross errors.

Probabilities seem to baffle people even when no calculation whatever is required. Here is an example, again from medicine, provided by Baron. Subjects were told that 'a patient has a .8 probability of umphitis. A positive Z-ray result would confirm the diagnosis, but a negative result would be inconclusive; if the result is negative, the probability would drop to .6. The treatment for umphitis is unpleasant, and you feel it is just as bad to give the treatment to a patient without the disease as to let a patient with the disease go untreated. If the Z-ray were the only test you could do, should you do it?'

Many subjects thought the test should be performed. In fact, it should not. Even if its results are negative, the patient is more likely to have the disease than not (the probability is at least .6), so clearly all patients should be treated for the disease regardless of the outcome of the test. Baron tells an anecdote of a physician who wanted to perform an expensive CAT-scan on a patient's back even though he already knew that the only treatment was rest. He said he 'wanted to confirm a diagnostic impression', but such zeal to obtain a useless truth can be damaging to the patient's body if it is unpleasant or to his pocket if it is expensive. Lest you think (rightly) that it is not enough to rely on anecdotes, in 1990 the British Royal Society of Radiologists and Anaesthetists published a report concluding that 250 people a year die in Britain as a result of unnecessary X-rays. Unless the results of a medical test can affect treatment, it should not be administered.

Here is a problem that requires virtually no knowledge of probabilities to solve. You are told there are three cards of which one has
two white faces, one two red faces and the third is white on one side
and red on the other. You are shown one of these cards placed on a
table with a red face upwards. What is the probability that it is the
card with red on both faces? Try to answer before reading on. The
vast majority of people (including myself), when first presented with
this problem, answer 1/2 – it clearly cannot be the white-white card,
so it must be one of two cards, either the red-red or the red-white.
They are wrong. The visible red face could be one of *three* red faces.
It could be the red face of the red-white card, or one or other of the
two red faces on the red-red card. Out of these three possibilities, in
two the hidden face is red, in one it is white. Therefore, the probability of the other face being red (the red-red card) is 2/3 not 1/2. Just
why people make this mistake is unclear. Perhaps the number of possible cards (two) is more available to them than the number of possible red faces (three).

It could be argued that people are better at combining different
pieces of evidence when the result can be known with certainty than
when it can only be assigned some degree of probability and so the
lapses set out in this chapter do not matter that much. Unfortunately,
almost all important judgements involve elements of uncertainty.
Think, for example, of a general trying to determine what strategy is
most likely to succeed, of a doctor trying to infer the patient's illness
from a set of symptoms, or of a jury deciding whether the accused is
guilty after having heard much conflicting evidence. Before turning to
some further cases from real life, it is worth commenting on the use
of statistics.

Most people's knowledge of statistics is either rudimentary or
non-existent. For many, 'statistics' is a dirty word: one hears such
allegations as 'Anything can be proved by statistics', but this is only
true if they are misused. Indeed, decrying statistics is usually merely a
device used by the ignorant to protect their self-esteem. Many readers
may feel that people cannot be expected to know about statistics or
elementary probability theory, but all of us make intuitive statistical
judgements much of the time and our false intuitions lead to grievous
errors. Although many people could not undertake the sort of calcu-
lations that have appeared in the previous pages, they would think
more rationally if they realised they must take base rates into account:
even if they did not arrive at precise answers, they could get much
nearer to the truth. It would surely be possible to sensitise people to

the general ways in which probabilities should be combined and to the requirements for concluding that there is an association between two events, as set out in Chapter 12, without their learning formal statistics or probability theory (on which all statistics are based). It will be shown later that in many circumstances rational thought – that is, thought that leads to the conclusion most likely to be correct – must be based on the manipulation of numbers. As Poincaré remarked, 'Mathematics is the language in which one cannot express nebulous or imprecise thoughts.'

The lack of any intuitive understanding of simple statistical reasoning is further illustrated by the following two experiments. Subjects were told that in a certain town there are two hospitals, a large one with an obstetric ward in which there is an average of forty-five births a day, and a smaller hospital which averages fifteen births per day. Over a period of a year roughly as many boys are born as girls. Subjects were asked which of the two hospitals would have more days on which 60 per cent of the births are boys. Most of them thought there would be no difference. In fact, male births will be 60 per cent of all births on about twice as many days in the small hospital as in the large one. This illustrates an important principle – when different events occur with a certain probability, the larger the sequence of events the more closely the actual frequency of the different events will approximate to their true frequencies. To see this, consider tossing a coin four times. There are sixteen possible sequences of heads and tails (four 1/2s multiplied together). Only one of these sequences is all heads so the chance of getting 100 per cent heads is one in sixteen. Now consider tossing a coin ten times. There are now 1,024 possible sequences of which only one is all heads; the chance of getting all heads is therefore reduced to less than one in 1,000. For simplicity I have considered an extreme case, 100 per cent heads, but exactly the same considerations would have applied if I had chosen, say, 75 per cent heads. The smaller number of tosses would again be much more likely to yield this percentage of heads. The rule that the bigger the sample the more likely it is that the frequency of events within it will approximate to the true frequency is known as 'the law of large numbers'. It has implications for everyone, including squash players. As Kahneman and Tversky point out, a game of squash may contain either nine or fifteen points. The better player is more likely to win in a fifteen-point game.

The second example of faulty reasoning is based on ignorance of the law of large numbers. Subjects were asked to imagine an urn which contains red and white balls. Two-thirds of the balls are one colour and a third the other. They are further told that person A has drawn five balls, of which four were red. Person B has drawn twenty balls of which twelve were red. Subjects were asked to decide whether person A or person B should feel more confident that two-thirds of the balls are red. Most of them believed that person A should be more confident because he has drawn a higher proportion of red balls. They were wrong. Because of the law of large numbers and the bigger sample drawn by person B, his guess that the urn contains two-thirds of red balls is twice as likely to be correct as the same guess made by person A.

Before drawing conclusions from information about a limited number of events (a sample) selected from a much larger number of events (the population), it is important to understand something about the statistics of samples. Opinion polls make carefully calculated use of samples to discover voting intentions. It can be determined in advance how big a sample of the population is needed in order to obtain a result with no more than a small and fixed probability of having an error no bigger than some chosen figure – say, nineteen times out of twenty accurate to within 1 per cent either way. Of course, several factors outside the pollsters' control, such as respondents lying or changing their minds before voting, can still produce sizeable errors.

There are many experiments demonstrating the failure to take sample size into account. In one, American students were either read a table giving a set of ratings on courses provided by dozens of senior students or they met just two or three senior students who had taken the courses and who orally provided their own ratings, adding a few brief comments supporting their judgements. The students' choices of what courses to take were much more affected by the face-to-face talk with a few of their seniors than by reading ratings collected from a large number of other students. Here, as so often, the availability error distorted judgement: it made the students forget the importance of sample size. Talking to a few senior students, who could hardly form a representative sample, made a much deeper impression than reading dry data collected from many such students.

Nisbett and Ross point out that this error permeates the American judicial system. Statistics on murder rates in states that have abolished capital punishment and those that have not are rarely quoted in the US Supreme Court. Instead, decisions are based on a small number of case histories. It is all reminiscent of the remark frequently made by smokers, 'My father lived to be ninety-nine and he smoked a hundred cigarettes a day' or the equivalent for heavy drinkers, 'My grandfather always drank a bottle of gin for breakfast, and he never knew a day's illness.' Such cases are always easy to find; and because they are dramatic they are readily available and may persuade some people that smoking or drinking is harmless. What matters, however, is not the individual case, which may or may not be exceptional, but the probability of dying or becoming ill through smoking or drinking. This can only be established by examining a large and representative sample of smokers and drinkers.

Irrational judgements, then, are often the result of paying too much attention to small samples, which are likely to yield atypical results. But there is a second way in which judgements based on samples often go wrong. Even when the sample is large enough, insufficient care may be taken to ensure that it is not biased. I have fallen victim to this error myself. Most of the Australian men one meets in bars along the Earls Court Road in London are loud and hearty, while the women are strong and long-legged. In addition, the British media usually portray Australian men as slightly uncouth and given to wearing hats with corks dangling from them. When I visited Sydney for the first time, I found to my amazement not a single cork dangling from a hat. Moreover, the Australians there, both men and women, turned out to be extremely courteous and gentle people. Clearly the sample I had met in London was biased, that is to say, not representative of most Australians. Perhaps it is a country that exports its roughnecks, while the rest stay at home.

Several experiments substantiate people's failure to take into account how far a sample is representative. In one, subjects were shown a videotape of an interview with someone pretending to be a prison guard. Half the subjects saw a guard who was completely inhumane: he described the prisoners as animals, beyond redemption. The other subjects saw a humane guard who thought prisoners could be rehabilitated. Within each of these two groups of subjects some were told the guard they had seen was typical, others that he was not at all typical, and yet others were given no information about him. The information on how typical he was made little difference to the influence of the videotape on subjects' opinions of the prison service. Most of those who had seen the nice guard thought guards as a whole treated prisoners fairly and were concerned with their welfare, while those who had seen the nasty one thought just the opposite. So even when people are warned that a single striking case is not typical, they still tend to assume that it is and to make judgements on a large population of people (in this case prison guards) accordingly. Basing judgements on too small a sample or on a biased sample plays a considerable part in sustaining irrational beliefs and, as has already been shown, is in part responsible for prejudicial stereotypes.

Unfortunately insensitivity to sample size and to how far a sample is representative is not limited to individuals: it is often displayed by organisations that should know better. A striking example was the prediction, based on a questionnaire sent through the post by the *Literary Digest*, that Roosevelt would lose the election for the 1937 presidency by a massive margin. In fact only 23 per cent of people returned the questionnaires and they tended to be among the better-off American citizens. As John Paulos points out, one can have little faith in the figures given by columnists like Shere Hite on the number of people having affairs. Apart from flagrant lying, people having affairs are more likely to read her column than those who are not and even among her readers those having affairs may be more likely to reply.

The main consumer body in Britain, the publishers of *Which?*, usually fails to recognise the importance of sample size. They publish comparative figures on different makes of products, rating them in various ways with no mention of how many of each model they have tested: one has the strong impression that often if not always they have only tested one. They then proceed to evaluate each model on a number of different criteria. For example, in the May 1990 edition of *Which?* there is a report on forty-three different vacuum cleaners. Each model is rated on, among other things, dust pick-up, fibre pick-up, bag clogging, working of bag-full indicator, blocking of tubes, suction power, dust in exhaust, noise and durability. *Which?* takes no account of the possibility that there may be as much variation between different instances of the same model as between models. Their 'best buys' may simply be the result of a lucky dip. When similar ratings are applied to different models of car, the possibility of error due to differences in individual cars of the same make and model is magnified further since cars are extremely complex and a small fault somewhere can have many ramifications. In none of these cases can anything be concluded about differences in the characteristics of the different models by testing merely one or even just a few instances of each.

moral

1. Do not judge solely by appearances. If something looks more like an X than a Y, it may nevertheless be more likely to be a Y if there are many more Ys than Xs.
2. Remember that a statement containing two or more pieces of information is always less likely to be true than one containing only one of the pieces.

3. Guard against believing a statement is true because you know that part of it is true.
4. Remember that if you learn the probability of X given Y (for example, the probability that a cab is green if a witness claims it is), to arrive at the true probability of X you must take into account the base rate (the frequency of green cabs).
5. Remember that the frequency with which a given attribute or event is observed is likely to deviate more from its frequency in the population as a whole in small samples than in large ones. Don't trust small samples.
6. Beware of biased samples.
7. Don't trust *Which?*

16 inconsistent decisions and bad bets

People are highly inconsistent about the bets they are prepared to place. Before demonstrating this, it is necessary to define the 'expected value' of a bet. It is simply the amount you expect to win or lose per bet if you make the bet a large number of times. For example, if someone offers to pay you £10 with a probability of .4 while you have to pay him £5 with a probability of .6, on average out of every ten bets he will pay you £10 four times and you will have to pay him £5 six times. In ten bets, therefore, you stand to win £40 and to lose £30: you are therefore likely to gain £10. To calculate the expected value of a single bet, the £10 must be divided by ten (the number of bets) and the answer is £1. This is rather a cumbersome method of calculation. The same result can be achieved by multiplying the amount to be won by the probability of winning and subtracting the amount that can be lost multiplied by the probability of losing. The expected value is, therefore, £10 x .4 minus £5 x .6 = £1.

Now clearly it is impossible to win exactly £1 on a single bet: either £10 will be won or £5 lost. The expected value is based on the most likely result of a large number of bets over which the luck will even out because of the law of large numbers discussed in the last chapter. You may say this is irrelevant to a single bet, in which you may be lucky and come away with £10 in your pocket. But this is a poor argument: you cannot know that you will win, and indeed in this example you are more likely to lose. Even if you only take this particular bet once, life can be regarded as a series of gambles and if you want to achieve your goals to the maximum possible extent, you had better make sure you always take the gamble with the highest expected value: because your luck will even out, this maximises your chance of satisfying your wants. (I shall show in a later chapter that expected value does not have to be couched in monetary terms.) The rule for calculating expected value, then, is to multiply the possible gain by its probability of occurring and subtract the possible loss multiplied by its probability. Of course the result may turn out to be negative, in which case it is a bad bet: you expect to lose money.

I now turn to human irrationality in deciding which bets to accept. In practice, people often make bets where the odds are loaded against them. The very same person who will not accept an evens bet of £10 on the toss of a coin will happily spend the same money on a lottery or sweepstake where the expected value is considerably less than zero because of organisational costs and any rake-off that the promoters take. Assume that the stake is £1, the prize is £500,000 and that the chances of winning are one in a million, then the expected value of the lottery is 50p minus £1 or minus 50p. In other words, if you enter this lottery or similar ones many times, you expect to lose on average 50p per entry. Why do people indulge in such transparently bad bets? It may be that they are impressed by the largeness of the prize and argue that the cost of entering means little to them whereas the prize would mean a great deal. Its size makes them put to the back of their minds the low chance of winning. The bet is irrational only if the person's goal is making money. But if the pleasure of thinking he may possibly win £500,000 is worth 50p to him, it becomes a rational bet.

Inconsistency in betting cannot, however, be rational. Of course the same bet may be accepted one day and rejected the next as a person's mood varies, but, of more interest, a person can be induced to accept or reject exactly the same bet, depending on how it is phrased. In one experiment, most subjects chose to bet on receiving £45 with a .2 probability (expected value £9) rather than betting on receiving £30 with a .25 probability (expected value £7.50): this decision is clearly rational. These two gambles only have one stage, but subjects took a different decision when the same gambles were presented in two stages: with a probability of .75 the gambler may be eliminated after the first stage thus winning nothing, or he may move to the second stage with a probability of .25. If he does get to that stage, he is offered either £30 for certain or £45 with a probability of .8. A glance at Table 5 should help to clarify all this. The subjects had to decide before entering the first stage which option they would take at the second. Most elected to have the £30 for certain if they reached the second stage. But in terms of expected value the two options are exactly the same as those in the one-stage gamble, as can be seen from the table. Because players only have a .25 chance of reaching the second stage, one option is worth .25 x .8 x £45 or £9 and the other .25 x 1.0 x £30 or £7.50. Why did the subjects behave so inconsistently? Presumably they were too impressed by the certainty of winning £30 if they got through the first stage of the two-stage gambles.

Table 5

	Probability of moving to second stage	Probability of winning	Amount to be won	Expected value
One-Stage				
Option A	N/A	.2	£45	£9
Option B	N/A	.25	£30	£7.50
Two-Stage				
Option A	.25	.8	£45	£9
Option B	.25	1.0	£30	£7.50

There are many further demonstrations that people are irrationally influenced by certainty. In one such experiment, subjects were told that a new virus had been discovered that was expected to afflict 20 per cent of the population. The vaccination could have unpleasant but not lethal side effects. Some of the subjects were told that it would protect half of those receiving it, the rest learned that there were two strains of the virus each of which would infect about 10 per cent of the population and that the vaccination would offer full protection against one strain, but none against the other. Note that in both cases the vaccination provides the same chance (50 per cent) of providing complete protection against the virus. But considerably more of the second group of subjects said they would be vaccinated than of the first. What amounts to the same problem had been posed in two different ways. More of the second group chose to be vaccinated, because they were influenced by the *certainty* that the vaccination would protect against one of the two strains of virus, just as in the previous example subjects were wrongly influenced by the certainty of obtaining £30 if they got through the first stage of the gamble. In a very simple study subjects were offered a choice between receiving 100 Dutch forms with a probability of .99 or 250 with a probability of .5. Despite the fact that the second option has a considerably higher expected value (125 forms as against 99) most of them chose the first, whose outcome was almost but not quite certain.

In fact people have great difficulty in combining probabilities and possible gains or losses. An everyday case in which people attach too much weight to probabilities and not enough to costs is fault-finding. Consider a garage mechanic confronted with a car whose engine will not start – the fault might be in the plugs, the leads, the distributor and so on. Now he should have learned from previous experience (or even better a manual issued by the manufacturer) the probability of each fault and he should know the length of time it takes to check each fault. The question is which of the possible faults he should check first. This must clearly depend on how long it takes to check each and on the probability for each possible fault that it really is the fault. The higher the probability, the more sensible it is to check it first, but similarly the less time it takes to check it, the more sensible it is to examine it first. In other words, the expected time to find a given fault depends both on its probability and the time to find it, just as the expected value of a bet depends on the amount to be won and the probability of winning it. However, it has been shown that in locating faults, people tend first to test those that are most probable: they do not take sufficient account of the time to test for a given fault. Presumably, they are concerned about finding the fault and hence they pay more attention to the probability of finding it than to the time it will take. Such behaviour is time-wasting and irrational: one would expect all organisations involved in fault-finding to calculate the optimal sequence in which possible faults should be examined and to issue the information to those actually doing the job. Sadly, this is rarely done – yet another irrational organisational failure.

Another curious incapacity to appreciate probabilities can be illustrated by the following experiment. Subjects were shown a series of black and red cards and were told that they would earn money every time they said yes to a card of a particular kind and every time they said no to a card not of that kind. In fact they were rewarded at random 80 per cent of the time for saying yes to black cards and 20 per cent for saying yes to red ones. They proceeded to distribute their guesses in the same proportion – 80 per cent black, 20 per cent red – but if they had wished to obtain the maximum reward they should always have said yes to black and no to red, thus securing reward on 80 per cent of guesses instead of 68 per cent. This behaviour may not be as irrational as it seems since they might have been trying to work out what the rule was – except that they could have done that equally well by concentrating all their yes's on black and observing the results.

One problem on which people take inconsistent decisions depending on how it is put is as follows. Subjects were told that a rare disease had broken out, which was expected to kill 600 people. There are two possible methods of combating it, but they cannot both be used. The consequences of each programme are known and are:

Programme A – 200 saved with certainty.
Programme B – 600 saved with a probability of .33.

When the problem was put like this, most subjects said they would choose Programme A, presumably because they did not want to run the considerable risk of not saving *any* of the 600 who were liable to die.

The experimenters put exactly the same problem in a different form to other subjects:

Programme A – 400 die for certain.
Programme B – 600 die with a probability of .67.

When the information was given in this way, most subjects chose Programme B, presumably because 600 deaths do not seem that much more than 400 and the difference does not offset the opportunity to save everyone with a probability of .33.

The outcomes of both Programme A and Programme B under the two descriptions are of course identical. The only difference in the descriptions is that one is framed in terms of gains (people saved), the other in terms of losses (people who die). To convince yourself of this examine the following statement of the two programmes in which their descriptions in terms of people saved and people killed are put together.

Programme A – 200 saved with certainty. Therefore 400 die for certain.

Programme B – 600 saved with a probability of .33. Therefore 600 die with a probability of .67.

The inconsistent switch from one programme to the other occurs because people are more prone to take risks to save losses than to make gains. To demonstrate this, consider which options you would choose in the following situations:

Situation 1
Option A: Accept £50 with certainty.
Option B: Accept a gain of £100 with a .5 probability.

Situation 2
Option A: Accept a certain loss of £50.
Option B: Accept a loss of £100 with a .5 probability, with a .5 probability of losing nothing.

When asked to choose between the two options, most subjects selected Option A in the first situation and Option B in the second. They were less willing to risk a certain gain of £50 to make a possible gain of £100 than to risk losing an extra £50 to prevent a loss of £50. People, therefore, are averse to risks in making gains (Situation 1), but prepared to accept them when dealing with losses (Situation 2).

The example of the two programmes for treating the disease is in line with this general finding: far more subjects chose the risky programme (B) when it was presented as possibly avoiding *losses* (by deaths) than when it was presented as yielding *gains* (people saved), but it cannot be rational to make different decisions on the same problem depending on how it is posed. It is not known with any certainty why people should behave this way. It may be that they feel they will obtain some satisfaction by making a certain gain and the additional satisfaction they would secure by making a larger but uncertain one is not sufficient to compensate for the disappointment of making no gain at all if the gamble does not come off. They therefore run the risk of regretting their decision. In the case of losses, if they opt for taking a certain loss, that in itself will cause dismay: hence, they may think it worth risking a larger loss with the compensating chance of avoiding any loss at all and therefore avoiding any dismay. The chance that they will lose nothing compensates for the possibility of being a bit more upset if the gamble does not come off. It cannot be said that these attitudes are rational, but then as soon as one enters the realm of the emotions, it makes little sense to talk about rationality. What is irrational is taking different decisions about the same problem depending on how it is presented.

It is presumably because people count a loss as more important to themselves than the equivalent gain that they are prepared to run more risks to avoid losses than to make gains. This was nicely demonstrated in the following experiment. Some subjects were given a mug costing about $5. They were told it was theirs to keep. They were then told they could sell it at a price to be determined later and were asked what price would be acceptable to them. Other subjects who had not been given a mug were shown one and asked how much they would pay to buy it. The average price named by sellers was $9, whereas buyers only offered $3.50. People are reluctant to part with what they have: they will only part at a price higher than the price they would be prepared to pay to acquire the same object.

It should be noted parenthetically that there is one everyday instance when people are actually risk-averse in the realm of losses: they sometimes take a certain loss to avoid the possibility of a larger one (that is, they act in the opposite way to that just described). Taking out insurance is the best example. In terms of expected value, insurance is not a good gamble – its cost is more than the expected loss (the probability of the loss occurring multiplied by its amount), since the insurance companies take their cut. Insurance is, however, rational in most cases. The possible disruption to one's life caused by being unable to replace a burnt-out house or even a wrecked car justifies the comparatively small sums spent to guard against such disasters.

Although in general we may be willing to take risks ourselves in order to avoid a loss, it seems likely that we are less willing to take risks on behalf of others. Oestrogen therapy for post-menopausal women considerably reduces the risk of their bones degenerating, a condition that can cause fractures, which in turn can lead to death. Unfortunately, oestrogen causes cancer of the womb in a very small percentage of women. A careful calculation made by medical research workers shows that oestrogen would save many more women from death as a result of bone fractures than it would (eventually) kill through cancer of the womb. Nevertheless, many doctors are reluctant to use it. Presumably they feel that if they administer it, they are responsible for the deaths of the few women who die of womb cancer, whereas they are not responsible for deaths through bone fractures, which occur from natural causes. It is now known that giving progestin with oestrogen obviates the risk of cancer, but many doctors are still giving the combination of the two drugs far too infrequently: old traditions, particularly bad ones, die hard.

There is a further irrational error in thinking that can lead to inconsistency. In making predictions, people tend to ignore small differences in the evidence with which they are presented and to focus on relatively large ones. In one study subjects were asked to decide which member of various pairs of applicants should be preferred for entry as a university student. They were presented with the figures shown in Table 6, which are ratings for five students on intelligence, emotional stability and social ability. It is clear that intelligence is likely to be the best predictor of academic success, but it will be noticed that the difference in intelligence between successive applicants was small, while the difference on the other two variables was quite large. Accordingly, the subjects thought that A should be preferred to B, B to C, C to D, and D to E. When asked whether A or E, who have a large difference in intelligence, should be preferred, subjects chose E. This is clearly inconsistent: logically one cannot prefer A to B, B to C, C to D, D to E and E to A. The first four choices imply that A is to be preferred to E: A is the best and E the worst. Yet confronted with A and E, subjects thought E better than A.

Table 6

Applicant	Intelligence	Emotional Stability	Social Facility
A	69	84	75
B	72	78	65
C	75	72	55
D	78	66	45
E	81	60	35

You may feel that this experiment was cunningly rigged in order to bamboozle the subjects into making contradictory decisions and you are of course right. Nevertheless, in real life we ignore small differences at our peril. In taking decisions, whether about a career, a house or a car, there are not just three sets of differences between the different options, but a great many and it is always possible that when the small differences are added up they will outweigh the more salient ones.

Parenthetically, there is evidence that very low odds are disregarded. When American drivers were told that the chances of being killed in a single car trip were .0000025, only 10 per cent said they would wear seat belts. When they were told that the chances of being killed in a car crash over a lifetime were .01 (which is based on the same figure per trip), 39 per cent said they would use seat belts. Once again, the answer depends on how the question is put.

Here is a final experiment demonstrating inconsistency of yet another kind. Once again subjects were offered two options.

Option A: Win $2 with a probability of 29/36.
Option B: Win $9 with a probability of 7/36.

The expected value of the first bet is $1.61 and of the second $1.75 so there is not much to pick and choose between them. In fact when asked which bet they *prefer* to accept, most subjects go for Option A. But when asked *how much money* they would put up in order to be allowed to bet on these terms, they offered more for the second option than for the first (for example, they might offer $1.25 for the first and $2.10 for the second). Why should subjects say they prefer Option A, but be prepared to lay out more money to take Option B? The answer appears to be the availability error at work again. When asked which bet he would prefer to accept, the subject thinks of winning and compares the figures for the probabilities, which are higher in Option A. When he is asked how much the bets are worth, he focuses on the possible payment he could receive in each bet, which is higher in B, and he therefore chooses that option.

This section ends with some instances from real life of inconsistent decisions that are irrationally affected by the context in which they are placed. Suppose someone wants to buy a particular make of refrigerator costing just over £200. He goes to a shop with his wife and finds the refrigerator priced at £210, but she tells him there is a shop a few miles away where it is on sale for £205. He cannot be bothered making the journey and buys the refrigerator on the spot. The same afternoon, the couple go to another shop to look at radios and decide on one that costs £15. The wife, who is clearly a knowledgeable shopper, says the same set can be bought a few miles away for £10. They drive to the other shop to buy it. This behaviour is extremely common and is wholly irrational: in both cases the gain that would be made by going to the second shop is £5. It is either worth the expense of time, effort and petrol to save £5 or it is not, but people are influenced not by the absolute amount saved but by the amount as a percentage of the cost of the article being bought. Although the above example is imaginary, the effect has been demonstrated in experimental studies. It is safe to conclude that the amount of effort people are prepared to put into saving a given sum of money depends on the context within which they see it.

It has been argued that it is for this reason that discount figures on car prices both in Britain and in the US are separately displayed. There may seem little difference in price between a £12,000 car (or more probably £11,999) and an £11,500 car. But if the discount figure is displayed separately as £500 it appears to be a sizeable sum, as indeed for most people it is. Moreover, expectations are all-important. If you see a car priced at £11,500 you are likely to believe you are paying the proper price for that car. But if you see the same car priced at £12,000 but with a £500 discount separately displayed, you are likely to feel that you are saving money. Few people can resist a bargain, no matter how little of a bargain it is.

Here is a final example of people taking different and inconsistent decisions as a result of receiving the same information in numerically different forms. Suppose you smoke cigarettes and are told by a doctor that smoking increases your chance of death over the next twenty years by 30 per cent. You might well consider giving up. But suppose the doctor had put the same risk differently and told you that if you went on smoking, your chance of dying over the next twenty years would increase from 1 per cent to 1.3 per cent. Would you still give up? Once again people's reactions are determined not simply by the information, but by how it is put.

* * *

The next set of studies demonstrates that it is easy to manipulate the conclusions people draw from the same evidence even when no numbers are involved. In a classic experiment Elizabeth Loftus showed subjects a videotape of a car accident. Some subjects were then asked, 'How fast were the cars going when they smashed into each other?', others were asked, 'How fast were the cars going when they hit one another?' The average speed given by the first group was 41 miles per hour and by the second 34 miles per hour. A week later subjects were asked whether they had noticed any broken glass resulting from the accident. The presence of broken glass was incorrectly reported by twice as many of the first group as of the second: the suggestion that the cars had been travelling fast had made subjects confabulate the occurrence of broken glass.

Loftus followed this up by showing other subjects a video of a car accident in which a pedestrian was knocked over. A green car drove past the accident without stopping. Some subjects were then asked about an (imaginary) blue car that drove past. Later on they falsely remembered the colour as blue not green. Loftus even managed to make them confabulate a non-existent barn near the accident by slipping a mention of it into her questions. The subjects were not merely trying to please the experimenter by going along with her suggestions, since when offered a large reward for accurate reporting (which could be checked against the video) they still made the same errors.

The notion of the power of suggestion is of course not new, but this is a particularly convincing demonstration of it. These results not only suggest that people are without knowing it irrationally influenced by the way a question is put, but they call in question the rationality of the adversarial system used in British and American justice. The outcome of a trial may largely depend on the skill of each counsel in phrasing questions.

There is another kind of error that affects people's estimates of the most probable number of items of a particular kind or the most probable value along a particular continuum. Subjects were asked what percentage of African countries were in the United Nations, but before answering they were given a percentage and asked whether it was higher or lower than the actual percentage. The average estimate by subjects who were started at 10 per cent was 25 per cent, while those started at 65 per cent averaged 45 per cent. By sticking too closely to the starting point, these subjects behaved in a particularly irrational way since they had seen the initial numbers being determined by spinning a wheel of fortune: they therefore knew that they could have no possible bearing on the real percentages that they were trying to estimate. In a similar experiment, some subjects were first asked to assess the probability that the population of Turkey was more than S million, others that it was less than 65 million. Both groups then had to guess the actual size of the population. They gave very different estimates – 17 million and 35 million respectively. Once again they were loath to depart too far from the figure with which they started.

A similar error occurs when people are asked to specify their attitude by selecting a point on a scale. This error, which has been confirmed by many experiments, can lead to large inaccuracies in data gathered by questionnaires. For example, a questionnaire on the number of headaches people experience in one week was given to two different groups of subjects. One group had to indicate whether the number was 1-5, 6-10, 11-15, and so on, while the other was presented with the numbers broken down into 1-3, 4-6, 7-9, etc. The first group reported many more headaches than the second. Moreover, almost everyone is influenced by the two end points of a scale, tending to pick a number that is near the middle. So if people are asked to indicate how often they brush their teeth per week by ringing a number in a consecutive series that runs from 0 to 15, they are likely to claim that they brush their teeth considerably less often than if they are given numbers running from 0 to 40. Presented with two numbers at either end of a scale, people tend to opt for a number that is near the middle, regardless of whether it is correct.

These human failings can be and are exploited by government agencies and by advertising firms in order to produce misleading statistics. The claim that most people are satisfied with Mrs Thatcher or President Bush is meaningless if it is arrived at by asking people to tick one of the following items:

Dissatisfied   Satisfied   Very satisfied   Extremely satisfied

They will tend to tick one of the two items in the middle of the scale.

These phenomena are known as 'anchoring effects'. In picking a number, people tend to pick one close to, or anchored on, any number with which they are initially presented or in the case of a scale one close to the midpoint. The cause of the anchoring effect is probably people's reluctance to depart from a hypothesis. If they start with a number, even one determined by the random spin of a wheel, they adopt that number as a working hypothesis and although they do move away from it, usually in the right direction, they are reluctant to move too far. Similarly, when picking a point on a scale or selecting a number from a series of consecutive numbers, they are reluctant to depart too far from either end point and hence plump for a point near the middle. They unconsciously assume that the end points are likely to be approximately equidistant from the true value. Allowing one's judgement to be influenced by the initial anchoring point causes inconsistency: different judgements are given with different anchoring points although the anchoring point has no bearing on the correct judgement.

The anchoring effect makes people incapable of estimating the result of multiplying or adding a set of numbers together. I give two examples: the first is trivial but it demonstrates the point. The second can seriously affect people's pockets and also the safety of large-scale projects.

One group of subjects was asked to estimate quickly the product of

8 x 7 x 6 x 5 x 4 x 3 x 2 x 1

and another group the product of

1 x 2 x 3 x 4 x 5 x 6 x 7 x 8.

The average answer given by the first group was 2,250; that given by the second was 512. The first group had presumably been influenced by the large numbers they encountered at the beginning of the series, the second by the small numbers there: each group may have multiplied a few of the numbers on the left-hand side and then made an estimate based on the number so far obtained. Moreover, both groups' judgements were far too low: the correct answer is 40,320. Presumably their answers were anchored on the eight small numbers they saw.

Of more consequence, people are very bad at estimating the probability of a series of events where the probability of each is known. If you place an accumulator bet on three horses each of which has a .2 chance of winning (odds of 4 to 1, except you won't be offered that), the chance of your collecting from the bookie is only .008 (8 chances in 1,000). Since bookies can do arithmetic and know that many of their customers either can't or won't, the accumulator odds offered are likely to be far worse than this. It has been repeatedly shown that unless people work out the arithmetic, they tend to overestimate the probability of an event that is determined by a sequence of other events each occurring with its own probability. Because of the anchoring effect, people stick too close to the probabilities of the individual events, failing to realise that when combined by multiplication to yield the probability of a given outcome, that probability will be very much smaller. It is partly for a similar reason that people who think Linda is very likely to be a feminist and very unlikely to be a bank teller, tend to think she is more likely to be a feminist bank teller than a bank teller, as discussed in the previous chapter.

A similar mistake is made when there are several probabilistic events, any one of which could produce the same outcome. For example, suppose that there are 1,000 possible structural causes of an aircraft crashing over a five-year period and that each has a probability of occurring within that period of one in a million. The chance of any given aircraft of that type crashing through structural failure within five years now becomes approximately one in 1,000. Yet when confronted with problems like this, people stick much closer to the probability of failure of the individual parts, thus grossly underestimating the probability of an outcome that depends on the failure of any one part. This tendency contributes to the unrealistic estimates of the time needed to complete a large-scale project – although the chances of any one thing going wrong may be small, there are many things that might go wrong, such as hurricanes, strikes, shortage of essential components, and so on. In determining the safety of nuclear reactors, the probabilities are worked out mathematically, but here a different question arises, namely, that of assessing all the risks, which range from material failures to terrorism, and of putting an accurate figure on everything that might go wrong.

The reader may protest that he cannot be expected to go around doing mathematics all the time. There are two answers to this. First, it is possible to have a feeling for what happens when probabilities have to be multiplied and for what happens when they are added (as in the aeroplane example). Since people make consistent mistakes in each case, they have not developed a good intuition for approximately where the correct answer lies. Second, and more important, mathematics is a tool to rational thinking: it is impossible to be rational without it whether you are going to the horse races, designing an aeroplane or, as will be shown, selecting an employee.

moral

1. Always work out the expected value of a gamble before accepting it.
2. Before accepting any form of gamble decide what you want from it – high expected value, the remote possibility of winning a large sum with a small outlay, a probable but small gain, or just the excitement of gambling usually earned at a cost.
3. Remember that whether you save £5 on the cost of a house or on the cost of a radio, the saving is equally valuable to you.
4. If you are making a numerical estimate and have a given starting value, remember that the correct estimate is likely to be further away from the starting value than you may at first think.
5. Remember that many small independent probabilities may add up to quite a large probability.
6. Equally, if an event is determined by the occurrence of all of several other events, the probability of the event occurring will be very much lower than that of any one of the other events.

17 overconfidence

One aspect of overconfidence is hindsight: it takes two forms. One is believing that an event that has already happened was inevitable and could have been predicted, given the initial circumstances; the other is the belief that if you had taken a decision that was in fact made by someone else, you would have taken a better one.

An ingenious experiment to demonstrate hindsight was performed by Baruch Fischhoff in Israel. Subjects read descriptions of historical events, for example that of a battle between the British and the Gurkhas in India in 1814. Here is an extract from the account they read.

[1] For some years after the arrival of Hastings as Governor-General of India, the consolidation of British power involved serious war. [2] The first of these wars took place on the northern frontier of Bengal where the British were faced by the plundering raids of the Gurkhas of Nepal. [3] Attempts had been made to stop the raids by an exchange of lands, but the Gurkhas would not give up their claims to country under British control, [4] and Hastings decided to deal with them once and for all. [5] The campaign began in November 1814. It was not glorious. [6] The Gurkhas were only some 12,000 strong; [7] but they were brave fighters, fighting in territory well suited to their raiding tactics. [8] The older British commanders were used to war in the plains where the enemy ran away from a resolute attack. [9] In the mountains of Nepal it was not easy even to find the enemy. [10] The troops and transport animals suffered from the extremes of heat and cold, [11] and the officers learned caution only after sharp reverses. [12] Major-General Sir D. Octerlony was the one commander to escape from these minor defeats. (pp. 383-84)

Some subjects were given four possible consequences of the battle – a

British victory, a Gurkha victory, a military stalemate with no peace made, and a stalemate with a peace settlement. They were then asked to assess the likelihood of each on the evidence presented to them. Not surprisingly, there was little difference in the rated probability of these four consequences. Since there had been an equal number of statements favouring a British and a Gurkha victory, victory to either side was about equally likely and so was an inconclusive outcome to the battle. Other subjects were told after reading the passage that a particular outcome had occurred: each of the four possible results was given to different subjects. These subjects were then asked to rate the four possible outcomes in terms of their likelihood given the information they had received. Their estimates of the likelihood of the outcome they believed had occurred were much higher than those for the same outcome given by subjects who had not been told that it had happened. Of more interest, subjects justified their hindsight to themselves by seeing the statements supporting the supposed outcome as more relevant to predicting what would happen than the other evidence. Those told that the Gurkhas had won would emphasise that they were brave while those told that the British had won stressed that the Gurkhas were numerically inferior. This is yet another example of people distorting evidence to support a hypothesis.

This kind of experiment has been repeated several times using different material: for example, subjects were asked about the most probable result of a scientific experiment that had been described to them either after being told the result or not knowing what it had been. The former group thought the result they had been given was much more probable than did the latter.

In another study Fischhoff used contemporary events, for example Nixon's visit to China. Subjects were asked before the event about possible outcomes, such as whether he would meet Chairman Mao or how successful the visit would be. After Nixon's return to America, the subjects were asked to recall how likely they had thought the different outcomes were before the visit. Their memories were extremely fallible and heavily biased in the direction of believing they had made good predictions: they consistently but wrongly remembered having thought that the outcomes that did occur would occur and that those that did not occur would not occur.

These experiments demonstrate that people's misplaced confidence in their own powers of judgement not only makes them believe they are able to predict the future from the past far better than they in fact can, it also makes them distort past events and their recollection of their previous opinions. In the studies described subjects were set clearly defined problems. For example, in the experiment on the battle in India, they were presented with a tidy set of evidence that they only had to carry in their heads for a few minutes and with only a small number of possible outcomes. For several reasons hindsight in real life is likely to be much greater than in these experiments. In everyday life people's attention is not drawn to outcomes that are possible alternatives to those that actually took place: hence, they are unlikely to consider other alternatives and this will raise their confidence that only the actual outcome could have occurred. Second, the events from which they claim to be able to predict may have taken place a long time ago: their memories are likely to be even more fallible than they were in the experiments, and they are likely to remember just those events that are connected with the actual outcome. This tendency can be compared with people's selective memory for evidence that agrees with their own attitudes, as set out in Chapter 11. Finally, people do not normally make systematic predictions about what will happen in the future: this must make it easier for them to feel that had they made predictions, they would have been the right ones.

The world is a complicated place and chance factors play a major role in determining what will happen, whether it be the future of a business, the fluctuations of the Stock Exchange, or political events. People fail to take chance into account when judging in retrospect how likely a given event was. As the historian, R. H. Tawney put it, 'Historians give an appearance of inevitability to an existing order by dragging into prominence the forces which have triumphed and thrusting into the background those which they have swallowed up.' As we have seen, people are adept at inventing causal explanations for what has happened: it is after all an easy task, given the multiplicity of possible causes.

In so far as it distorts the past and exaggerates the ability to predict from it, hindsight is clearly irrational, but it is also dangerous. As Fischhoff puts it, 'When we attempt to understand past events, we implicitly test the hypotheses or rules we use to both interpret and anticipate the world around us. If, in hindsight, we systematically underestimate the surprises which the past held and holds for us, we are subjecting those hypotheses to inordinately weak tests and, presumably, finding little reason to change them. Thus, the very outcome knowledge which gives us the feeling that we understand what the past was all about may prevent us from learning anything from it.' Not only does it stop us learning from the past, it is likely to make us generate wrong predictions about the future and to feel too confident about those predictions. As Bernard Shaw said, 'We learn from history that men never learn anything from history.'

* * *

In view of the fallibility of human judgement, it is desirable that people should have some feeling for how likely they are to be wrong, particularly if they are taking important decisions. It has repeatedly been shown that, as in hindsight, people tend to err on the side of overconfidence. Here are two simple examples. In a recent survey of British motorists, it was found that 95 per cent thought they were a better than average driver. How can that be? Almost half the drivers questioned must have exaggerated their skill at the wheel. Again, most people think they are likely to live longer than average.

In one experimental study subjects were asked, among other things, to spell words and to rate their confidence in having spelled each one correctly. When they were 100 per cent confident of their spelling, they spelled the word correctly only 80 per cent of the time. In another study undertaken in Hong Kong, Asian subjects were asked questions like, 'What is the capital of New Zealand? Auckland or Wellington?' Since there were only two alternatives they could have scored 50 per cent by guessing. On items where their actual score was just above chance (65 per cent), they were 100 per cent confident that they were correct. British subjects were also tested in the same way: they were a little more cautious than the Asians, but their estimates of their ability to answer correctly still showed gross overconfidence: they were 100 per cent certain that they were right on items on which they were correct only 78 per cent of the time. This overconfidence is not caused merely by a form of boastfulness, for in another study, subjects were prepared to bet with the experimenter that they were right, when he offered better odds than those they themselves had given to the probability of their being correct. Had they made a true estimation of this probability they would have made money. In fact they lost it.

In another interesting study, clinical psychologists and students were shown a six-page account of the history of a real patient, who had been treated for adolescent maladjustment. It was given in four stages – a very brief description of the patient, and then successive accounts of his childhood, his time as a student, his service in the army and his subsequent career. After each of the four stages, subjects were given twenty-five sets of statements about him; each set contained five alternative statements, only one of which was true. The same statements were used at each of the four stages. After each stage, the subjects had to decide which statement in each set of five was most likely to be correct. All performed very poorly, getting only about seven statements right in the twenty-five sets (they could have scored five right by chance alone). The important point is that their performance did not improve over the successive batches of additional information they received. In contrast, their *confidence* that they were right rose steadily as they received more information. They clearly believed that the extra information was helping them, even though it was not. One can conclude that a lot of knowledge is a dangerous thing – it may not increase accuracy, but it does lead to false confidence (a theme to which I will return).

Although the vast majority of studies on the topic have shown that people are overconfident about the correctness of their judgements, there are two exceptions. When asked a mixture of easy and difficult questions, subjects sometimes underestimate how often they give correct answers to the difficult ones. They may estimate that they are never right on such questions, when they are in fact right about 30 per cent of the time. This is in reality another example of overconfidence. The subjects believe their answers to the difficult questions are likely to be wrong and they hold this belief too confidently, so they underestimate their ability to answer correctly. In addition, they may have judged the difficult questions to be even more difficult than they really were, by contrast with the majority of questions which they found very easy. However this may be, overconfidence is the rule, underconfidence the exception.

Consider some examples from real life. It has been found that doctors, engineers, financial advisers and others have an unwarranted confidence in their judgements. The dangers of such overconfidence are obvious. A patient may die in an operation which should never have been undertaken, but which the doctor was confident would succeed. Financial advisers on average do considerably worse than the market in which they are investing: if you buy securities by sticking a pin in the stock market listings, you will on average do better than investing in unit trusts run by securities advisers if only because you will save the monstrously high commission charged for their non-existent expertise. If you speak to any financial adviser, he will be aware of the findings but claim that he is an exception, another example of overconfidence. The building industry and the defence industry both consistently underestimate the time to complete a project and also underestimate the costs. The time underestimation cannot be made merely in order to obtain the contract since it occurs even when there are heavy penalties for being late. Kahneman and Tversky suggest that it happens because engineers look only at the project under consideration without comparing it with previous projects of a similar kind. In fact they may allow a slippage factor, but they do not systematically estimate the probabilities of different mishaps, for example, a strike, unusually bad weather, failure to receive supplies from other firms on time, and so on. Looking at similar projects might alert them to the effects of something unexpected going wrong. Even if people estimate the correct probability of such a series of individual events, they tend to underestimate the combined probability of any one of them occurring as was shown in the previous chapter. Finally, one of the most irrational instances of misplaced confidence in one's judgement is the widespread belief that the interview is a useful selection procedure, a mistake that will be discussed in more detail later.

It has been repeatedly shown that people are overconfident not merely about their own judgements, but about their ability to control events. If a subject can press one of two buttons whereupon a sign is illuminated telling him whether he has scored or not, after a number of presses he comes to believe that he has some control over the appearance of the 'score' light even though it in fact appears randomly regardless of which button is pressed. The extent of this 'illusion of control' can be illustrated from gambling. In Las Vegas, croupiers are sacked after a run of bad luck. Many croupiers actually think they can influence the number at which the ball comes down in roulette by the way they throw it, a false belief often shared by the players. Many dice players are known to throw dice softly if they want a low number and hard if they want a high one, although of course it makes no difference. Even more extraordinarily, it has been found that subjects bet more money on the throw of a dice before it has been tossed than if they are asked to bet after the toss. Perhaps they thought they could influence the result even though they were not tossing themselves.

The main reasons for overconfidence are almost certainly the same as those for the maintenance of false belief in the light of contrary evidence. First, people fail to look for evidence that would reduce their faith in their own judgement. This was confirmed in an experiment in which, after answering a question but before announcing how confident they were about having given the right answer, subjects were asked to give reasons why their answers might have been wrong. Making them search for contrary evidence did reduce overconfidence, though it still existed. Second, in many if not most cases, it is impossible to discover what the consequences of a different decision would have been. If you select a particular candidate for a post, there is no way of knowing whether a different candidate would have been better. Provided the candidate selected does tolerably well, you are likely to think you have made a good choice, which will of course boost your confidence in your ability to take such decisions. Third, as we have seen, people are likely to distort both their memories and any new evidence received in such a way as to fit in with their beliefs and decisions: again, this will inevitably produce overconfidence. Fourth, people will build up a causal story in their heads that explains why their judgement is right. As Nisbett and Ross point out, this may develop into a vicious circle in which the existence of the story makes them distort the evidence to fit it and the distortion of the evidence goes to confirm their explanatory story. The availability error may enter into the stories people build: if one is thinking along a particular line, the material most closely associated with that line of thought is likely to be called to mind and will serve to confirm one's beliefs, thus producing overconfidence. Our extraordinary facility at forming explanations to support our beliefs results in our placing too much faith in them instead of carefully examining alternatives. Finally, self-esteem may play a part: nobody likes to be wrong. But as we saw in Chapter 11, self-esteem alone cannot be a complete explanation. All these factors may also contribute to the illusion of control, but in addition illusory correlation is operating. The croupier rolling the ball at roulette notices the occasions when the ball goes to the desired spot (the positive event), but dismisses the plays on which the ball falls into the wrong hole.

moral

1. Distrust anyone who claims to be able to predict the present from the past.
2. Be wary of stockbrokers (or anyone else) who claim to predict the future.
3. To avoid disappointment, try to control your own overconfidence: think of evidence or arguments that are contrary to your beliefs.
4. If you are a casino owner losing money, don't sack the croupier: it's not his fault.

18 risks

As we have seen, many advanced military projects are cancelled after the expenditure of vast sums of money because they turn out to be impractical, but misplaced confidence on the part of experts can lead to worse damage than that. In the case of nuclear power, overconfidence and faulty reasoning caused the Three Mile Island and Chernobyl disasters. Of all dams built in the USA, one in 300 fails when the reservoir is first filled. In one study, seven eminent geotechnical engineers all failed to estimate the maximum height of an embankment that could safely be built on a clay foundation. Disasters can be caused by irrational decisions made on the part of the management, the engineers, the operators or the general public. Usually more than one of these factors is involved, but the main responsibility lies, as we shall see, with management and engineers for failing to foresee the reactions of the operators and of the general public.

Engineers are notorious for their failure to take into account the limitations of the human operator and to provide displays and control equipment that are easy for him to understand and use. The President's Commission on Three Mile Island concluded that the operators were badly trained and the control room was badly designed. Hence, they repeatedly misdiagnosed the problem and took the wrong action. As was shown in Chapter 9, when under stress, people become fixated on the first idea that comes to mind: unless displays can be correctly read intuitively and unless the operation of the controls is intuitive, when faced by a crisis the operators are likely to misread gauges and to mismanage the controls. Until quite recently altimeters were designed in such a way that they could easily be misread by a factor of ten. Pilots could believe that they were flying at 1,000 feet when they were actually only 100 feet above the ground. It is likely that the three crashes of the Airbus A-320 that have occurred since its launch in 1988 were caused at least in part by poor layout of the VDUs conveying information to the pilots. One Air France captain commented, 'I have always thought that this craft posed a real problem of interface between the pilot and the machine. The futurist plane sends heavy volumes of information that pilots have to sift . . . On classic aircraft, we receive what we call more primary information. And only that is essential.' The A-320's cockpit layout is now being altered.

Again, in a monotonous task, the operator may miss the significance of important information. In the history of railways, there have been hundreds of accidents caused by drivers failing to slow down or stop at signals, or exceeding speed restrictions on stretches of line that they knew well. British Rail tried to improve rail safety by having a klaxon sound in the cab if a driver had acknowledged a danger signal by pressing a button within three seconds of passing it: if he fails to press the button the brakes are automatically applied. Yet in 1989 in South London a driver went through two danger signals pressing the button each time but failing to apply the brakes: he collided with another train killing five people. The designers of the system had not recognised that pressing the button in response to the danger signal could become an automatic response and did not necessarily mean that the driver had consciously noticed the danger signal.

It is admittedly difficult to make allowance for the sheer daftness (irrationality) of people. Operators may fail to follow laid-down procedures in unpredictable ways. For example, a fire at the Brownes Ferry reactor was caused by a technician who was checking for an air leak with a candle. The fire came close to causing a melt-down, which would have had disastrous consequences. Again, the near melt-down of the reactor at Three Mile Island was partly caused by the fact that the operators simply refused to believe the monitors which showed that the core was overheating (as a result of the failure of a coolant pump).

Engineers not only fail to take into account the limitations of the human operator, they sometimes ignore the reactions of the public even when they are predictable. It has been shown, for example, in the USA that after a dam has been built as a protection against flooding, there is a tendency to develop the area threatened. In consequence, although the number and severity of the floods are reduced, the damage done may be increased. Again, in Britain, making seat belts compulsory has reduced the fatality rate of people in cars but only at the expense of more cyclists and pedestrians being killed: the security of a seat belt encourages reckless driving. In one experiment in the US, it was found that people wearing safety belts drove go-karts faster than people driving go-karts not fitted with a belt. The British high-speed train may have been safe but it proved a fiasco because the engineers were so engrossed with its design that they quite forgot that once in service it would carry passengers. The train was designed to run on conventional track by making carriages tilt on bends. When, after an expenditure of millions of pounds, the train was first tested, the tilting motion made the passengers sick: the elaborate food provided for the distinguished travellers was wasted. The train never entered service.

Apart from failing to take account of how operators and the general public will react, engineers sometimes design devices that are inherently unsafe, by not thinking hard enough to take the possibilities of failure into account, a fault again caused in part by overconfidence. Many modern devices are very complex and the designer may not appreciate the impact of a failure in one part on others. The early crashes of DC-10 aircraft occurred because the designers had not realised that decompression of the cargo compartment caused by its door flying open would wreck the control system of the aircraft.

A related error is the failure to recognise that a single cause can result in the simultaneous failure of two or more systems intended to complement one another. The five emergency core cooling systems at the Brownes Ferry reactor in Alabama were intended to act independently so that the failure of one or two would not be disastrous. In fact, all were damaged simultaneously because the electric cables supplying them were close together and were burnt by a fire.

When there are a great many crucial components, even if the probability of any one failing is very slight, the probability of the system as a whole failing may be quite high if it is the sum of the probability of failure of each individual part. Unless this sum is computed mathematically, people are, as we have seen, likely to underestimate it grossly. Moreover, in nuclear reactors the parts and the interactions between them are new, there is often no objective method of determining their true probabilities of failure: the evidence already quoted suggests that engineers' estimates are likely to be too optimistic. It may be impossible to ascertain whether the probability of failure per year of a new part is one in 10,000 or one in 1,000,000, but when there are many such parts, the difference becomes crucial.

It is often difficult to foresee all the possible chains through which a risk could develop, particularly if the damage is insidious rather than dramatic. The effects of acid rain or of lead in the air are examples. So are the greenhouse effect and the destruction of the ozone layer. The difficulty can also be illustrated by a more recent blunder, this time over oil seed rape plants. Rape plant genes were modified to protect them against herbicides; genes for an antibiotic used with people were also included. Since people do not eat rape seed, the British government's Advisory Committee for Release into the Environment passed the mutated rape seed for commercial cultivation. They had, however, overlooked the fact that bees collect honey from rape flowers and that people eat the honey together with any pollen it may contain. There is, therefore, a danger that the new genes might be transferred to micro-organisms in the stomach, causing allergies and producing strains of bacteria resistant to the antibiotic. The Government's Advisory Committee was irrational in so far as it failed to examine in sufficient detail all the chains through which the mutant plants could have adverse effects. It subsequently resorted to that time-honoured defence for making a mistake – passing the buck: honey is a foodstuff and therefore outside its remit, being the proper concern of the Ministry of Agriculture and Fisheries.

As a further example of a disaster caused by irrationality at all levels consider the recent sinking of the car ferry, the *Herald of Free Enterprise* in calm seas outside Zeebrugge with the loss of 180 lives. The immediate cause was water entering the car decks because the ship sailed with the bow doors open. The following factors contributed to the disaster: 1. Although the captain had asked for an automatic signal on the bridge showing the state of the doors, none had been supplied. 2. The assistant bosun who should have closed the doors was fast asleep. 3. The officer who should have checked that they were closed had been called away on other duties, because of a shortage of crew. 4. The *Herald* had originally been designed to ply between Dover and Calais: since the ramp at Zeebrugge was lower than that at Calais, the ship had to take on ballast water to lower it sufficiently to load the cars at Zeebrugge. Because the captain had been ordered to save twenty minutes on the crossing, there was no time to pump out the ballast before leaving, so that the ship was unduly low in the water. 5. Because of the time pressure, the captain left at full speed, thus creating a bow wave which swept into the car decks.

Two points should be made. First, had any one of these factors been absent, the ship might well not have sunk. Second, as Willem Wagenaar points out, the main responsibility must lie with the managers. They endangered the ship by insisting on a very fast crossing, by refusing an earlier request made by the captain for an automatic signal reporting the state of the doors, and by failing to provide sufficient crew. The captain was to a lesser degree at fault for not ensuring that the ship was ready to depart. He and the master took the absence of any warning from the assistant bosun that the doors were open as meaning that they were closed: for obvious reasons it is always safer to insist on a positive indication than to rely on the absence of an indication. To some extent the captain and even the first officer were merely obeying orders. As to the bosun, he clearly should have invested in an alarm clock. Wagenaar rightly says that this combination of events could not have been foreseen. On the other hand, the danger of leaving harbour with the bow doors open could have been foreseen and indeed had been by the captain. In the light of a large series of case histories, Wagenaar argues that most major accidents are caused by bad management. Those actually operating the system simply obey the rules management lays down. Whether or not this was the case with the *Herald*, management has a tendency to act out of greed or sloth: in this case there was no warning system, the schedules were too tight and the ship was undermanned. Although Wagenaar describes the accident as an 'impossible' one because of the elaborate combination of circumstances that caused it, it could have been prevented by more rational action on the part of management.

These failures to estimate risks correctly stem partly from overconfidence and partly from people's inability to think hard enough to envisage all possibilities. Engineering systems are becoming more and more complex: hence it is increasingly difficult to take into account all the possible interactions between their components. The most complex system of all is of course the human body: it was the failure to realise that a drug that was harmless to the person to whom it was administered might have adverse effects on the foetus that led to the thalidomide tragedy.

In estimating risks, engineers may suffer from overconfidence and an inability to take account of all important factors, but the general public's attitudes towards risks are even more irrational. It has been repeatedly shown that warnings about risk have little or no effect on behaviour, for example, campaigns in several US states completely failed to persuade more drivers to wear seat belts. It is not only on the roads that people ignore risks. Wagenaar took a stand at a home products fair and invited people to try out four different products ranging from insecticides to a new fuel for fondue sets. All carried instructions on the label, for example the fuel bottle carried warnings to wear gloves, not to sniff at the bottle, to extinguish the fire before using, and to close the can after using. Visitors to the stand were invited to try out these products and were provided with the means of doing so such as a mock-up kitchen. Despite the conspicuous danger warnings fewer than one in three read them before use. Wagenaar argues that much behaviour, including that of drivers, becomes automatised. This automatic behaviour persists even when people are made aware of the risk they are running. He points out that of his subjects 77 per cent confessed to not reading the label out of some sort of habit ('I forgot'; 'I never read labels'; 'I did not see the label'). The behaviour of his subjects contrasted with that of people whom he interviewed: 97 per cent claimed to read labels of potentially danger-ous products. There would appear to be a large gap between what people think they do and what they in fact do.

The public's estimation of risks is also irrational. In particular, because of the availability error, they vastly overestimate the dangers of dramatic accidents that kill several people simultaneously in one place as compared to the more insidious killing of many people at dif-ferent times and over wide areas. They are also afraid of new devices to which they are not accustomed. I shall illustrate these forms of irra-tionality by a comparison of the likely dangers of nuclear and fossil fuels. Despite the design errors already discussed, there have been very few deaths from nuclear power in the West where nuclear sta-tions are subject to careful inspection and control. Yet the layman is reluctant to believe that they are safer than fossil fuels.

The risks of fossil fuels include those to the workers extracting and transporting them. One in 10,000 miners die in the pits per year and the risk to workers on oil platforms is much higher; the transport of oil by road causes twelve deaths a year in Britain. Moreover, burning fossil fuels releases hydrocarbons into the air, some of which are a cause of cancer. It also releases various acids, particularly sulphuric acid, which cause widespread damage to trees and other vegetation. In Britain there is an excess death rate of 10,000 a year in people liv-ing in towns over people living in the country. The great majority of these deaths is almost certainly caused by the toxic products of fossil fuels. Finally, the burning of fossil fuels is exacerbating both the greenhouse effect and the depletion of the ozone layer: the long-term effects on humanity of either could make the melt-down of several nuclear reactors appear to be trivial incidents. The effects of burning fossil fuels are, therefore, widely scattered, insidious and long-term. Hence, they are largely ignored in contrast to those of nuclear fuels which are concentrated in area and for the most part sudden and immediate. And all this despite the fact that it has been estimated that the likely fatalities per unit of electricity produced are between ten and hundred times greater from coal-fired stations than from nuclear reactors.

The public's main worry about nuclear reactors is the escape of radiation. Even when it occurs on a small scale, it is a fairly dramatic event limited in locality and widely reported in the newspapers. It is highly available and hence causes concern. It has been argued that radiation is more dangerous than fossil fuels because of damage done to the genes: successive generations suffer. It has, however, been found that the proportion of babies born in Hiroshima with genetic defects was no higher than in Osaka, a comparable Japanese city that had not suffered irradiation from the atomic bomb. In fact the risks from radiation caused by burning coal are almost certainly far higher than those from nuclear power. Coal contains several radioactive substances, some of which on combustion are released into the air. A bigger danger, however, is that they occur in higher concentrations in coal ash which is deposited on the earth's surface: it has been calculated that (at present levels) their release into ground water and the air will cause 40 million deaths before the earth becomes uninhabitable through the enlargement of the sun.

A further factor which predisposes the general public to misperceive the dangers of different systems is the power of association. Whereas coal is associated with cosy fires burning in the hearth, nuclear power calls to mind the atomic bomb, thus producing a halo effect. The average risk of current nuclear reactors in Britain on life expectancy has been estimated as equivalent to being overweight by one gram – a weight one could not even feel in the palm of the hand. Moreover, the risks of reactors have to be seen in the light of other risks that are accepted. The risk of a major accident (killing 10,000 people) in the chemical plants and refineries at Canvey Island has been calculated as one in 5,000 per year. The Thames barrier was designed to have a one in 1,500 chance per year of being overtopped by a freak tide which could cause devastation and thousands of deaths in the area upstream. In contrast the risk of death per annum from a nuclear reactor has been calculated as one in a million to people living nearby and one in ten million to the public at large. One in a million is about the chance of being electrocuted at home. Most of the figures I have quoted are from a report by the British Health and Safety Executive, a body that is not biased either for or against nuclear reactors. Nevertheless, because the technology is new some of them may be wrong by a considerable margin. I have discussed nuclear reactors at some length not in order to defend them, but to show the irrationality of people's attitude to risk. The only valid argument against nuclear energy is that its production may contain more unknown risks than does that of fossil fuels.

There are two final forms of irrationality that affect risk assessment, particularly in laymen. It is not sufficiently recognised that any form of technology whether new or old carries risks. Although there are unfortunately no statistics on stage coaches and hansom cabs, it seems likely that horse-drawn vehicles caused more deaths per mile than does motor transport, which at present slaughters about 5,000 people a year in Britain. A connected point is that people fear anything novel. When electric lighting was introduced, people thought it so dangerous that they would not have it in their houses. In fact, it was far safer than the candles and oil lamps then in use. The first railways were greeted with a similar storm of terror with prognostications that travelling at speeds over 40 miles per hour would be lethal for the passengers. Whether such fears are rational must depend on how far the effects of a new technology have been investigated before it is introduced.

The irrationality of the extreme fear of nuclear reactors can be illustrated by contrasting it with people's attitudes to X-rays. Each radiologist in Britain administers to his patients annually a dose of radiation equivalent to the entire output of the Sellafield reprocessing plant. This is equivalent to about 1,600 reactors spread over Britain 'disguised as hospitals' as *The Independent* newspaper puts it. Although X-rays cause 250 unnecessary deaths a year (and many others, which may be warranted because of the benefits of diagnosis), there is no public protest about the overuse of X-rays. The reason is that people are familiar with X-rays and associate them with better health, whereas nuclear power is new and associated with the atomic bomb.

In short most people's attitudes to risks are based not on true probabilities, or rather on the probabilities that in our current state of knowledge are thought to be approximately correct, but on such irrational factors as the availability error and the halo effect.

moral

1. If you are an engineer, take into account the limitations of the human operator and the likely reaction of the general public to your project.
2. If you are a manager, remember that you are ultimately responsible for safety. Your operators are likely to act according to your directions, without showing initiative of their own.
3. Remember that insidious dangers may kill more people than dramatic disasters.
4. In evaluating new devices, remember that what matters is not that they are new but whether they could present unknown dangers.
5. If you have a choice, work in a nuclear reactor rather than on a North Sea oil rig.

19   false inferences

We can rarely know with certainty the full consequences of a decision. Hence, most decisions are based on an intuitive estimate of probabilities. The general cannot know what is the best strategy: he has to pick one that is likely to be the best. The doctor often cannot be certain, particularly in the early stages of diagnosis, what is the illness: has the patient with a pain in his chest got angina, in which case he should be referred to a cardiologist, or has he merely got a hiatus hernia when he should be given some medicine and packed off home? Is the probability of Winged Pegasus winning the 3.30 at Ascot greater or less than the odds offered? For all these cases there are many different factors that must be taken into account. Winged Pegasus has a very good pedigree, but he tends to run badly in wet weather and it is raining; his form has been excellent this year, except that he failed to finish his last race; moreover, to assess his chances the rest of the field must be considered. Not one of these factors on its own can predict whether he will win – they must all be taken into account and, even worse, combined to get at the true probability.

Confronted with several objectives and many courses of action, a person suffers from information overload. He cannot systematically examine all the possible actions to decide which is the best. In these circumstances, he attends only to those aspects of the options that occur to him (usually those with very different outcomes) and he settles for a course of action that is 'good enough', but may be far from optimal; Herbert Simon, the Nobel prizewinning economist, termed this way of taking decisions 'satisficing'. The person making an important decision ceases his search through the possible options when he has found one that is 'good enough' but not necessarily optimal. Even someone engaged on a very important decision does not begin to evaluate the full range of options and their possible consequences. Apart from failing to consider all jobs that he is equipped to do, someone deciding on a career will rarely take into account all the different advantages and disadvantages of a given job, such as pay, prospects, pension provisions, the number of hours of work, holidays, the probable congeniality of the company he is likely to meet at work, job security, level of responsibility, travelling time to work, status, benefits to society, chance to be creative, the basic interest of the job, the stress involved and so on. Instead, he may be reduced to seizing on one aspect in which the jobs clearly differ, such as the provision of a company car.

One could argue that the satisficing policy is to some extent rational. The consequences of a given decision can rarely be known with certainty and there comes a time when seeking further information or indulging in more thought is just a waste of time. This is true, but on the admittedly rather high standards of rationality I am setting, the resulting decision is likely to be irrational. All factors, certainly all important factors, should be taken into account, but it is a limitation of the human mind that it can only cope at one time with a very small number of ideas. Moreover, the few factors a person does consider in forming a major decision may not be the most important ones: they are likely merely to be those that are most available. It is surely foolish to let the provision of a company car outweigh everything else. One might expect that people would devote more time to considering what decision to take if it were important rather than trivial. Oddly enough, it has been shown that this is not so: people devote the same amount of time to thinking about large purchases as small ones, yet another curious piece of irrationality.

The following chapter will demonstrate that when many factors have to be considered people make poor predictions, and – since an element of prediction is involved in making all decisions – bad decisions. This chapter will show that in dealing with uncertain outcomes people may make poor predictions and decisions even when they only need to take one or two factors into account. Previous chapters have demonstrated that people go badly wrong in collecting and assessing evidence; this one examines the mistakes they make in using it. For the sake of simplicity, I will assume that the person making predictions knows the true value of the evidence at his disposal.

In what follows, 'prediction' refers to any inference about the likelihood of an event that is based on evidence, not merely to predictions about the future. The errors made are the same whether we are inferring from the evidence before us something about the past, the present or the future. If a student's IQ and capacity for hard work are known, one can 'predict' his academic performance in the past as well as in the future. The word 'predictor' will be used to mean any part of the evidence on which a prediction is based.

* * *

Kahnemann and Tversky record the following true story. Israeli Air Force officers engaged on training pilots complained that praising their trainees when they flew exceptionally well did not help: in fact, they always flew worse after being praised. They found, however, that when they reprimanded trainees for flying badly, they nearly always flew better next time. They therefore suggested to their superior officers that they should blame pilots for poor performance but not praise them for flying well. There is a subtle error behind this reasoning. Exceptionally good flying and exceptionally bad flying are both rare. It follows that regardless of praise or blame, if a pilot flies very well or very badly on one occasion, he is likely to revert towards his average performance on the next flight, just because an average performance is more usual than an extremely good or bad one. Hence the pilot who has flown well on one occasion will probably do worse on the next, and the pilot who has flown badly is likely to fly better next time. The principle that if an event is extreme (either way), the next event of the same kind is likely to be less extreme is known as 'regression to the mean'. It affects all events in which chance plays a role. For example, parents who happen to have very high IQs – whether because they have an exceptionally favourable collection of genes or have had an exceptionally favourable environment – are likely to have children of considerably less intelligence. Since the children receive only half of each parent's genes, they are unlikely to have exactly those that helped to make the parents intelligent, while if the parents had an exceptionally favourable environment, the children are likely to have a less favourable one, because that is closer to the average.

As a further illustration, here are two instances from everyday life, the first provided by Nisbett and Ross. In American baseball there is a phenomenon that is so common that it has been given a name – 'the sophomore effect'. In one season a player hits an exceptionally large number of runs. He is widely acclaimed as a star, but the next season his performance slumps and he plays just a little bit better than average. Numerous explanations appear in the newspapers for this effect – the pitchers had learned how to deal with him, he was spoiled by success, he gained weight, lost weight, got married, got divorced, and so on. In fact no explanation is necessary: chance is bound to play a large part in how many runs a player hits and if he has been favoured by chance one season, it is likely that this will not happen the following one and his performance will revert towards his own average level.

Baron provides another illustration from an experience we have all had. Someone goes to a restaurant for the first time and finds the food excellent, but on going back, finds the second meal disappointing. Chance plays a considerable role in cooking and if the food was exceptional on one occasion, it is likely to revert towards the norm on the next. As Baron points out, if you have a bad meal at a restaurant, you do not return there, so you never discover whether the second meal would have been better, which it is likely to be.

The effect of regression to the mean has been put to practical use by a securities adviser. A range of unit trusts is often offered by the same firm. He started by buying the worst-performing unit trust of a particular firm. Every year he then sold this trust and transferred the money to another one belonging to the same firm: he always bought the trust that had done worst in the previous year. At the end of the ten years he had made ten times as much money as he would have made by investing each year in the unit trust that had done best. Yet financial advisers persist in advising their clients to buy unit trusts with 'a good track record'.

Most people, then, fail to see that anything that is exceptional on one occasion is likely to revert towards average on the next, at least where chance plays a role. Hence, they make a prediction that is too extreme and therefore likely to be wrong. So far we have considered the prediction of one event (or quality) from another of exactly the same type. But the principle of regression to the mean applies just as much to the case where the evidence used to predict is completely different from the event being predicted. The rule here is that the worse the predictor, the more regression to the mean must be expected. This can be illustrated by the following experiment. Subjects were asked to predict a student's Grade Point Average. Different groups were given different kinds of evidence – either his Grade rank compared to other students (from which the Grade Point Average expressed as a number can be accurately deduced), or his score on a mental concentration task (from which it is possible to infer the Grade Point Average with only moderate accuracy), or a measure of his sense of humour (which has little if any bearing on the Grade Point Average). The three groups of subjects were respectively told that Grade Point rank was a perfect predictor, mental concentration was only a moderately good one and sense of humour was valueless. The first group, as one might expect, performed well. But the second two groups did not allow for regression to the mean: if the person they were judging had a very high (or very low) score on mental concentration or sense of humour, they allocated him an equivalently high (or low) score on the Grade Point Average. They did not take into account the fact that they were dealing with an imperfect predictor and that since most scores cluster around the mean, the student being judged was far more likely to have a Grade Point Average score near the average than an extreme score equivalent to a very high or very low score on measures of mental concentration or sense of humour. Economists have wasted much time and paper trying to explain why a business that does exceptionally well one year does worse the next. Had they made use of the principle of regression to the mean, they could have saved themselves and their readers a great deal of time.

The cause of this mistake is debated. The availability effect may play a part. People have before their minds a high or low value of the predictor and without thinking they tend to assign the corresponding value to whatever they are trying to predict. Even when people know that the predictor is imperfect, they cannot disabuse themselves of the idea that the value they are predicting should correspond to the predictor's value, as of course it always does in the case of a perfect predictor. The mistake is not dissimilar to the failure to take into account the base rate when assessing probabilities, as in the green and blue cabs problem discussed in Chapter 15.

A further mistake made in connection with regression to the mean concerns people's confidence in their judgements. As we have seen, when an imperfect predictor score is high, the estimate of the variable being predicted should be adjusted downwards towards the average, and similarly it should be adjusted upwards if the predictor score is low. Not only do people fail to do this, but they express more confidence in their mistaken judgements when they are based on high and low predictor scores than when these scores are near the average value. Extreme predictor scores engender extreme confidence even though these scores are the very ones likely to result in the biggest errors. It is as though people unconsciously think that if one thing (the predictor score) is extreme, then anything connected with it (their confidence in the prediction) should also be extreme.

A further curious error of confidence can be illustrated by a simple example. Suppose that before the days of calculators an accountant was trying to assess whether an applicant would make a good clerk. The accountant might test his speed at addition and subtraction. He would of course want to take other considerations into account such as how tidy the applicant's work was, how conscientious he was and so on. Now it is highly likely that ability at addition is completely correlated with ability at subtraction: if we have a measure of someone's ability to add, it will predict almost exactly how well he can subtract. It follows that in predicting how good a clerk the man will make, it does not help to take into account measures of his skill at both addition and subtraction. Since the two are completely correlated, we need use only one measure. On the other hand, since tidiness and conscientiousness are likely to correlate poorly with ability at addition and subtraction, using these two factors (as well as skill at either addition or subtraction) will help to predict whether he will be a successful clerk.

In practice, as the following experiment shows, people actually do the opposite of what they ought to do: they place more faith in correlated qualities than in uncorrelated ones. Subjects were told that students' academic success could be predicted by four tests, each of which was only moderately reliable as a predictor, and all of which had exactly the same reliability as one another. The tests were divided into two pairs: the first was 'mental flexibility' and 'systematic reasoning', the second 'creative thinking' and 'symbolic ability'. Subjects were told that the scores on the first pair were highly correlated with one another (that is, the score on 'mental flexibility' could be accurately predicted from that for 'systematic reasoning'), while the scores on the second pair of tests were uncorrelated (that is, one could not infer the score on 'creative thinking' from the score on 'symbolic ability'). The subjects were then given the fabricated scores of imaginary students on all four tests, arranged in keeping with what they had been told: for example, if an individual student's score on 'mental flexibility' was 16, his score on 'systematic reasoning' would lie between say 15 and 17, whereas a score of 16 on 'creative thinking' was randomly paired with a score of say 1 to 20 on 'symbolic ability'. The subjects had to make their predictions of individual student's academic success either from the correlated or from the uncorrelated pairs. When asked how much faith they had in the accuracy of these predictions, they expressed much more confidence in those based on the correlated pairs: this is the reverse of a rational judgement. If one score reliably predicts another, knowing the second score gives no new information, whereas when two scores are not correlated making use of both can improve prediction.

The error described presumably occurs because the correlated scores are consistent with one another and this makes people think that they must be consistent with the score being predicted, while the uncorrelated scores are usually inconsistent with one another and hence people think they cannot reliably predict the target score.

* * *

This chapter ends with a few disparate examples of failing to draw the right conclusion from limited evidence. Suppose a selection committee is deciding whether to accept someone on a postgraduate course in clinical psychology. The committee relies on two pieces of evidence – his examination performance in a special examination and the amount of time he has spent working in a psychiatric hospital. These two figures are uncorrelated, that is, it is impossible to predict one from the other. In fact, this particular candidate had spent much longer working in a psychiatric hospital than most students admitted to the course. The committee naturally views this very favourably, but his examination results are missing. When they are found, they prove to be only slightly better than average for candidates applying. Try to decide whether the committee should raise their opinion of him or lower it. Most people think they should lower it, but in fact they should raise it. This error is again related to failure to take into account regression to the mean. Since experience with mental patients is not correlated with examination results, the best estimate for his results is that they will be average. So when the committee discovers that he is in fact above average, they should raise their opinion of him. The mistake arises in part because people tend to average scores when they should be adding them, just as they do with probabilities as was shown in Chapter 16.

Suppose you are playing roulette and the ball comes down on black six times running. Most people including seasoned gamblers think it is more likely to come down on red than black on the next throw. They make this prediction because on average over a large number of throws it will come down about equally often on black and red. Returning to an idea introduced earlier, the sequence BBBBBBR is more representative of the typical sequence than are seven blacks in a row. But the ball has no memory: it does not matter how many times in succession it has already come down on one colour, the chance of it falling on the same colour on the next throw remains equal. For obvious reasons, this error is called the 'gambler's fallacy'.

As Fischhoff points out, the same mistake can occur in more serious contexts than gambling: even the eminent American historian, Morrison, fell for it. He recalled that at the beginning of his fifth year in office Roosevelt announced that he would pack the Supreme Court with judges of his own choosing. Morrison goes on to argue that since no judge had retired during the first four years of Roosevelt's presidency, and taking into account the rate at which judges normally retire, 'the odds were eleven to one in [Roosevelt's] favour that he would be able to name one or more justices by traditional means that very year'. Fischhoff comments, 'The past four years were history, and the probability of at least one vacancy in the coming year was still .39.'

A related fallacy is to see a pattern in a set of events when they are in fact random. One instance that has often been cited is the pattern of German bombs on London during the Blitz. Londoners developed elaborate theories about the targets at which the Germans were aiming and hence where they should take cover. Many drew the false inference that the East End of London had received more than its fair share of bombs and that the Germans were trying to alienate the poor from the rich. When, after the war, the pattern of German bombs was submitted to statistical analysis, it was found to be completely random. The human desire to make sense of things – to see patterns where none exists or to concoct theories that explain why someone is particularly good at spotting suicide notes – can lead people badly astray.

Finally, here is an example of people being completely blind to the fact that any prediction made from very poor evidence must be tenuous. Subjects were given an account of a graduate student based on projective tests. The subjects believed that projective tests, such as the Rorschach or Draw-a-Person test described in Chapter 12, had almost no predictive value: we have already seen that they were right, at least in this respect. They were given a list of nine courses that the graduate student might be studying and asked to pick the right one. Because of the projective test description ('. . . lacking in true creativity . . . need for order and clarity and for neat and tidy systems . . . little feel and little sympathy for others . . .'), most of them plumped for his being an engineer. They were then told that he was in the Graduate School of Education working in a special programme on handicapped children. They were asked how they reconciled this with the description given as a result of the projective tests. Most of them did so by picking out aspects of the description that fitted someone in education ('deep moral sense'). Almost none of them rejected the profile given by the personality tests. We consistently overvalue bad evidence.

moral

1. Remember that when anything extreme happens, whether it is very good or very bad, the next happening of the same kind is likely to be much less extreme for purely statistical reasons: it reverts to the mean.

2. When drawing predictions from imperfect evidence, make your prediction closer to the average value of whatever you are predicting than the value of the predictor.

3. If two pieces of evidence always agree, you need only take account of one in making a prediction.

4. Learn some elementary statistical concepts and some elementary probability theory, particularly if you are in a profession. It should not take more than a few days. An enjoyable start is J. A. Paulos, *Innumeracy* (referred to in the Further Acknowledgements).

5. Falling for the 'gambler's fallacy' won't make you win money, nor come to that will it make you lose.

20   the failure of intuition

One of the most prized human faculties is intuition. Many people find it more hurtful to be accused of having poor intuition than of being slovenly, lazy or selfish. As Rochefoucauld said, 'Everyone complains about the badness of his memory, nobody about his judgement.' There are only a few dissenting voices – for example, it has been said that intuition is that strange instinct that tells a person he is right, whether he is or not.

In the last chapter we saw that people are prone to make errors when making predictions based on a small number of factors. In real life many different factors must be taken into account, each of which predicts more or less reliably; that is to say, the prediction made by each has a given probability of being correct. Consider the following passage from a medical book on cancer, which was quoted by David Eddy: the italics are his and are used wherever there is a phrase that indicates a degree of uncertainty. The passage is intended to help physicians to differentiate a benign cyst from cancer of the breast.

Chronic cystic disease is often confused with carcinoma of the breast. It *usually* occurs in parous women with small breasts. It is present *most commonly* in the upper outer quadrant but *may* occur in other parts and eventually involve the entire breast. It is *often* painful, particularly in the premenstrual period, and accompanying menstrual disturbances are *common*. Nipple discharge, *usually* serious, occurs in *approximately* 15 per cent of the cases, but there are no changes in the nipple itself. The lesion is diffuse without sharp demarcation and without fixation to the overlying skin. Multiple cysts are firm, round and fluctuant and *may* transilluminate *if* they contain clear fluid. A large cyst in an area of chronic cystic disease *feels* like a tumour, but it is *usually* smoother and well delineated. The axillary lymph nodes are *usually* not enlarged. Chronic cystic disease *infrequently* shows large bluish cysts. *More often* the cysts are multiple and small.

This quotation demonstrates that a great many different symptoms may have to be taken into account in making a diagnosis and that their reliability varies from 'may' through 'usually' and 'most commonly' to 'is' (complete certainty) with many other probabilistic terms thrown in. It is unlikely that any physician examining a patient could carry all of the dozen symptoms listed in his head giving each its due weight and intuitively come to the diagnostic decision that is best given the evidence.

This chapter will demonstrate that human intuition is in fact remarkably bad: indeed it is so poor that when the same data used by people in making intuitive judgements are submitted to a formal mathematical analysis, the resulting judgements are consistently much better than those of people. I shall call the two methods of making predictions intuitive and actuarial, and for want of a better word I shall call the person who makes an intuitive prediction a 'judge'.

To assess the performance of human judges, we need to discover how well they might do if their judgements were optimal: they can never be perfect, if the predictors are not perfect. Fortunately, there is a mathematical method that assesses the validity of different predictors and puts them together in such a way as to make the best possible prediction from the evidence available (with rare exceptions that require other mathematical techniques).

As Robyn Dawes, one of the leading workers in the field, points out, this method was to some extent anticipated by Benjamin Franklin, who wrote the following letter to his friend, Joseph Priestly.

I cannot, for want of sufficient premises, advise you *what* to determine, but if you please I will tell you *how* . . . My way is to divide half a sheet of paper by a line into two columns; writing over one *Pro* and over the other *Con*. Then, doing three or four days' consideration, I put down under the different heads short hints of the different motives, that at different times occur to me *for* or *against* the measure. When I have thus got them all together in one view, I endeavour to estimate the respective weights . . . [to] find at length where the balance lies . . . And, though the weight of reasons cannot be taken with the precision of algebraic quantities, yet, when each is thus considered, separately and comparatively, and the whole matter lies before me, I think I can judge better, and am less liable to make a rash step; and in fact I have found great advantage for this kind of equation, in what may be called *moral* or *pru-*

dential algebra.

It has in fact been shown that the use of Franklin's technique enables people to take into account more evidence and more alternatives before reaching a decision.

The mathematical technique to be described puts the best possible weights (in Franklin's terms) against each of the separate pieces of evidence that are relevant. It can be illustrated by a study predicting the success of graduate students at Oregon University. The staff members responsible for their admission had access to their undergraduate grades, to their performance on a special examination for intending postgraduate students (the Graduate Record Examination) and to reports from referees. The references were given numerical ratings by the four members of the admissions committee. The approximate numbers for the three pieces of evidence about the candidates ranged from 3.0 to 4.9 on undergraduate grades, from 70 to 90 on the Graduate Record Examination and from 1 to 5 on the references. In summary, each candidate was allotted three numbers, one for each of the three pieces of evidence. Finally, the admissions committee on the basis of these numbers placed each candidate in one of six categories which indicated their judgement of his potential as a graduate student.

It is always difficult to decide whether a selection committee is performing its job well, because one cannot know how rejected candidates would have performed had they been selected. But one can compare the actual performance of those selected after they have completed their course (or towards the end of it) with the category (1-6) in which they had been placed by the admissions committee. This gives a measure of how far the committee's ratings predict performance in graduate school. In fact, their predictions were poor but better than chance. Now obviously the three pieces of evidence might not be of equal importance in predicting the students' ultimate success. For example, grades might predict much better than references, in which bias on the part of the referee may occur. To arrive at the best ratings the admissions committee must attach the right importance to each of the three pieces of evidence. But we have already seen how difficult it is for most people to judge connections. How is the committee to decide whether previous university grades are more important than references and if so, by how much? They do so by using their intuition.

The actuarial method to be described is known as multiple regression analysis. It takes the initial ratings on the three bits of evidence for each candidate and systematically compares them with the final assessment of his performance. It calculates the reliability with which each of the three pieces of evidence predicts the student's performance as judged towards the end of his university career. The predictive value of each of the three factors is represented by a decimal lying between 0 and 1 – a weight. To obtain a prediction for a given student, all that needs to be done is to take each of his three scores, multiply it by the appropriate weight and add the resulting three figures. (This procedure not only takes into account the relative value of each factor in predicting the outcome, it also corrects for the fact that the range of the three predictor numbers is very different – for example, 3 to 4.9 for undergraduate grades against 70 to 90 for the Graduate Record Examination). The mathematical analysis yields approximately the best prediction that can be made from the three pieces of evidence supplied.

You may rightly object that there is an element of cheating in all this. Because the mathematical analysis makes use not just of the three predictors but also of the outcomes to be predicted, it could hardly fail to do better than the judges. To overcome this, the results of the initial analysis are tested by applying them to a different batch of students and a calculation is made of how well the predictions work for these students: these predictions can then be compared with those made by human judges using intuition. It is not possible to compare in everyday terms the difference in the accuracy of the mathematical model and that of the human judges, but in this study the best estimate (based, in technical terms, on the amount of variance in the students' progress accounted for by the two methods) was that the actuarial method predicted with an accuracy four times as great as that of the human judges.

It must be remembered that even the actuarial method is not perfect: it merely makes predictions that are as good as possible given the evidence received. It is, of course, never possible to predict human performance with perfect accuracy: in the case of the students some will fall in love and be distracted, others will be left by their partners and be even more distracted, some will choose a project for a doctoral thesis that by pure luck yields interesting results, others will choose one that proves recalcitrant to all their efforts. Nor is it merely human performance that cannot be predicted with complete certainty. The weather, the location of geological sites containing oil and the nature of an illness given a set of symptoms can be predicted only with a certain degree of probability. In these and many other cases actuarial prediction has been shown to do better than human judges.

Indeed, out of more than a hundred studies comparing the accuracy of actuarial and intuitive prediction, in not one instance have people done better, though occasionally there has been no difference between the two methods. In the great majority of cases, the actuarial method has been more accurate by a considerable margin. Here are a few randomly selected instances in which it has been more successful than the intuitions of experts (the type of prediction is placed first, followed by the kind of expert with whose judgements the actuarial method is compared): the extent to which people on parole will show good conduct or will violate their parole – three separate studies on over 3,000 parolees (psychologists and psychiatrists); pilot performance after training predicted before training (US Air Force personnel officers); adjustment to a reformatory (psychiatrists); job satisfaction in engineers predicted before they left college (counsellors); recidivism in criminals (physicians); suicide attempts in psychiatric patients (psychiatrists); amelioration of mental illness in schizophrenics (physicians); whether to classify a mental patient as psychotic or neurotic (psychiatrists and psychologists); the growth of corporations (securities analysts); horses' performance at the races (tipsters).

It will be noted that in all but one of these examples the predictions are made about people, whether it is their behaviour, their attainments, their capacities or their state of mental health that is in question. It is of course precisely about other people that we claim to have intuitions. Most people already acknowledge that the external world is best understood and its states best predicted by using scientific methods rather than intuition. If you want to predict the weather, rather than consulting Old Moore's Almanac or noticing a red sky at night, you would do better to read the weather forecast or to compile, as the Weather Office does, detailed records that enable moderately accurate forecasts to be made with the use of mathematical analysis. And if you have a car that won't start, you examine the leads, the plugs, the distributor and so on, applying knowledge but not intuition. The rationality or otherwise of human intuition is therefore best tested by predictions about people.

Although prediction by actuarial methods is in the great majority of cases much more successful than prediction by intuition, three caveats should be made. First, the evidence (or at least some of it) used in actuarial prediction must be relevant to the prediction and it is people who in the first instance decide what is relevant. The admissions committee decided that undergraduate grades, performance on the Graduate Record Examination, and references were relevant, but one can think of many other kinds of evidence that might possibly be helpful, for example, the candidate's state of health, or judgements by those who know him about how conscientious or persistent he is. Now, it is extremely difficult for a human judge to know whether such additional evidence has any bearing on the student's ultimate level of success. Part of the beauty of the actuarial method is that if any predictor is added to the computation, it will automatically determine whether it is relevant or not. If the evidence is completely unconnected with the prediction to be made, it will be assigned a weight of zero, which means that in the final calculation it is simply disregarded. As we have seen, people often make connections that do not exist, and actuarial prediction is a safeguard against their use. Although the data fed to the mathematical crunching machine must be suggested by people, the actuarial computation determines accurately what use to make of it.

The second caveat is that comparing human and actuarial judgement is only valid if the same data are available to the mathematical analysis and to the human judge. This is not always possible since people often do not know what are the bases of their judgements. To take an extreme example, in one study photographs of men and women were touched up so that their pupils were either very large or very small. Photographs of the same person with small pupils and with large ones were shown to members of the opposite sex. A person shown with big pupils was judged to be much more sexually attractive than when shown with small pupils, but the people looking at the photographs had no idea that they had been influenced by pupil size. Nevertheless, although judges may acquire a general impression of a person from an interview without knowing exactly how they do it, it is possible to have them rate a candidate on the basis of an interview and to feed that rating into the mathematical analysis. In fact, as we shall see, interviewing does not improve prediction: it tends to make it worse.

The third caveat is that the data fed to the mathematical model must be in numerical form. This does not present a problem. Human judges can readily assign numbers to pieces of evidence. In the example given, the admissions committee rated how good references were on a scale of 1 to 6. If people are averse to assigning numbers, then they can simply be asked to tick a graded series of adjectives, for example, 'very bad, poor, indifferent, good, excellent', and numbers ranging from 1 to 5 can subsequently be assigned, depending on which category is ticked. There is of course no guarantee that an individual judge will be consistent in his ratings: presented with the same reference on different days, he may assign it a 1 on one day and a 2 on another. To the extent that judges are fallible in this way the value of the predictor they are assessing will be reduced. But if a judge is

inconsistent in his evaluations that will of course lower his own predictive success as well as that of the mathematical model. One way to
overcome this problem is to have several people make judgements of
the score on a predictor and to average their results: their mistakes
tend to cancel out and more consistent figures are produced.
Moreover, it seems likely that being compelled to categorise a quality
in numbers will actually make judges more consistent. Suppose that
two of the qualities sought in a salesman are charm and self-confidence and that these are assessed in an interview. Most interviewers
simply carry away a global impression of the interviewee (highly
coloured by the halo effect): if they were forced to allot numerical ratings to charm and self-confidence, they would surely be more likely
to isolate such qualities from their general impression. The predictive
value of their ratings can be assessed by the mathematical analysis
once there have been enough cases and provided the success of the
salesmen selected can be ascertained.

The final caveat is that the actuarial method can only be applied
when we are making the same type of prediction and have the same
kinds of knowledge (the predictors) about a reasonably large number
of similar cases, for example, the performance of graduate students
given their records or the type of disease given the symptoms. Except
in special cases it is hard to predict the outcome of a battle or a
courtship. Oddly enough, however, the actuarial method has proved
successful in predicting happiness in marriage, simply by subtracting
from the average number of times a couple makes love a week, the
number of rows they have a week.

So far then, we have established that when applicable the actuarial
method almost always does better than human judges. But there is
something even more extraordinary to come. It is possible to take the
predictions for a number of cases made by the same judge and to calculate the weights he has implicitly assigned to each of the predictors,
such as undergraduate grades, Graduate Record Examination, and
strength of references. Although he may not know it, he is implicitly
assigning weights to each predictor and the weights assigned can be
established by comparing the scores on the predictors for each candidate with the judge's assessment of that candidate's potential as a
graduate student. Notice that no account is taken of how well the
candidates actually perform. Now when the judge's weights are calculated in this way, it turns out that the mathematical formula using
these weights actually predicts better than the judge himself. How can
this be? L. R. Goldberg answers the question: the judge 'is not a

machine. While he possesses his full share of human learning and hypothesis-generating skills, he lacks a machine's reliability. He has his days. Boredom, fatigue, illness, situational and interpersonal distractions, all plague him, with the result that his repeated judgements of the exact same stimulus configuration are not identical . . . If we could remove some of this human unreliability by eliminating the random error in his judgements, we should thereby increase the validity of the resulting predictions.'

Once again, by averaging judgements over many cases, random variations cancel out and we arrive at the judge's average weights, from which too often he departs. The mathematical model does not depart from these weights and hence does better than the judge. Although the procedure just described, which is known – appropriately – as 'bootstrapping', does not normally predict as well as a formula based on the optimal weights calculated by comparing the individuals' predictor scores with their final performance, it often falls not far short. The implication is that the judge has implicitly developed quite a reasonable set of weights, but he does not use them consistently. It should be stressed that bootstrapping yields the weights the judge (or judges) actually use, not those they think they use. In fact they are usually unaware of how they make their judgements. When the judgements of stocks made by thirteen individual stockbrokers were analysed, it was found that the weights they actually attached to predictors were almost the reverse of those they thought they attached.

We can now consider why intuitive prediction is so much worse than actuarial prediction. First, the human judge does not attach an optimal set of weights to the predictors, for all the reasons laid out in the previous chapters. As we have seen, people are very bad at making the right connections: they may attach too much importance to a predictor that bears little or even no relationship to the outcome being predicted. Second, people are very bad at combining different pieces of information. Indeed they do not consciously assign values to the predictors at all. What is a judge to do if a candidate has done astoundingly well in the Graduate Record Examination, but has very poor college grades? He resolves the dilemma by 'intuition', but the intuition is unfortunately not based on evidence: it is likely to be derived from just one more of those misleading expectations. Third, as we have seen, his mood will alter from day to day, making his judgements inconsistent. If he has just discovered that his wife is having an affair, he may well take a gloomy view of a candidate's potential in graduate school, while if he has just been promoted to a full professorship he may feel beneficent to all and give even quite weak candidates a chance. Fourth, he may be too heavily influenced by which predictor he accidentally comes across first and indeed may interpret the values of other predictors by his assessment of the first (the primacy effect). Finally, if there are many predictors (more than about three or four) he will find it impossible to keep them all in his head at the same time and to give appropriate weights to each.

People, then, are irrational in the way they take intuitive decisions. Of course, in the case of predictions about something fairly trivial, the time spent on making the prediction by actuarial methods could not be justified. It is not worth keeping careful records of the characteristics of steaks in order to predict how long it will take to cook a new one: it is simpler to keep an eye on it and possibly taste it when it is about done.

Moreover, the method only works if there has been a fairly large number (about thirty or more) of previous cases and if a complete record has been kept of the values of the predictors for each case and of the outcome. Nevertheless, where these conditions are satisfied and where the decision is of importance, one might expect to see the actuarial method being used. Once the optimal weights for predictors have been established, the analysis for each new case can be performed in a fraction of a second by computer. It is a further example of irrationality that people are strikingly resistant to using this method rather than their own intuitions even in cases where its use unquestionably does better than unaided human judgement.

Robyn Dawes notes how little actuarial prediction is in fact used. He points out that at the time he was writing only four major American universities used it for admissions, and even they did not use it for final selection, but merely as a means of weeding out wholly unsuitable candidates: the rest were interviewed. An actuarial method was used for a time at one hospital in America in order to decide whether patients were psychotic or neurotic. Although it performed better than any psychiatrist, it was abandoned on the grounds that it made obvious mistakes. It is not clear whether the mistakes made by the psychiatrists were as obvious, but it is certain that there were more of them. Dawes points out that the use of actuarial methods would not only improve the decisions taken, it would save much time and money: he estimates that if this method were used just for all admissions to graduate schools in the US, a saving of $18 million a year would be effected.

Why are people so resistant to the actuarial technique? The reasons that follow are in part based on Dawes. First, people remember successes particularly if they are unusual. A member of an admissions committee may remember accepting on a hunch a candidate who had very bad scores on all predictors, and who subsequently performed exceptionally well. Clearly, the actuarial model would never have accepted him. The problem with this argument is that human judges are likely to forget all the other candidates accepted on hunches who fared extremely badly. I have already shown that it is the odd man out who is remembered.

Second, professional judges want to believe that they have special skills and talents: they are reluctant to accept that their own expertise can be outshone by a computer. Moreover, for the reasons set out in Chapter 17, they are likely to suffer from overconfidence in their own abilities. They could perhaps comfort themselves by the thought that they select the predictors – all the mathematical analysis does is to put them together in an optimal way.

Third, an illusion of good judgement may be fostered through a self-fulfilling prophecy. A staff member who admits a student who is slightly out of the ordinary may subsequently devote a great deal of time to helping him, partly to show that he was right to admit him, partly because he is likely to be interested in that student's progress. Dawes provides an analogy with a waiter who thinks he will not be tipped by certain customers: in consequence, the waiter is offhand with them and this in turn causes his expectation to be fulfilled – he receives no tip.

Fourth, people have argued that, at least in most cases, even actuarial prediction is far short of perfect. This is an extraordinarily obtuse argument, for no prediction about human performance can ever be perfect. All that matters is that actuarial prediction is better than human judgement. If it is used to select students, more students who will succeed will be selected than if the selection is made by intuition. If it is used to classify patients into neurotics and psychotics, mistakes will of course be made but they will be fewer than if the classification is performed by a psychiatrist.

Fifth, people feel that the actuarial procedure cannot deal with the unexpected. For example, one might want to relax normal admission standards for someone with a very poor background. But this sort of factor can be built into the analysis. One can evaluate whether type of background is a predictor: do those from a poor background perform better than others with the same scores on other predictors? If this is true, type of background can itself become a predictor. If, on the other hand, the reason for wishing to relax admission standards for people with a poor background is to give them a chance even if they risk failing, it is easy enough to reduce the score on the mathematical model at which they will be admitted. The only contingencies that actuarial prediction cannot take into account are those that are totally unforeseen. Suppose, for example, someone had been quite ill when taking the Graduate Record Examination: the human judge might want to make allowances, but such illness might not have been incorporated as a predictor in the actuarial method in use. The answer to this is not to throw away the actuarial method, but to examine candidates' records for such eventualities. If they are admitted as a result, their performance can be followed through and a decision taken as to whether to incorporate the eventuality in question as a predictor in the actuarial model.

Sixth, some people persist in believing there is some magical quality about intuition that cannot be replaced by formal calculations, or by careful counts of what has happened in the past. To see how wrong this is, ask yourself what the human judge relies on. He relies on his experience, but that can only consist of the individual cases he has encountered. In other words, the judge is without realising it using an actuarial method: the trouble is that he does not use it very well.

Finally, some consider it soulless to have decisions that will affect their whole lives taken by formal mathematical models rather than by people. One student complained that she had been rejected from a Californian university without an interview. 'How can they tell what I'm like?' As Dawes writes, 'The answer is that they can't. Nor could they with an interview.' Dawes points out that it is presumptuous to assume that one can learn more about a student's abilities in a half-hour interview than by examining his grade point average, which is based on four years of assessment.

The worry about not knowing the candidate could in principle be overcome by assigning a score to the results of an interview and feeding that score into the mathematical analysis. In practice this would be unhelpful, since the analysis would almost always yield a weight of zero for the interview. It has repeatedly been shown that in personnel selection interviewing is not merely unhelpful, it can be harmful. Neal Schmitt begins an article on interviewing by stating that four separate reviews each of dozens of studies 'have concluded that the interview as employed in many employment situations lacks both reliability and validity', that is to say, the judgements of different interviewers do not agree with one another and they bear no relationship to the suitability of applicants for a job.

There are many reasons why interviewing is such an unsatisfactory method of selection, of which the halo effect is one. An applicant who is well turned out, pleasant and self-confident without conceit is likely to be thought to have the skills needed for the job whether he has or not. Moreover, interviews have been shown to be subject to the primacy effect and to a phenomenon not yet mentioned, the 'contrast effect'. If the selection committee interviews some exceptionally pre-possessing or intelligent-sounding applicant, they are likely to under-estimate the next one interviewed. Of course the effect works in reverse: if an applicant who puts up a very poor performance is fol-lowed by someone about average, the committee will think the latter is much better than he is. This effect has been repeatedly demonstrat-ed: it distorts human judgement in many different situations. It has been argued that the interview is the only way to detect something unusual about the candidate, for example, a disabling stammer or the habit of dressing in leather and chains. In fact, it seems unlikely that the candidate's referees would have failed to comment on such qual-ities. Some have argued that interviews are needed in order for the firm to sell itself to the candidate. Plausible though this is, research shows that it is wrong: applicants usually think worse of the firm after an interview than before. Perhaps they arrive with expectations that are too high and are inevitably disappointed. It should be added that there is some debate about the value of what is called the struc-tured interview, in which exactly the same pre-set topics and ques-tions are put to all candidates, but it seems likely that even here one would do better to present the questions in writing, thus avoiding the bias introduced by meeting the candidate.

The predictor that has consistently done best in personal selection is cognitive ability, as determined by a series of verbal and spatial tests. These tests have been administered to candidates for jobs of all description, including thousands of US recruits and hundreds of US businessmen: the tests have been found to be the best-known predic-tors of their future progress. There are of course many more spe-cialised objective tests, but there is less information on how useful they are.

It is curious that, despite the many published papers showing that in personnel selection the interview is useless, firms continue to employ it. Its use is one of the more curious acts of irrationality in the Western world and the fact that interviewers continue to have faith in their own erroneous judgements is just one more example of over-confidence.

It is interesting to contrast the extent to which actuarial prediction is used in medicine and in commerce, for it works in both cases. In one study, doctors were asked to estimate how long 193 patients with Hodgkin's disease would live. There are ten different predictors yield-ed by biopsies. It was found that although the doctors had faith in their ability to predict, their judgements were in fact completely random – they would have done just as well by pulling a number for each patient out of a hat. When, however, a mathematical model was constructed by systematically comparing the values of the predictors with the patients' longevity over a series of cases, the model did considerably better than chance.

A second example from medicine is MYCIN, a computer program developed at Stanford to diagnose bacterial diseases of the blood and to suggest the best antibiotic. It is largely based on the sort of mathematical analysis I have been discussing, but is slightly more elaborate. The knowledge and the probabilities incorporated in the program come entirely from doctors. All the information about a given case is of course also obtained and fed in by people, but the program can request more information or further tests on the patient whenever they are needed. In one study, the computer program diagnosed 65 per cent of cases correctly, whereas different doctors were correct between 42.5 per cent and 62.5 per cent of the time. MYCIN has been followed by many similar medical programs ranging from the diagnosis of gastric disorders to assessment of the risk of sudden death in newborn infants.

Turning to commerce, a few years ago if you wanted a bank loan, you arranged to see your bank manager, who would either assent or courteously decline. Nowadays 90 per cent of loans (and all credit cards) are given or refused by a computer program: the programs take into account whether the client has a house and a telephone, his marital status, the nature of his job, the history of his bank account and so on. When experienced bank officials were asked to rate the creditworthiness of a set of clients, more of the people they selected for loans defaulted than did those chosen by computer.

For many years, insurance companies have of course been using the actuarial method to assess risks and hence to offer a realistic premium. Nowadays, there are many other examples of the actuarial method being employed in commerce, but the medical programs are still comparatively little used. It would appear that where money is at stake, the best method of taking decisions is often employed, but when it is merely a human life at risk, we continue to rely on a discredited ability – human intuition. Most businesses, however, fall far short of acting rationally. They continue to employ useless methods of selection. For example, large firms often employ at considerable expense 'head hunters' to find personnel for posts paid at more than £50,000 a year. Head hunters are normally untrained and rely on interviews and other subjective methods. Astonishingly, two such firms use astrology. Andrew Dickson, director of one of the biggest

British agencies, stated recently, 'There is no point in trying to make a science out of something that clearly is not a science. How can one predict with 100 per cent accuracy how a person is going to perform in a new job?' That statement encapsulates the irrationality of many businessmen. Of course one cannot always be right, but might it not be worth Dickson's while acting on the existing evidence in order to raise his success rate from 5 or 10 per cent to 60 or 70 per cent?

moral

1. Suspect anyone who claims to have good intuition.
2. If you are in a profession, don't hesitate to take decisions by using a mathematical model if it has been shown to be better than human judgement.
3. If you are an applicant, instead of being indignant at not being interviewed, reflect that the organisation is almost certainly ahead of its time.
4. If you are a head hunter, try not to make asinine remarks.

21 utility

The last chapter showed that there is a mathematical procedure that will (almost always) yield the best possible prediction, when there are a number of known predictors none of which predicts with certainty: this sets a standard by which one can judge the rationality of intuitive predictions made by people. A second model specifies the ways in which people should act in order best to attain their goals. It is known as Utility Theory.

At the beginning of Chapter 16 I showed how to calculate the expected value of a bet: you multiply the monetary value of each possible outcome by the probability of its occurring and add the resulting figures. This yields the expected value and if all you want to do is to maximise your monetary winnings, you should always choose the bet in which the value is highest. In theory, one could take all decisions in life by placing one's own cash value on each of the possible outcomes, calculating their expected values and choosing the action whose outcomes have the highest. Unfortunately, there is a snag. £10 million is not normally ten times as desirable as £1 million, just as owning 1,000 pairs of shoes does not confer 1,000 times the benefit of owning one pair. For many people, £1 million is enough to satisfy almost all their needs, certainly all the most important ones. In terms of gratifying their desires each extra million is of much less importance than the first: hence, how much a given sum of money means to a person (its utility) varies with how much he has already. The diminishing benefit of increasing amounts of money is known as 'marginal utility'. It is the justification for progressive taxation: paying a small percentage of earnings in tax may hurt a poor man more than paying a larger percentage hurts a rich man.

Consider as an illustration the following two bets.

Option A: £10 million with a probability of .2.
Option B: £1 million with a probability of .8.

The expected value of the first option is £2 million and of the second £800,000, so the monetary expected value of the first bet is far higher than that of the second. But almost everyone would choose the second and they would be rational to do so, because in terms of satisfying their desires £10 million is simply not worth ten times £1 million. Utility Theory overcomes this problem by using an arbitrary number for the desirability of different outcomes (their utilities). In terms of utility, people might judge that £10 million was only twice as desirable as £1 million: hence they might arbitrarily assign the utility value of 20 to £10 million and 10 to £1 million: the expected utility of the first option then becomes four (20 x .2) and that of the second eight (10 x .8) and in terms of their utility, people should choose the second option, as most do.

Utility Theory prescribes how best to achieve one's goals to the maximum possible extent and given that that is what you or an organisation want to do its principles should be followed. Its limitations will be discussed after it has been described. Since it is impossible to give a simple exposition of Utility Theory, the next two pages may present some difficulty, but after that the going gets easier. It may be useful to begin with four definitions, to which the reader may refer back.

Option   One of several courses of action open to an individual or organisation.

Outcome   Any of the possible consequences of taking a given option.

Utility   A number representing the desirability (or undesirability) to an individual of a possible outcome of an option.

Expected utility The sum of the utilities of all possible outcomes of an action, each multiplied by its probability of occurring.

Utility Theory is similar to the procedure for evaluating the expected value of a bet, but utilities are substituted for money. The application involves the following steps.

Step 1   List the possible outcomes of each option.

Step 2   The person making the decision assigns a number (a utility) to each outcome representing how desirable (or undesirable) it is for him.

Step 3   Because some outcomes are not completely certain, the utility for each is multiplied by its probability of occurring,

	yielding the 'expected utility' of that outcome.
Step 4	The expected utilities of the outcomes for each option are added, yielding its expected utility.
Step 5	The expected utilities of all options are compared and the option with the largest expected utility is chosen.

The utilities assigned by the person taking the decision are arbitrary numbers, but they must be consistent: if he regards one outcome as twice as desirable as another it does not matter whether he assigns values of 30 and 60 or 300 and 600. For convenience he is usually asked to represent a neutral outcome (one neither desirable nor undesireable) by the value zero. Negative utilities will then be attached to costs and positive utilities to benefits. Note that the values do not merely represent his estimated happiness: they are based on how far the possible outcomes meet his ends, which may include benefiting someone else at his own expense. Now, since there are usually many outcomes of a given decision, one must be able to add and subtract the values of each to assess its ultimate value. If I assign a utility of +40 to seeing a play, -20 to the price of the ticket, -10 to the nuisance of the journey to the theatre, and -10 to curtailing my supper in order to get there, the result is zero: I am completely indifferent as to whether I go or not. As we have seen, most outcomes will be uncertain: they will occur with a probability less than 1.0. To take this into account, we must multiply the utility of each outcome by its probability and then add together for each option the expected utilities of all its possible outcomes.

Here is an example (modified from Baron) of a difficult but important decision facing many women in which Utility Theory could be used. A forty-five-year-old woman is pregnant and wants a child: on the other hand, given her age she is worried about Down's syndrome. To determine whether she is carrying a Down's syndrome child, she could have amniocentesis: if the result were positive, she could have an abortion and therefore avoid having a child with Down's syndrome. Unfortunately, this test carries about a 1 per cent risk of causing a miscarriage, in which case as a result of taking the test, she would have lost the chance of having a perfectly normal child. The approximate probability of her carrying a Down's syndrome child is also known. What should the woman do? A rational decision depends on her utilities for the four possible outcomes – a Down's syndrome child (which could only happen if she does not have the test); a normal child (which could happen whether or not she has the test, but with a lower probability if she has it because of the risk of a miscarriage); a miscarriage caused by the test; and an abortion if the test is positive. The utility for each outcome of each of the two options (having or not having amniocentesis) should be multiplied by its probability and the results added: whichever option yields the higher total should be chosen.

There is a further version of Utility Theory known by the formidable name, Multi-Attribute Utility Theory. In this theory each outcome is broken down into independent attributes. For example, if you were wondering which car to buy you might consider several in the price range you could afford. You would then list the attributes that interested you and give a weight to each that represented how important it was for you: your list might start: 'reliability (.7), acceleration (.4), comfort (.6), road-holding (.7)' and so on. You would then allocate a score between, say, 1 and 100 to each attribute for each car and multiply it by the weight for that attribute. The resulting scores are added up for each car and you buy the one with the top score. You will have used a rational method of selecting a car, but it will have cost you a good deal of time and as with so many personal decisions you may decide the possible gain is simply not worth it. Remember, however, that it will save you from buying a car merely through the blandishments of a salesman or because of one salient characteristic such as its colour. To use this method of calculating utility, each attribute must be independent of all the others, that is to say, the utility to you of any one attribute must not depend on the utility of another one. To understand why this should be so, think of a dinner as having three attributes – first, second and third courses. You allocate a number to each dish offered on each of the three courses, but because you like fish you may end up with smoked salmon, turbot, and anchovies on toast. Few would regard this outcome as satisfactory – the utility of a given dish on each course depends on what you are having on the other two: the three attributes of the meal are not independent and therefore Multi-Attribute Utility Theory gives you the wrong result.

Utility Theory has two practical limitations. First, a formidable difficulty is to get people to estimate their preferences correctly and to assign consistent utility values to outcomes. There are in fact various cunning tricks for ensuring that people are consistent in their judgements of utility. If, for example, someone thinks that outcome A has twice the utility of outcome B, and outcome C has the same utility as B, then – to be consistent – when comparing A and C, he must believe that A has twice the value of C. It should be remembered that to the extent that people cannot consistently value outcomes in terms of how desirable they are, decision-making in everyday life will be erratic: forcing them to make such evaluations explicit can only help them to take the best decision. Second, Utility Theory does not tell us how to list possible outcomes of a decision let alone how to assess their probabilities; intuitive decision-making is, however, subject to the same limitations – we cannot take into account an unforeseen consequence. Even if the figures that are cranked into the mechanism of Utility Theory are not completely accurate, it is still likely to be useful since it combines them rationally rather than in the haphazard way that characterises most human thought. Although almost nobody uses Utility Theory for taking personal decisions, it sets a standard for rational decision-taking: its use ensures that your desires will be maximally fulfilled, given the knowledge you have.

It has been demonstrated that using Utility Theory can help people to overcome their own irrationality and in particular it can force them to take account of evidence against their own views. One study showing this was undertaken in California, where the right to develop land by the sea is granted in each area by a California Coastal Commission. These commissions contain a mixture of people, including would-be developers, environmentalists and state planners. Needless to say, they normally find it hard to reach agreement on the applications. Vast amounts of time are often wasted on a single case. For each application, so many facts and statistics are gathered and marshalled that no one individual can possibly take them all in. Peter Gardiner and Ward Edwards, who performed the following study, argued that decisions were often arrived at not on their merits but through chance or guile. For example, an application discussed late in the meeting was more likely to be passed in order to save time; other applications were passed because one or two key members of either side were not present.

To compare the results of intuitive estimates with those obtained through Multi-Attribute Utility Theory, fourteen people involved in coastal planning gave ratings based on each procedure. To use Utility Theory, the possible value of the projects was broken down into eight separate attributes, such as number of square feet occupied by a project, its distance from sea level, and so on. The subjects then assigned a weight to each attribute, representing their estimate of its importance. For example, one subject might think area and distance from the sea equally important, but the aesthetics of the development of no importance. For each project, the subjects were then presented with the raw scores on each of the eight attributes, for example, the number of feet from sea level. From these scores they estimated how well each project ranked on each attribute, using figures from 0 to 100. These values did not correspond in a simple way with the raw scores. For example, one subject's utility value for density of population in a development fell off sharply from 100 for zero density to 40 for twenty dwelling units per acre and then tailed off much less steeply to zero utility at 200 units. In other words he saw a large advantage in a small decrease in the number of dwelling units when there were not very many, but little advantage when there were a lot. Finally, for each project each subject's utility value for each attribute was multiplied by the weight he had previously assigned to that attribute and the eight resulting figures were added to give his total utility value for the project.

On the intuitive ratings of a project's worth, there was little or no agreement between the subjects who in general favoured development and the environmentalists who were against it, but when both groups were forced to use Multi-Attribute Utility Theory, their results were very similar to one another. Although the environmentalists rated the desirability of giving planning permission as slightly lower than those who in general favoured development, the rank order in which the projects were placed was now exactly the same for both groups. The use of Utility Theory had made each group pay attention to factors that were contrary to their own overall view, which they simply ignored in their intuitive judgements. Multi-Attribute Utility Theory, then, can save much dispute and might vastly shorten the time spent on committees. The only reservation is that agreement must first be reached on what are the relevant dimensions to be judged, but given that each member is free to ignore a dimension (by attaching to it a weight of zero) this is unlikely to be a major problem.

A second application of Utility Theory that shows its value concerns the bullets used by the Denver police. They found their conventional bullets lacked 'stopping effectiveness' – they failed to prevent the person hit from firing back. The police wished to replace this bullet by one with a hollow point, which would flatten on impact, in order to increase stopping effectiveness and to reduce the chance of injuring bystanders through a ricochet. The American Civil Liberties Union opposed the new bullet on the grounds that it was no different from a dum-dum bullet and could cause massive injury. A deadlock ensued, until two psychologists suggested that Utility Theory should be applied. There were three critical dimensions on which bullets could vary – stopping effectiveness, risk of serious injury to the target and risk of injury to bystanders. The policy-makers could not agree on their relative importance so the psychologists gave them equal weight. They then turned to ballistic experts and asked them to say which bullet was equally effective in all three respects (other bullets might of course be more effective in a single respect). This led to the adoption of a bullet that satisfied both the police and the Civil

Liberties Union.

There are some clear-cut cases mainly from medicine and from time and motion studies that demonstrate the usefulness of Utility Theory. One example concerns growths in the kidneys. An X-ray can reveal the presence there of a cyst or a tumour, but the radiologist can rarely be certain which it is: to find out it is necessary either to perform an aspiration of the site or an arteriography. The former procedure can establish that the mass is a cyst, the latter that it is a tumour: however, a negative result on one does not establish that the other is present, for the abnormality may be neither. Aspiration is a comparatively harmless procedure in which a needle is inserted through the back to discover whether the lump contains fluid. Arteriography, on the other hand, is unpleasant since it involves the insertion of a tube through the artery of the leg into the kidney; it requires at least two days in hospital and carries the risk of causing a blood clot. At one hospital it was discovered that arteriography was given whenever the radiologist's estimate of the probability of a tumour was greater than .5. However, on being questioned both patients and doctors agreed that arteriography was at least ten times as bad a procedure as aspiration. If the disutility (negative utility) of arteriography is ten times as great as that of an aspiration, their *expected utility* will be equal when the probability of a tumour is 10/11. An arteriography should therefore only be performed if the radiologist's estimate of a tumour being present is above this fraction. Putting this another way, the performance of ten aspirations has the same utility as the performance of one arteriography: hence when the probability of a cyst being present is greater than 1/11, aspiration should be performed first. This calculation if followed up could save many patients from having distressing arteriographies.

In the last chapter, we saw that multiple regression analysis when tested against human intuition was always superior or no worse. In most cases, similar tests are not available for Utility Theory for two reasons. First, if a decision is taken using that theory on a large-scale project, we cannot be certain how the project would have fared had all the decisions been made by human intuition. Second, all large projects are different: one cannot therefore compare the success of Utility Theory with that of intuition across different projects. Although, then, there is evidence that the use of Utility Theory can bring a considerable measure of agreement on issues about which people strongly disagree, there is less empirical evidence that better decisions are taken by Utility Theory than by intuition except in problems in which there are only a few clearly defined outcomes with known probabilities, such as the decision whether or not to give arteriography or aspiration first. Nevertheless, Utility Theory must be the best way of taking important decisions: it avoids or minimises many of the errors detailed in this book and by taking into account both the probability of outcomes and their desirability, it will in the long run maximise the fulfilment of aims. In practice, Utility Theory is too complex and its application too time-consuming for it to be useful in most personal decision-making. However, even if it is not used *in toto*, writing down all possible outcomes of a decision, taking account of their probabilities and assessing their desirability should help people to make more rational decisions.

There are, however, some more fundamental limitations to Utility Theory than any yet discussed. Although a person cannot be wrong about what he wants, he may be wrong in believing he will be happier if he gets it. As Bernard Shaw remarked, 'There are two tragedies in life. One is not to get your heart's desire. The other is to get it.' Many lives have been ruined by winning large lotteries or the football pools: people cannot adjust to the publicity and the possession of a large sum of money. Again, it has been shown that promotion often brings stress and unhappiness. It is also clear that marriage does not always confer the domestic bliss to which the partners had so eagerly looked forward. Neither Utility Theory nor any other method of thinking can take account of the fact that people rarely know exactly how they will feel in a new situation no matter how devoutly they have wished for it. A further problem is that a person may simply not know what he wants, hence he cannot take rational decisions – unless of course he knows what he doesn't want, in which case he can concentrate on avoiding that.

Another consideration is that maximising utility is not the only rational end. Instead, one can take an option that is safe, that is to say, it precludes one from obtaining the maximum benefits, but it ensures that nothing dreadful happens. We have already seen this tendency at work in accepting bets – people often prefer a small safe gain to a large but uncertain gain, even when its expected value is higher. A business might well adopt a strategy that ensured it would not become bankrupt at the cost of forgoing the probability of making very large profits. Or again, someone may aim at improving his situation a little rather than risk no improvement while forgoing the possibility of a large improvement. Provided the overall aim is precise enough there are prescriptive mathematical models (variants of 'decision theory') that will handle it (given that utilities and probabilities are known), but in real life it seems likely that people have a mixture of overall aims – at one and the same time they want to maximise utility, ensure at all costs that they do not make a disastrous loss, and also ensure that they at least come out ahead of the game. Unless they have clearly thought out their overall aims, it becomes impossible for them to act rationally in many circumstances, though in so far as they can act in ways that defy all these aims they still have the prerogative of acting irrationally.

Utility Theory must then be treated with caution as a model of how the rational individual should act, but in many circumstances it should be regarded as an approach that will provide the optimum solution. Moreover, for many large-scale projects in which the stakes are high enough to justify the expenditure of time and effort and in which the aims are clear it remains the most rational approach. Utility Theory is in fact being increasingly used by government, business and the military. Some examples are: where to put the airport in Mexico City; where to place radioactive disposal sites; and even how school desegregation should be implemented in Los Angeles. One version of it is, as we will see, increasingly being used to take decisions in medicine.

Utility Theory is completely general, but there are two more specific ways of taking decisions which may be regarded as its offspring. The first, called cost-benefit analysis, was devised by economists: it is sometimes used in irrational ways. The second is a technique that has recently been introduced in medicine, which although potentially rational is irrationally rejected by many people.

Cost-benefit analysis is usually used to assess the expected benefits or costs in monetary terms for a firm thinking of undertaking a particular project. This use is straightforward: the potential costs and gains are estimated and on this basis a decision can be taken. If it does nothing else, it forces management to think of all the costs of a project, some of which may not be obvious, for example, loss of profits in the firm's other activities caused by redeploying labour on the project in question or the provision of extra car-parking space and toilet facilities if additional labour is engaged. Where there are several possible outcomes, their monetary gains and costs are once again multiplied by their estimated probability of occurring.

Cost-benefit analysis is, however, quite often used to assess the benefit or cost to society as a whole of undertaking large-scale engineering projects, like building a dam or constructing a supersonic plane. Employed in this way it can lead to irrational decisions. Once again a monetary value is assigned to all the costs and benefits of the project that are of any significance; the value of each cost and each benefit is then multiplied by the probability of its occurring, and the figures added to give the total expected value of the project. If the costs outweigh the benefits, the project is not worth undertaking, but, it is argued, if the benefits outweigh the costs then it should be carried out.

The following criticisms of cost-benefit analysis when used to assess a project's value for society are largely derived from Fischhoff. One problem is the difficulty of putting a cash value on a human life. Many people think this value should be infinite, but in practice we do not act as though this is so. There is no question that if in Britain government funds at present directed to the arts were instead given to the National Health Service, some lives would be saved. And in theory there is no limit to the additional safety systems that could be incorporated in planes, in trains and on the roads. The actual expenditure on safety is determined by what people are prepared to pay to use these forms of transport. In practice, airlines and airline authorities determine which safety devices to employ by comparing the cost per life that each is likely to save. Although this conclusion may be repugnant to many people, we do not value a human life as worth an infinite amount of money. Indeed, people often act as though they set quite a low value even on their own life. In a survey undertaken in 1973, it was found that most Americans would work in a dangerous job to earn an extra $200 a year, when the increased risk of death by accident in any given year was .001: this is equivalent to valuing a life at $200,000 per year. One of the most dangerous occupations is deep-sea fishing: although the chance of being killed on the job is one in 1,000 per year (or about 4 per cent in a lifetime), the pay ensures that there is no shortage of recruits. Since, then, we constantly put implicit values on human life, it is irrational to argue that it does not have a monetary value even if most people are too squeamish to admit it.

Cost-benefit analysis, however, often tackles this problem by assigning a value to a life that corresponds to what the person might be expected to earn had he lived (sometimes making a deduction for the value of the resources he might be expected to consume). Similar figures are also used by courts of law, where they are simply a way of arriving at the financial loss to dependents for deaths caused by negligence. But this is an unsatisfactory way of estimating the costs of a project. If carried to extremes, the death as the result of a project of someone on social security would be counted not as a cost but as a benefit, since the state saves money by his death. It also fails to take into account a fair distribution of income. Many would regard it as wrong simply to offset financial losses to many poor people against huge gains to a few rich ones. And is the value of a cathedral or church that might be demolished to make way for an engineering project to be equated with the voluntary donations made by those who visit it? A country footpath torn up in the course of a project may have no economic value, but give pleasure to many.

Unlike Utility Theory, whose application does not have these pernicious consequences, cost-benefit analysis deals only in monetary values and fails to take into account other benefits and costs. To this extent using it to estimate the value of a project for society as a whole is unlikely to provide a rational evaluation of its true expected utility.

Nevertheless, its use by government and by local authorities could have prevented some disastrous errors. It might have stopped Camden Council building the brutal blocks of new council flats which replaced so many pleasant Georgian streets: it was discovered too late that the new 'living units' (the council's name for houses and flats) cost more than three times as much to erect as the cost of refurbishing older properties.

For all its shortcomings, cost-benefit analysis highlights the fact that if we are to take rational decisions, a value must be placed on the cost of a life. One area in which the cost of saving a life is increasingly under scrutiny is medicine. Since there are not enough medical resources to go round, doctors have to decide after considerable but probably undisciplined and highly intuitive thought who shall live and who shall be left to die. In Britain alone, more than 1,000 kidney patients die a year because of a shortage of renal units. The problem has two aspects. First, who will be given access to a limited treatment that cannot be made available to all who need it, such as a by-pass operation on the heart or a kidney transplant? Second, on what medical resources should the available money be spent? Should one increase the number of clinical psychologists or buy another scanner?

As far as I know, no rational scheme has been put forward for deciding which individual gets access to a given facility. Clearly earning power is an insufficient guide. Do penurious writers, schoolteachers and academics contribute less to society than rich businessmen? One could base the judgement on the patients' potential contribution to society and on their worth to themselves. People contribute to society in many ways that are uncorrelated with earnings; they may be kind, amusing or interesting, and they may have many relations and friends who will miss them or they may have none. Nor is it just the present contribution that is important: Van Gogh's paintings were not appreciated in his lifetime, but have given joy to future generations. And a person's value to himself should be considered: a happy person has more to lose by death than a miserable one and a young person more than someone older.

Now, even leaving probabilities out of account, it is obviously very difficult to assign numbers to all these aspects of a person. Yet despite all the uncertainties and there are many other considerations I have not listed – a systematic method of allowing for the factors mentioned would surely result in fairer decisions than those at present made by doctors merely on the basis of intuition, if only because whether they know it or not they are likely to be influenced by how far they personally like a patient and how similar he is to them in terms of social class, outlook and so on.

Many readers will undoubtedly rebel, thinking that decisions about life and death should not be taken by rule: they would rather they were taken by chance, which admittedly plays so large a part in everyone's life. But doctors' decisions are not chance and if these matters ought really to be determined by chance, one should hold lotteries for by-pass operations. The refusal to face the fact that implicit decisions about the value of human life are being made all the time, not just in medicine, but in all forms of transport and in every aspect of engineering, is a prime form of irrationality.

Because people shy off the problem, the ways in which decisions are taken are rarely examined. A more rigorous system would be open to debate: it would of course have flaws but they might well be fewer than in the present system, which is based on intuition. Perhaps the worst feature of the type of system proposed is that the judgements of a person's worth would have to be made by others. Although in deciding whom to employ or with whom to form a friendship, we consistently judge others, there is something repugnant about taking decisions about life and death. Few people would care to condemn someone to death, even in order to save several other lives.

There is, however, under development a rational method of taking such decisions that depends not on a patient's worth but solely on the benefits (or costs) to him of a particular treatment. The method is based on the QALY – a 'Quality Adjusted Life Year'. Many medical treatments have unpleasant side effects. For example, radiotherapy and chemotherapy sometimes eliminate cancer but at a considerable cost in suffering to the individual. It would clearly be irrational to subject a ninety-year-old woman who was blind, deaf and arthritic to such treatment, but how does one decide when to treat and when not to? One answer is to discover how many years of life with a given disability members of the general public would trade off against a smaller number of years with no disability. Almost everyone would prefer forty years of normal life to forty-two years spent in a wheelchair: similarly they would prefer forty years in a wheelchair to one year's normal life. To establish QALYs, one tries to determine how many years with a given disability are equivalent in terms of people's preferences to one year of normal life. That number of years is then called one QALY for the disability in question. To arrive at the total number of QALYs yielded by a given procedure, the life expectancy must be divided by the number of years of the disability that make up one QALY (assuming the disability will last until death). For example, suppose that three years of life while suffering severe angina are thought to be equivalent to one year of normal life. If a patient has a life expectancy of twelve years, angina reduces this to four QALY years. This figure can be compared with the expected number of QALYs, if he is given a by-pass operation (taking into account the probabilities of death or complications resulting from the operation). Using these measures one can calculate the probable benefits (or costs) to the patient of a given treatment and of no treatment and hence decide whether to treat or not.

Potentially, then, the use of QALYs could prevent treatments that do the patient more harm than good, thus combating doctors' refusal to obey one of Clough's ten commandments:

> Thou . . . need'st not strive
> Officiously to keep alive.

Moreover, where resources are insufficient to treat everyone, the same measures can be, and increasingly are, used to decide who should receive treatment. The probable QALYs gained through treatment can be used to determine an order of priority for people needing a form of treatment that cannot be given to everyone who might benefit from it.

In Britain QALYs have mainly been used to determine not the fate of the individual patient but the ways in which the available money is spent within the health regions. The North Western Regional Authority did such an exercise with QALYs. To determine the desirability of investing more money in a given medical procedure, they calculated the extra QALYs it would provide per patient and divided this number by the cost per patient. Surprisingly, it turned out that on the QALY criterion the replacement of a shoulder joint was about twenty times as cost-effective as dialysis for kidney failure.

Unfortunately, as Lesley Fallowfield points out, the QALY technique is at present far from satisfactory. In Britain only a very small number of people have been questioned on how they would make the trade-off between years of healthy life and years with a given disability. Moreover, preferences change with age and the preferences of those who are already ill are different from those who are well. It has been found that before labour begins women say they do not want an anaesthetic when giving birth, but they change their minds when actually in labour, subsequently reverting to their previous belief after parturition. Nevertheless, QALYs are a potentially useful approach to problems that are at the moment treated irrationally: the use of operating theatres should not depend on whether the cardiac surgeon has stronger lungs than the colorectal one. Despite the technique's existing imperfections, it makes explicit some of the criteria that can be used in making unpleasant decisions. It may also force people to confront what are real and distressing problems, rather than refusing to adopt a rational approach to matters of life and death. And it may help to dispel the prevalent but wholly irrational notion that all that matters in medicine is keeping people alive.

moral

1. When the importance of a decision merits the expenditure of time, use Utility Theory or a watered-down version of it.
2. Before taking an important decision decide what your overall aim is, whether it be to maximize the attainment of your goals, to save yourself from loss, to make at least some improvement in your position and so on.
3. Don't value everything in terms of money unless you're an accountant.

22   the paranormal

At a rough count, about a hundred different systematic causes for irrational thinking have been described: it would be tedious to conclude by reviewing them all. Instead, I will illustrate some of them by showing how they explain the widespread belief in the paranormal. In more primitive countries, such belief is universal, while in the Western world three-quarters of adults accept at least some psychic phenomena as genuine. For example, the majority of people both in Britain and the US think there is something in astrology.

By way of preamble, I should say why I personally do not believe in such phenomena. One of the strongest reasons is that by definition they defy all the known laws of physics: these laws have held up extremely well, in view of some of their pernicious by-products some might think too well. Psychic events – the transfer of thought between people with no intervening physical events, the effects of the position of the constellations at a person's birth on his personality, or the movement of objects without the application of physical force – would, if proven, require a complete revision of the laws of physics. From this viewpoint, they are highly unlikely and the more improbable something is, the better the evidence needed to accept it as shown in Chapter 15. In fact, the evidence is not there: nobody has ever made a fortune on the stock exchange through clairvoyance and it has proved impossible to repeat psychic events to order under controlled conditions. Moreover, there is a long history of fraud, running from the nineteenth-century medium Margery Crandon to Uri Geller. Interestingly, such frauds have usually been detected not by physicists nor by psychologists but by magicians, like Harry Houdini and the Great Randi, who repeatedly offered to reproduce any 'psychic' happening using their own ingenious but non-psychic tricks. Finally, where claims about paranormal events have been subjected to careful scrutiny, they have been found to be false. For example, the thirty best-known American astrologers were given the birth date of a client and three personality profiles, one of which was the client's: they completely failed to match the client's profile with his date of birth. Again, it was found that the distribution of astrological signs for the birth dates of 16,000 of the best-known American scientists were completely random.

One must distinguish two different questions about belief in the paranormal. First, how do such beliefs originate in someone's mind? Second, having started, how are they maintained? There are perhaps three reasons for their origins. As I have shown, people are unwilling to suspend judgement: they seek explanations. If they cannot satisfactorily account for a door slamming, a breath of cold air or a strange rustling sound, they may be tempted to give a paranormal explanation rather than no explanation at all. Second, young children, and many primitive tribes, think animistically. Their own movements are the causal agents of which they are most immediately aware: hence, they think of all movement as animate. Belief in the paranormal may in part be a hangover from this stage of development, though this is pure speculation. Third, most known cultures have believed in supernatural and immortal agencies inhabiting a different world and possessing powers superior to those of mortals. There are several reasons for inventing gods. Fear of death has played a role, as has people's desire to find some significance for their own petty lives. Belief in the paranormal may in part simply be an escape from our own mundane existence. Moreover, the invention of gods can help to remove the mystery of the creation of the universe. Because everything we know has been created, people irrationally believe that the universe as a whole must have been created.

In what follows, I shall go into more detailed reasons for belief in the supernatural, all based on the irrational errors described in this book. The availability effect must play a strong part. There are many newspaper headlines of the kind 'Poltergeist Disrupts Rectory', while no news editor who values his job would pass a story with the headline 'Attempt at Telepathy Fails'. The paranormal is news, its absence is not. In 1979 an excellent book (by David Marks and Richard Kamman), which debunked Uri Geller's tricks and other alleged paranormal phenomena, was turned down by over thirty American publishers, all of whom were competing to publish books endorsing psychic phenomena. The paranormal is therefore available. The fact that alleged paranormal events are unusual also draws attention to them and adds to their availability.

Although in the absence of statistics the point cannot be proven, I have the impression based on personal experience that belief in the supernatural runs in families. If this is correct, it is partly a product of conformity, and in-group pressures. Moreover, there is a tendency, already described, for strong emotion to spread in a small group or crowd: mediums have used this phenomenon for their own purposes. The atmosphere of séances was (and still is) distinctly spooky, since they were held in dim light, usually with long curtains concealing most of the room, and were often accompanied by mysterious thumps or the intermittent sound of musical instruments. Under heightened emotion both thought and the ability to observe carefully are impaired and those attending séances may well mistake a piece of muslin for the apparition of their dear departed. Parenthetically, it may be observed that the form the supernatural takes is as much determined by fashion as women's clothes. Séances are – at least for the most part – out, the Bermuda Triangle and flying saucers are in.

Faith in the predictive power of tea-leaves or of the stars' influence on your life is easily explained. There will always be some truth in a set of vague predictions and if you are a believer, you are likely to seize upon the few that happen to be correct. Moreover, if the prediction is sufficiently vaguely worded, you will distort its meaning to suit your own situation (distorting the evidence). Luckily, there is some remarkable confirmation for this assessment. Subjects were asked to complete a bogus personality test. The experimenter then gave them all exactly the same sketch of their personalities, which he claimed was based on their test results. When asked about the accuracy of the sketch, 90 per cent of the subjects thought it a very good or excellent description of themselves. People are so good at distorting material to fit their expectations that the identical sketch was thought by each of nearly fifty subjects to apply specifically to him or her. In addition to trying unconsciously to confirm his or her beliefs, anyone who pays to see a fortune teller will have invested time and money: unless he has just gone for a lark, he will therefore want to feel he has got something out of it (misplaced consistency) and hence will be predisposed to believe what he hears.

There will also be a strong tendency to make the wrong connections. We have seen how readily this occurs, particularly when someone has preconceived notions of what the connections between events will be. Suppose that you can remember ten incidents from a night's dreaming, at least when prompted by a similar incident occurring the following day. Now consider how many incidents occur during a day, including those you read about in the paper, watch on television or hear from your friends. There are a vast number and it is highly probable that from time to time one of them will, at least to some extent, resemble one of those from your dreams. When one or more of these coincidences occur, people are likely to conclude that dreams foretell the future.

Most of us are very poor at calculating the chance of a coincidence. For example, if there are twenty-three people in one room, the probability of at least two of them having a birthday on the same day of the year is over a half: because of the 'anchoring effect' people tend to think of twenty-three *pairs* of people, but altogether there are (23 x 22/2 = 253) such pairs and the members of any of them can have the same birthday. People vastly underrate the probability of coincidences of this sort. Arthur Koestler sought to establish the truth of the paranormal by pointing to fifty coincidences that had occurred in his life, which he claimed could not be given any normal explanation, but Marks and Kamman point out that in a lifetime he would have been exposed to over 18 billion pairs of events: it would be most unlikely if some of the members of a pair did not match. Another example concerns a woman who won the New Jersey lottery twice in four months: since journalists are as innumerate as anyone else, the newspapers reported that it was a one in a trillion chance. That may be true of that woman in those two lotteries, but it has been calculated that if all the different lottery winners in the US are included, then over a seven-year period there is a better than evens chance of a double winner. People focus on the specific coincidence that occurs: they do not take into account all the other occasions on which a similar 'coincidence' could have occurred but did not. They neglect the negative cases, which is of course one of the prime causes of irrationality.

Belief in telepathy can be explained in the same way. Most stories about this phenomenon concern people who are close to one another – husband and wife or brother and sister. Since such people have much in common, it is highly probable that they will sometimes think the same thought at the same time. When a soldier is wounded in battle and the wife simultaneously has a stab of anxiety, she does not ask herself how often she had similar stabs when he was not being wounded: in terms of making the right connections she ignores the negative cases. Moreover, her memory for the exact time when she felt the anxiety is likely to be fallible.

People who believe in the paranormal almost certainly base their faith on too small a sample: a single unlikely happening sets them off and the resulting expectations do the rest. However that may be, they certainly, like everyone else, suffer from overconfidence in their own beliefs. They also concoct elaborate but plausible stories in order to maintain them: 'Telepathy cannot be controlled, you have to be in the right mood. It just sort of happens,' or in the case of a medium, 'I cannot summon the departed. There's a disbeliever in our midst.'

In explaining belief in the supernatural, I have not been able to use more than a small proportion of the mistakes in thinking outlined earlier, but they include many of the more important ones. Belief in the psychic does not seem to be caused by fallacies based on how the question is put nor on people's inability to make rational predictions.

I have not attempted to deal with the so-called 'scientific' evidence for the paranormal, that is to say evidence carefully collected under controlled conditions. It seems likely that when positive results have been obtained they were due to fraud, as has been demonstrated in so many cases. In 1953, S. G. Soal, a respected mathematician at University College, London, startled the world by providing evidence for precognition. He may have been respected, but it was found after his death that he had faked his results, using a simple but ingenious method. In his experiments on telepathy, the sender transmitted one of five cards and the receiver had to write down which one it was. Soal had a prepared list of numbers ranging from 1 to 5 to determine which card should be sent on any one trial. The receiver's guesses were recorded as one of these numbers by an independent witness. When the experiment was over, Soal simply altered the '1's on his own pre-prepared list to '4's or '5's whenever the recipient's previous guess was a 4 or a 5. His chicanery was not discovered until after his death and then only by a careful analysis of his results, for inspection of the writing in his tables could not reveal the alterations he had made.

The Great Randi, the world's leading magician, dislikes the charlatans who use his tricks but pretend to have psychic powers, and like Houdini before him, he has made a hobby of unmasking them, but his remarkable findings, including his exposure of Uri Geller, are outside the scope of this book. It is perhaps worth recounting one comparatively recent episode. Randi sent two of his assistants to a laboratory of paranormal psychology in the States, instructing them to perform their magicians' tricks but not to say how they worked unless asked. They spent two years in the laboratory and their 'psychic' powers were duly written up in journals of the paranormal. Nobody thought to ask them how they obtained their effects. When they left, Randi blew the gaffe: to its credit the university closed down the laboratory.

Credulity is not limited to the layman. From Conan Doyle to Brian Josephson, a Nobel prize-winning physicist who holds a chair at Cambridge University, distinguished people have often been deceived. Nancy Reagan constantly consulted a woman astrologer, who claimed that she had determined through Nancy the times of President Reagan's speeches and his trips abroad, and that she influenced his views on Gorbachev. At one time the Russians spent millions of roubles on paranormal research because they thought it was of potential military importance: they held the curious belief that unlike messages sent by radio waves, communication by telepathy could not be intercepted by the enemy. Not to be outdone, the United States Air Force, Army and Navy all rushed to fund research on the topic. Cambridge University in its wisdom recently gave a doctoral degree for a thesis claiming to have demonstrated telepathy, while the University of Edinburgh has created a chair in parapsychology: its first incumbent was thoroughly up-to-date, for he announced his intention of investigating the 'role of psychic functions in unusual interactions between people . . . and computers'. Like other forms of irrationality, belief in the supernatural is not limited by class or creed, and it affects all institutions from the highest to the lowest.

23   causes, cures and costs

Having examined the many specific causes of human irrationality, it is time to consider some broader causes from which these more specific ones originate. Underlying the many different kinds of irrationality described are five basic causes. I should stress that the first three are speculative.

One stems from evolution. Our ancestors in the animal kingdom for the most part had to solve their problems in a hurry by fighting or fleeing. A monkey confronted by a lion would be foolish to stand pondering which was the best tree to climb: it is better to be wrong than eaten. It is probably for this reason that when under stress or high drive, people act and think in such stereotyped ways. Like the monkey they do not mull over alternatives, they act on impulse. Similarly, strong emotions, such as anger or fear, which can lead to highly irrational behaviour, were probably more useful at a time when confrontations between members of a species were solved by physical action not by more or less subtle verbal interchanges. Conformity and the emotion of embarrassment that keep people in line with the group's norms are also almost certainly partially inborn. Physically man is a defenceless creature and his survival depends upon being a member of a group. This is just as true today as in his early history when his only chance of enjoying a decent steak was to hunt antelopes in a group. Nowadays we are just as much dependent on others for our survival and our pleasures. It is the vast systems of factories, shops, roads, railways and aeroplanes that make modern life possible: they depend entirely on group co-operation. It is likely that without the appurtenances of modern living, many could not fend for themselves. But the allegiance to a group that makes modern society possible can readily be carried over into situations where it is inappropriate and hence leads to irrational behaviour.

The pervasiveness of irrational thinking and action raises the question of how the species survives. Why has not irrationality been eliminated or at least greatly reduced by evolutionary pressure? One answer is that in our society it does not require a great deal of rationality to find shelter and sustenance, and to rear a viable family. Indeed, anyone who spent their time learning probability theory and statistics and agonising over every decision in order to make it wholly rational would have little time (and possibly no inclination) for rearing a family. The bad effects of irrationality occur mainly when major decisions are being taken: mistakes made by engineers are revealed in accidents and those of doctors in avoidable deaths. Their decisions are enormously complex, particularly as compared to those made by our distant ancestors whose most formidable problems were which cave, spouse or antelope to choose. In short, because of a lack of evolutionary pressure to increase rationality, the sophistication of our technology has far outrun the evolution of our brains.

A second broad cause of irrationality is that parts of the brain appear to consist of networks of nerve cells initially connected together at random. Whenever anything is learned some of the connections between these cells are strengthened, others are weakened. A given concept, for example 'house' or 'daughter', is, after learning has occurred, represented not by the firing of one brain cell but by the simultaneous firing of many cells scattered over a wide area. Such systems have remarkable properties. The cells that are activated fire simultaneously rather than sequentially so that processing is very fast, as it is known to be in the human brain. Moreover, such systems of cells generalise readily. If presented with a number of different birds, they will classify as a bird a member of a species not previously shown. However, such networks have one problem: they tend to be sloppy. Because exactly the same cells are involved in learning different things, when something new is learned some of the connections made in previous learning can be altered and errors (usually small) can result. The existence of such systems in the brain would explain errors caused by the availability and the halo effect. Both depend on a person being unduly influenced by what is most salient, which in terms of neural networks would correspond to the activation of the cells having the strongest connections. Anything very salient would suppress other connections and hence prevent less salient material being taken into account.

It is likely that there is an input from systems of this kind into those parts of the brain associated with conscious thought, whose processes do not operate simultaneously, but proceed in a step-by-step fashion. We cannot think of more than a few items at any one time – at the very most seven. If the input to these higher levels comes from sloppy neural networks, it will contain errors: only if we are sufficiently persistent can these be removed by conscious thought. Everyone has had original ideas, probably produced by their neural networks, but everyone knows that many such ideas are useless: they have to be evaluated by careful thinking. But thinking – hard thinking – requires effort: people have to be trained or to train themselves to concentrate for enough time to solve whatever problems confront them. Contrast the speed and ease with which you recognise a face with the difficulty of working out a new geometric proof. Face recognition depends upon a system that is largely parallel, that is, many computations are undertaken by the brain simultaneously: its operations do not enter into consciousness. Understanding geometry, on the other hand, involves a conscious and laborious step-by-step process. Yet investigations of vision have suggested that the calculations made by the brain when we look around are more complex than those that led Einstein to the Theory of Relativity. We have evolved to be brilliant at seeing, we have not evolved to be brilliant physicists. All of this is admittedly rather speculative, but it remains true that the brain processes of which we are unconscious operate with enormous speed, efficiency and ease whereas most people have to force themselves to labour through the conscious thought processes needed to solve a difficult problem or to take a difficult decision. But unless this effort is made many decisions will be irrational and many problems will go unsolved.

A third general reason for irrational thinking also arises from mental laziness. To reduce the need for hard and prolonged thought, we have developed a number of tricks for taking quick decisions. These are called 'heuristics', that is, ways of thinking that will usually produce a passable but not perfect result quickly. This book has been devoted to showing among other things where such heuristics lead us astray, but it should be remembered that they often produce the right answer. If you buy a particular model of car because a friend has told you how good it is, the chances are that you will be satisfied with your purchase, even though you did not use the optimal method of making a decision. And if you select a job applicant because you are greatly impressed by his fluency at interview (the halo effect), he is unlikely to be totally unsatisfactory even though he might not be the best of those applying.

A fourth contribution to human irrationality is our failure to use elementary probability theory and elementary statistics and the concepts to which they have given rise. The root cause here would appear to be ignorance, which can in turn be largely attributed to our educational system. This failure can cause errors that superficially have nothing to do with numbers, for example, the Israeli pilots' failure to use the concept of regression to the mean or the judgement that Linda is more likely to be a feminist bank teller than a bank teller. The mathematics needed to solve every numerical problem posed in this book is much easier to acquire than is elementary geometry or calculus. H. G. Wells believed that statistics was as important to an educated citizen as reading or writing and that it would soon be taught routinely along with these subjects. His belief in its importance was undoubtedly correct, even if his faith in the rationality of our educational system was misguided. Given that its intellectual content is no less than that of these other branches of mathematics and given that for most people it would be more useful in their daily lives and jobs, it is hard to see why it is rarely taught at school. The answer may lie in another piece of irrationality – the difficulty of breaking tradition.

I have not stressed the final general cause of irrationality – self-serving bias – mainly because it is so obvious. Although I have shown that other factors play a part, it is hard to believe that the desire to be right or the wish to support one's self-esteem do not play some part in people's reluctance to give up a hypothesis, to change a bad decision, or to see a house they have just bought for what it really is.

Given the multiple causes of irrationality, the question arises of whether anything can be done to reduce it. The most general approach would be to try to persuade people to keep an open mind, to come to a conclusion only after they have surveyed all the evidence and to realise that, when occasion merits, it is a sign of strength not weakness to change one's mind. They should also be taught to seek out evidence against their own beliefs and if they find it, to be on their guard against misinterpreting or ignoring it. Looking for flaws in arguments in favour of one's own view is always salutary. Taking decisions in a hurry or while under stress is a mistake, since one's thinking is too inflexible. Where the evidence does not point conclusively in one direction, people should suspend judgement, which most find hard to do. As Bertrand Russell put it, 'Man is a credulous animal and must believe something. In the absence of good grounds for belief, he will be satisfied with bad ones.' One could also draw people's attention to all the specific errors I have described, for example, to sunk costs or the failure to base inferences about connections between events on the four relevant figures. The above advice is rather abstract and therefore not readily available, but it could be presented in the context of specific examples, which are available. It would also help if people were merely induced to write down the pros and cons before taking any important decision, as recommended by Benjamin Franklin.

Several studies have evaluated the effect of encouraging students to act on the general principles outlined. For example, they have been encouraged to think about why an answer is wrong (or right); to take their time and not act on impulse; to be persistent; and to examine alternatives. Such advice, given in the context of specific problems, has for the most part produced some but usually not very marked improvements on tests purporting to measure rationality. Unfortunately, because there have been no long-term follow-ups, it is not known how long the effects last.

It has been demonstrated that learning statistics helps people to deal rationally with some problems drawn from everyday life. As I have shown, solving such problems often requires the use of statistical concepts, whether explicitly or implicitly. Perhaps surprisingly, learning logic failed to help students spot flaws (for example, the reversal of cause and effect) in arguments presented to them, but even here a knowledge of statistics was of some help.

Recently Richard Nisbett and his colleagues performed a series of cunning experiments demonstrating that the ability to use statistical concepts really does help people to take good decisions in everyday life, not merely when under test in a psychological laboratory. They found that the extent to which subjects could apply the law of large numbers (see Chapter 15) in everyday reasoning varied with the type of problem: they were given three different types. 1. When the events in the problem were clearly random, like the behaviour of a slot machine, they applied the law quite well. 2. They were less good at applying it to events that could be measured and in which there was an element of skill (such as athletic performance or examination results). 3. They were very poor at applying it to personal characteristics (such as honesty). For example, they understood that a small sample of a slot machine's behaviour was a poor guide to its general behaviour; they were less likely to be cautious in generalising from a small sample of an athlete's performance; and they completely failed to appreciate that if they briefly encountered someone who was friendly, they could not infer that he was a friendly person in general. Of more importance for present purposes, the subjects were trained on problems from one of these three types and then tested on all three types. The subjects were taught to make use of such concepts as sample size and regression to the mean. They improved not merely on the type of problem on which they had been trained but on the other two. This shows that a training in applying statistical concepts to one type of problem transfers to others.

A further paper provides evidence that the ability to take rational decisions in everyday life correlates with people's success at their work, in particular with their level of salary. One hundred and twenty-six professors at the University of Michigan were interviewed by telephone. It was found that the better they were at answering correctly sunk-cost questions and similar problems, the higher were their salaries age for age. This might be expected of economists since their work depends to some extent on a knowledge of theories prescribing how best to take decisions, but the finding was equally true for professors in arts subjects. The investigators also examined how far their subjects took rational decisions in ordinary life. For example, they asked each whether in the last five years he had ever left a movie before it finished. Given the number of bad movies on show, most people are likely to have been to one at least once in five years. People who do not fall for the sunk-cost trap will leave, those who do will see the film out. Twice as many economists said they had left a movie as did professors of biology or arts. In other words economists, who are presumably no cleverer than other professors but whose subject gives them a better knowledge of how to take rational decisions, act more rationally in at least some aspects of their everyday life. This would appear to be direct evidence that a knowledge of the theory of decision-making can improve the rationality of ordinary decisions. As far as I know it is the only existing evidence, but there is likely to be a spate of work on the topic in the next few years.

Apart from a knowledge of economics, an education in psychology and to a lesser extent in medicine has been shown to improve students' answers to the sorts of questions posed in this book. Both disciplines emphasise the traps in drawing inferences about causes from data and both give some training in elementary statistics. In evaluating the beneficial effects of psychology, one should perhaps bear in mind that almost all tests of rationality have been constructed by psychologists, though no knowledge of psychology is needed to answer them. The only other subject that has been shown to assist is law. Although it does not help improve arguments based on statistics, it increases the number of causal-type arguments that students produce, but as befits future lawyers, the increase is limited entirely to arguments in favour of the hypothesis being entertained. Other subjects such as chemistry and logic appear to have little or no effect on people's ability to reason correctly, at least as measured by the sort of problems set out in the second half of this book. Moreover, there is considerable evidence against the idea that learning one subject makes it easier to learn a second, unless the content of the two overlaps. Until recently, there was a widespread belief that learning classics was a training in thinking that would subsequently enable one to pick up any other subject with ease. Unfortunately, however, fluency in Latin and Greek will not help you to become a competent physicist or even a good historian.

If one believes that part of the purpose of education is to teach people to think, then the methods of examining used both in Britain and in the US are irrational. A-level teaching in Britain for the most part emphasises rote learning and lays little stress on rational thinking; in America, this system is often adopted even by universities where it is common to set multiple-choice questions that allow no scope for thought, but depend entirely on memory. Moreover, examinations with a fixed time-limit are likely to encourage impulsive and inflexible thinking.

I end by asking a question that must have been bothering many readers, 'Is rationality really necessary or even desirable?' In the case of decision-making by experts, there can be no doubts. General Montgomery, Admiral Kimmel, General Haig and Bomber Harris, by their refusal to change their minds in the face of the evidence, caused large numbers of unnecessary deaths. Some doctors, through their ignorance of probabilities, have submitted many women to unnecessary and unpleasant biopsies, while others have indirectly been responsible for the deaths of older women through bone fractures because of their unwillingness to administer oestrogen. Many refuse to use computer systems whose diagnostic capabilities are better than their own. Civil servants continue to squander public money because of an irrational system that permits laziness, adherence to tradition and self-aggrandisement. Engineers often fail to think sufficiently hard about the risks in the systems they produce, thus causing many deaths. Even the decision of a university to admit or not to admit a candidate is important, at least for the candidate, but it is still not taken in what is demonstrably the best way. One method of circumventing ineptitude is to substitute mathematical methods of taking decisions whenever they can be shown to be more effective than people's intensely fallible intuitions. This is almost certainly a better recipe for success in professional domains than any amount of training in statistics, though the training should still take place.

In personal decision-making, the effects of irrationality are less than in the professions and indeed in many cases they only marginally affect people's private lives. Most personal decisions are after all quite trivial. Does it matter whether we have spaghetti or baked beans for supper? Whether we spend an evening at home or go to the theatre? Whether we take our holidays in Paris, Munich or the Costa Brava? It does not even matter that much if we buy a dud car, though it is certainly annoying. In their private capacity, people take very few important decisions. For most there are only four: which neighbourhood to live in and which house to buy; which career to follow and which options to choose within that career; whom, if anyone, to live with and when to stop doing so; whether to have children (an outcome that is in any case often involuntary). In all these choices, there are usually many unknowns, which means that rational thinking may only marginally increase one's chance of a successful outcome. It is an open question whether the application of Utility Theory would lead to happier marriages.

One can even question whether it is desirable for everyone to be completely rational. We prize spontaneity but, as we have seen, rational decision-making often takes time. When lovers meet, a spontaneous kiss is more cherished than one delivered after careful reflection. There are two reasons for valuing such spontaneity. First, we regard emotional gestures as insincere unless they are spontaneous. If the person has the emotion he purports to have, it will show in the speed with which he displays it. If he stops to think, it suggests he does not really have it: his response is contrived not genuine. Second, very ruminative people, concerned only to take the best decision, can be rather boring. They may go through long silences while they ponder the right thing to say and their search for the rational decision may result in irritating vacillation. People can be too cautious to be likeable. Generosity to be true generosity has to come from the heart not the head: we dislike 'the lore of nicely calculated less and more'.

Spontaneity, however, has its problems: although we admire spontaneous good actions, equally we disapprove of spontaneous bad ones. Except under special circumstances the spontaneous display of anger, frustration, depression or envy is unwelcome: nor should we spontaneously give vent to impulses that will yield small short-term gains at the expense of large long-term costs. But how can we spontaneously act in good ways and not spontaneously act in bad ones? The difficulty is that it seems impossible to select without careful consideration which actions to perform spontaneously and which to repress: but it is impossible both to ponder and to be spontaneous.

To solve this dilemma we return where we began. Aristotle believed that the truly good man did good naturally: he did not have to force himself to do it. One can of course take the opposite line and reason that the truly good man is one who succeeds in fighting his evil inclinations – if you are good by nature, behaving well is easy and, so the argument goes, you can't expect much credit for it. But regardless of this issue, it is certainly true that the man for whom good comes naturally is better company than one who is always agonising over it, even if he succeeds in quenching his doubts. There is still a dilemma – few of us if any are born naturally good. To this Aristotle had a partial answer.

He believed that people form their own characters. Every time we resist a bad action, it becomes easier to resist, and every time we do something good it becomes easier to do again. By assiduous practice people can turn themselves into beings who spontaneously do the right thing and spontaneously avoid the wrong. If you have sufficiently rehearsed the reasons for being pleasant to your partner or for not sulking and if you have acted on them at whatever cost, the actions will come spontaneously in future. There is considerable evidence that practising a habit leads to its being run off without thought: think of the automatic way in which an experienced motorist drives. But Aristotle's advice could only be taken by the rational man, by someone whose end was to form his character in a certain way and who accepted that careful selection of what he did was the best means to that end. To put oneself in a position where one does the right thing without thought, that is without consideration of what is rational, one has to undergo a period of deliberately acting in the ways that mould one's character to one's desire: that is rationality indeed.

further acknowledgements and bibliography

I have used material from the following books and am grateful to their authors for the ingenuity of their research and ideas. I have not listed books on the social and emotional causes of irrationality, since as far as I know there is no book devoted exclusively to this topic. To help readers who want to go more deeply into the subject, I have added a comment on each book mentioned.

Nisbett, R., and Ross, L., *Human Inference: Strategies and shortcomings of social judgement.* Englewood Cliffs, NJ: Prentice-Hall, 1980.
An exceptionally clear, well written and in places original account of the cognitive causes of irrationality. It can be read with pleasure by non-specialists.

Baron, J., *Thinking and Deciding.* Cambridge: Cambridge University Press, 1988.
A textbook on the cognitive causes of irrationality. More up-to-date, but much more difficult than the previous book.

Kahneman, D., Slovic, P., and Tversky, A. (Eds), *Judgment Under Uncertainty: Heuristics and biases.* Cambridge: Cambridge University Press, 1982.
Thirty-two chapters by different authors, most fascinating, a few not; they vary greatly in level of difficulty.

Wagenaar, W. A., *Paradoxes of Gambling Behaviour.* Hove: Lawrence Erlbaum Associates, 1988.
A careful study of the irrational beliefs of gamblers.

Janis, I. L., and Mann, L., *Decision Making.* New York: Free Press, 1977.
A highly original study of the processes (many of them irrational)

underlying decision making, illustrated by examples drawn mainly from politics. Very readable.

Dawes, R. M., *Rational Choice in an Uncertain World*. Orlando: Harcourt, Brace, Jovanovich, 1988.
A readable, but occasionally slightly technical account of how and how not to make choices.

Dixon, N., *The Psychology of Military Incompetence*. London: Cape, 1976.
Dixon, N., *Our Own Worst Enemy*. London: Cape, 1987.
These two books make easy and entertaining reading: the first provides striking examples of irrationality by the military, the second concentrates on irrationality in different professions.

Paulos, J. A., *Innumeracy*. New York: Hill and Wang, 1988.
A very brief but highly entertaining account of the errors – sometimes comic, sometimes disastrous – perpetrated by people who can't be bothered to understand simple figures.

I have used many other books and many papers in learned journals: these are acknowledged in the Notes.

notes

The notes provide page and line numbers for the source material used. Normally it will be unnecessary to consult line numbers, since the connection with the text is usually obvious from the title of the reference cited. References are provided for the sources of almost all the experimental results mentioned in the text. Some of the incidents and one or two of the experiments recorded were taken from newspaper reports and no reference is given, where I could not check the original source. The notes serve not only as a guide to the reader, but as an acknowledgement to the many psychologists who have contributed to our knowledge of irrationality by their elegant research and theorising.

Chapter 1

Page
8,　line 6 Mandel, A. J., 'The psychobiology of transcendence', in Davidson, J. M. and Davidson, R. J., *The Psychobiology of Consciousness* (New York: Plenum, 1980).

Chapter 2

11,　line 9 Tversky, A., and Kahneman, D., 'Availability: a heuristic for judging frequency and probability', *Cognitive Psychology*, 1973, 5, 207-232. This paper made the concept of 'availability' available.

12,　line 14 Higgins, E. T., Rholes, W. S., and Jones, C. R., 'Category accessibility and impression formation', *Journal of Experimental Social Psychology*, 1977, 13, 141-154.

13,　line 39 Axelrod, R., *The Evolution of Cooperation* (New York: Basic Books, 1984).

14,　line 21 Hornstein, H. A., LaKind, E., Frankel, G., and Manne, S., 'Effects of knowledge about remote social events on prosocial behaviour, social conception, and mood', *Journal of Personality and Social Psychology*, 1975. 32, 1038-1046.

14,　line 32 Tversky, A., and Kahneman, D., op. cit.

15,　line 32 Bower, G. H., 'Mental imagery and associative learning', in Gregg, L. (Ed.), *Cognition in Learning and Memory* (New York: Wiley, 1972).

15,　line 37 Standing, L., 'Learning 10,000 pictures', *Quarterly Journal of*

Experimental Psychology, 1973, 25, 207-222.

16,   line 3 Enzle, M. E., Hansen, R. D., and Lowe, C. A., 'Humanizing the mixed-motive paradigm: methodological implications from attribution theory', *Simulation and Games*, 1975, 6, 151-165.

16,   line 38 Slovic, P., Fischhoff, B., and Lichtenstein, S., 'Characterizing perceived risk', in Kates, R. W., Hohenemser, C., and Kasperson, J. V. (Eds), *Perilous Progress: technology as hazard* (Boulder, CO: Westview).

17,   line 29 Elstein, A. S., Shulman, L. S., and Spralka, S. A., *Medical Problem Solving: An Analysis of Clinical Reasoning* (Cambridge, Mass: Harvard University Press, 1978).

17,   line 35 Dreman, D., *Contrarian Investment Strategy* (New York: Random House, 1979).

18,   line 14 Borgida, E., and Nisbett, R. F., 'The differential impact of abstract vs concrete information on decisions', *Journal of Applied Social Psychology*, 1977, 7, 258-271.

18,   line 27 Asch, S., 'Forming impressions of personality', *Journal of Abnormal and Social Psychology*, 1946, 41, 258-290.

19,   line 11 Jones, F. E., Rock, L., Shaver, K. G., Goethals, G. R., and Ward, L. M., 'Pattern of performance and ability attribution: an unexpected primacy effect', *Journal of Personality and Social Psychology*, 1968, 10, 317-340.

20,   line 12 Dawes, R. M., *Rational Choice in an Uncertain World* (Orlando: Harcourt, Brace, Jovanovich, 1988).

20,   line 41 Wagenaar, W. A., *Paradoxes of Gambling Behaviour* (Hove: Lawrence Erlbaum Associates, 1988).

21,   line 8 Nisbett, K. E., and Wilson, T. D., 'The halo effect: evidence for unconscious alteration of judgements', *Journal of Personality and Social Psychology*, 1977, 35, 250256.

21,   line 17 Broveman, I. K. D., Broveman, D. M., Clarkson, F. E., Rosenkrantz. P. S., and Vogel, S. K., 'Sex role strategies and clinical judgments of mental health', *Journal of Consulting and Clinical Psychology*, 1970, 34, 1-7.

22,   line 8 Peters, D. K., and Ceci, S. J., 'Peer-review practices of learned journals: the fate of published articles submitted again', *The Behavioral and Brain Sciences*, 1982, 5, 187-255.

Chapter 3

Most of this chapter is based on Milgram. S., *Obedience to Authority: An experimental view* (New York: Harper and Row, 1974, London: Pinter & Martin, 2006).

28,   line 39 Hofling, C. K., Brotzman, E., Dairymple, S., Graves, N., and Pierce, C. M., 'An experimental study in nurse-physician relationships', *Journal of Nervous and Mental Disease*, 1966, 143, 171-180.

29,   line 40 Green, R., 'Human error on the flight deck', RAF Institute of Aviation Medicine: unpublished report (Farnborough, England: 1991).

29,   line 40 Ennis, M., 'Training and supervision of obstetric Senior House Officers', *British Medical Bulletin*.

30,   line 43 Dixon, N., *Our Own Worst Enemy* (London: Cape, 1987).

Chapter 4

32,   line 9 for Asch's experiments on conformity, see Asch. S. E., *Social Psychology* (New York: Prentice-Hall, 1952); Asch, S. E., 'Opinions and social pressure', *Scientific American*, 1955, 193, 31-35; Asch, S. E., 'Studies of independence and conformity: a minority of one against a unanimous majority', *Psychological Monographs*, 1956, 70 (9, whole no. 416).

34,   line 37 Pollak, M. S., and Cummings, W., 'Commitment and voluntary energy conservation', paper presented at the annual meeting of the American

Psychological Association, Chicago, 1975.

35,　line 17 Kiesler, C., Mathog, P., Pool, P., and Howenstein, R., 'Commitment and the boomerang effect: a field study', in Kiesler, C. (Ed.), *The Psychology of Commitment* (New York: Academic Press).

37,　line 20 Brown, R., *A First Language: The early stages* (Cambridge, Mass: Harvard University Press, 1973).

37,　line 34 Hovland, C. 1., and Weiss, R., 'The influence of source credibility on communication effectiveness', *Public Opinion Quarterly*, 1951, 15, 635-650.

38,　line 23 For a review of panic behaviour and crowd violence, see Schneider, D. J., *Social Psychology* (Reading, Mass: Addison-Wesley, 1976) pp 298-305.

39,　line 4 Stouffer, S. A., Suchman, E. A., De Vinney, L. C., Star, S. A., and Williams, R. M., *The American Soldier: Adjustment during army life*, Vol. 1 (Princeton, NJ: Princeton University Press, 1949).

39,　line 25 Zimbardo, P. G., The human choice: individuation, reason and order versus deindividuation, impulse and chaos', in Arnold, W. J., and Levine, D. (Eds), *Nebraska Symposium on Motivation, 1969* (Lincoln: University of Nebraska Press, 1970).

40,　line 28 For a review of the bystander effect, see Latane, B., and Darley, J. M., *Help in a Crisis: Bystander response to an emergency* (Morristown, NJ: General Learning Press, 1976).

Chapter 5

44,　line 29 Newcomb, T. M., *Personality and Social Change* (New York: Diyden, 1943).

45,　line 11 Kogan, N., and Wallach, M. A., *Risk Taking: A study in cognition and personality* (New York: Holt, Rinehart and Winston, 1964).

45,　line 34 Moscovici, S., and Personnaz, B., 'Studies in social influence. V: Minority influence and conversion behaviour in a perceptual task', *Journal of Personality and Social Psychology*, 1969, 12, 125-135.

46,　line 9 Sniezek, J. A., and Henry, R. A., 'Accuracy and confidence in group judgements', *Organizational Behaviour and Human Decision Processes*, 1989, 43, 1-28.

46,　line 16 Janis, I. L., and Mann, L., *Decision Making* (New York: Free Press, 1977).

46,　line 38 Janis, I. L., and Mann, L., op. cit.

47,　line 29 Stein, M., *Stimulating Creativity: Individual differences*, Vol. 2 (New York:. Academic Press, 1975).

48,　line 39 Johnson, R. D., and Downing, L. L., 'Deindividuation and valence of cues: effects on prosocial and antisocial behaviour', *Journal of Personality and Social Psychology*, 1979, 37, 15321538.

49,　line 15 Sherif, M., *Group Conflict and Co-operation: Their social psychology* (London: Routledge and Kegan Paul, 1966).

51,　line 27 Brown, R. J., 'Divided we fall: an analysis of relations between sections of a factory work-force', in Tajfel, H. (Ed.), *Differentiation between Social Groups: Studies in the social psychology of intergroup relations* (London: Academic Press, 1978).

52,　line 15 On stereotypes, see the discussion in Nisbett, R., and Ross, L., *Human Inference: Strategies and shortcomings of social judgement* (Englewood Cliffs, NJ: Prentice-Hall), pp. 237-242, from which I have borrowed many of the ideas set out here.

52,　line 24 See evidence given in Chapter 12.

52,　line 42 Tajfel, H., Flament, C., Billig, M. G., and Bundy, R. P., 'Social categorization and intergroup behaviour'. *European Journal of Social Psychology*, 1971, 1, 149-178; Tajfel, H., and Wilkes, A. L., 'Classification and quantitative judgement', *British Journal of Psychology*, 1963, 54, 101-114.

53,　line 43 Hamilton, D. L., and Rose, I. R., 'Illusory Correlation and the Maintenance of Stereotypic Beliefs', unpublished manuscript, University of California at Santa Barbara, 1978.

Chapter 6

55, line 28 Chapman, L., *Your Disobedient Servant* (London: Chatto, 1978).
57, line 9 The examples of decisions made by businessmen are taken from Slatter, S., *Corporate Recovery* (Harmondsworth: Penguin Books, 1984).
57, line 24 Chapman, L., *Waste Away* (London: Chatto, 1982).
63, line 13 The remainder of this chapter is drawn from Dreman, D., *Contrarial Investment Strategy* (New York: Random House. 1979).

Chapter 7

65, line 1 For a classic account of the ways in which people attempt to resolve internal conflicts, see Festinger, L., *Conflict, Decisions and Dissonance* (Stanford: Stanford University Press, 1964).
66, line 6 Festinger, L., op. cit.
66, line 15 Vroom, V. H., 'Organizational choice: a study of pre- and post-decision processes', *Organizational Behaviour and Human Performance*, 1966, 1, 212-225.
66, line 28 Mann, L., Janis, I. L., and Chaplin, R., 'The effects of anticipation of forthcoming information on predecisional processes', *Journal of Personality and Social Psychology*, 1969, 11, 10-16.
67, line 15 Bettelheim, B., 'Individual and mass behaviour in extreme situations', *Journal of Abnormal and Social Psychology*, 38, 417-452.
67, line 36 Quoted in Janis, I. L., and Mann, I., op. cit.
69, line 6 Freedman, J. L., and Fraser, S. C., 'Compliance without pressure: the foot-in-the-door technique', *Journal of Personality and Social Psychology*, 1966, 4, 195-202.
69, line 23 Aronson, E., and Mills, J., 'The effect of severity of initiation on liking for a group', *Journal of Abnormal and Social Psychology*, 1959, 59, 177-181.
69, line 39 Axsom, D., and Cooper, J., 'Reducing weight by reducing dissonance: the role of effort justification in inducing weight loss', in Aronson, E. (Ed.), *Readings about the Social Animal*, third edition (San Francisco: Freeman, 1981).
70, line 23 Arkes, H. R., and Blumer, C., 'The psychology of sunk cost', *Organizational Behaviour and Human Decision Processes*, 1985, 35, 124-140.
70, line 35 Dixon, N., *The Psychology of Military Incompetence* (London: Cape, 1976).
71, line 4 Quoted in Baron, J., *Thinking and Deciding* (Cambridge: Cambridge University Press, 1988).
71, line 18 Tversky, A., and Kahneman, D., 'The framing of decisions and the psychology of choice', *Science*, 1981, 211, 453-458.
72, line 7 Thaler, R. H., 'Toward a positive theory of consumer choice', *Journal of Economic Behavior and Organization*, 1980, 1, 39-60.
72, line 32 Festinger, L., and Carlsmith, J. M., 'Cognitive consequences of forced compliance', *Journal of Abnormal and Social Psychology*, 1959, 58, 203-210.
73, line 4 Nel, E., Helmreich, R., and Aronson, E., 'Opinion change in the advocate as a function of the persuasibility of his audience: a clarification of the meaning of dissonance', *Journal of Personality and Social Psychology*, 1969, 12, 117-124.
73, line 19 For a review, see Tetlock, P. E., and Manstead, A. S. R., 'Impression management versus intrapsychic explanations in social psychology: a useful dichotomy?', *Psychological Review*, 1985, 92, 59-77.

Chapter 8

75, line 1 For a review of the undesirable effects of reward and punishment, see McGraw, K. O., 'The detrimental effects of reward on performance: a literature review and a prediction model', in Lepper, M. R., and Greene, D. (Eds), *The Hidden Costs of Reward* (Morristown, NJ: Lawrence Erlbaum, 1978).

75, line 9 Lepper, M. R., Greene, D., and Nisbett, K. E., 'Undermining children's intrinsic interest with extrinsic reward: a test of the overjustification hypothesis', *Journal of Personality and Social Psychology*, 1973, 28, 129-137.

75, line 21 Deci, E. L., 'The effects of externally mediated rewards on intrinsic motivation', *Journal of Personality and Social Psychology*, 1971, 18, 105-115.

75, line 29 Smith, W. E., 'The effects of anticipated or unanticipated social reward on subsequent intrinsic motivation', unpublished doctoral dissertation, Cornell University, 1957.

76, line 3 On token economies, see e.g. Greene, D., Sternberg, B., and Lepper, M. R., 'Overjustification in a token economy', *Journal of Personality and Social Psychology*, 1976, 34, 1219-1234.

77, line 15 Deci, F. L., op. cit.

78, line 17 Likert, R., *The Human Organization* (New York: McGraw-Hill, 1967).

78, line 28 Likert, R., op. cit.

80, line 9 *The Author* 1990, 101, no 2.

80, line 42 E.g. Zanna, M. P., Lepper, M. R., and Abelson, R. P., 'Attentional mechanisms in children's devaluation of a forbidden activity in a forced compliance situation', *Journal of Personality and Social Psychology*, 1973, 3, 355-359.

81, line 11 Quoted in Condry, J., 'The role of incentives in socialization', in Lepper, M. K., and Greene, D. (Eds), *The Hidden Costs of Reward* (Morristown, NJ: Lawrence Erlbaum, 1978).

81, line 22 Bell, S. M., and Ainsworth, M. D., 'Infant dying and maternal responsiveness', *Child Development*, 1972, 43, 1171-1190.

82, line 14 Langer, F. J., 'The psychology of choice', *Journal for the Theory of Social Behavior*, 1977, 7, 185-208.

82, line 24 Hammond, T., and Brehm, J. W., 'The attractiveness of choice alternatives when freedom to choose is eliminated by a social agent', *Journal of Personality*, 1966, 34, 546-555.

82, line 40 Liem, G. R., 'Performance and satisfaction as affected by personal control over salient decisions', *Journal of Personality and Social Psychology*, 1965, 31, 232-240.

83, line 8 Friedman, C., Greenspan, R., and Mittelman, F., 'The decision making process and the outcome of therapeutic abortion', *American Journal of Psychology*, 1974, 131, 1332-1337.

83, line 11 Morris, T., Greer, S., and White, P., 'Psychological and social adjustment to mastectomy: a two-year follow-up', *Cancer*, 1977, I. 40, 2381-2387.

83, line 16 Ferrari, N. A., 'Institutionalization and attitude change in an aged population: a field study in dissonance theory', unpublished doctoral dissertation, Case Western Reserve University, 1962.

Chapter 9

86, line 16 Miller, L. B., and Estes, B. W., 'Monetary reward and motivation in learning', *Journal of Experimental Psychology*, 1962, 64, 393-399.

86, line 32 Glucksberg, S., 'The influence of strength of drive on functional fixedness and perceptual recognition', *Journal of Experimental Psychology*, 1962, 63, 36-41.

86, line 37 McGraw, K. O., and Mcullers, J. C., 'Monetary reward and water-jar performance: evidence of a detrimental effect of reward on problem solving', paper presented at a meeting of the Southeastern Psychological Association, New Orleans, 1976.

87, line 16 Glucksberg, S., op. cit.

88, line 4 Schwartz, B., 'Reinforcement-induced behavioural stereotypy: how not to teach people to discover rules', *Journal of Experimental Psychology: General*, 1982, 111, 23-59.

88, line 27 Keinan, G., 'Decision making under stress: scanning of alternatives under controllable and uncontrollable threats', *Journal of Personality and Social Psychology*, 1987, 52, 639-644.

88,   line 39 Norris, W., *The Unsafe Sky* (London: Arrow, 1981).

89,   line 35 Goidsen, R. K., Gerhardt, P. T., and Handy, V. H., 'Some factors relating to patient delay in seeking diagnosis for cancer symptoms', *Cancer*, 1957, 10, 1-7.

91,   line 14 Quattrone, G. A., and Tversky, A., 'Causal versus diagnostic contingencies: on self-deception and the voter's illusion', *Journal of Personality and Social Psychology*, 1984, 46, 237-248.

91,   line 30 For a critical review of the evidence on wishful thinking, see Miller, O. T., and Ross, M., 'Self-serving biases in the attribution of causality: fact or fiction?', *Psychological Bulletin*, 1975, 82, 213-225.

91,   line 32 Janis, I. L., and Terwilliger. R., 'An experimental study of psychological resistances to fear-arousing communications', *Journal of Abnormal and Social Psychology*, 1962, 65, 403-410.

92,   line 10 Baron J., *Thinking and Deciding* (Cambridge: Cambridge University Press, 1988).

92,   line 29 Norris, W., op. cit.

92,   line 39 Hawkes, N., Lean, G., McKie, R., and Wilson, A., *The Worst Accident in the World* (London: Pan, 1986).

93,   line 17 Sutherland, S., *The Macmillan Dictionary of Psychology* (London: Macmillan, 1989).

Chapter 10

95,   line 5 Janis, I. L., and Mann, L., *Decision Making* (New York: Free Press, 1977).

98,   line 21 Wason, P. C., 'On the failure to eliminate hypotheses in a conceptual task', *Quarterly Journal of Experimental Psychology*, 1960, 12, 129-140.

99,   line 6 Popper, K. K., *Objective Knowledge* (Oxford: Clarendon Press, 1972).

99,   line 39 Wason, P. C., 'Reasoning', in Foss, B. (Ed.), *New Horizons in Psychology* (Harmondsworth: Penguin, 1966).

101,   line 29 Evans, J. St. B. T., 'Linguistic determinants of bias in conditional reasoning', *Quarterly Journal of Experimental Psychology*, 1983, 35A, 635-644.

102,   line 1 Snyder, M., and Swann, W. B., 'Behavioral confirmation in social interaction: from social perception to social reality', *Journal of Experimental Social Psychology*, 1978, 14, 148-162.

102,   line 21 For proof if proof be needed, see Lazarsfeld, P. F., Berelson, B., and Gaudet, H., *The People's Choice* (New York: Columbia University Press, 1948).

102,   line 28 Katz, J. L., Weiner, H., Gallagher, T. F., and Heilman, I., 'Stress, distress, and ego defenses: psychoendocrine response to impending breast-tumour biopsy', *Archives of General Psychiatry*, 1970, 23, 131-142.

102,   line 33 Janis, J. L., and Rausak, C. N., 'Selective interest in communications that could arouse decisional conflict: a field study of participants in the draft-resistance movement', *Journal of Personality and Social Psychology*, 1970, 14, 46-54.

Chapter 11

104,   line 3 The account of the battle of Arnhem is largely based on Dixon, N., *The Psychology of Military Incompetence* (London: Cape, 1976).

105,   line 29 The quotation from Francis Bacon was taken from Nisbett, R., and Ross, L., *Human Inference: Strategies and shortcomings of social judgment* (Englewood Cliffs: Prentice-Hall, 1980).

105,   line 36 Lord, C., Ross, L., and Lepper, M. R., 'Biased assimilation and attitude polarization: the effects of prior theories on subsequently considered evidence', *Journal of Personality and Social Psychology*, 1979, 2098-2109.

106,   line 4 Ross, L., Lepper, M. R., and Hubbard, M., 'Perseverance in self perception and social perception: biased attributional processes in the debriefing paradigm', *Journal of Personality and Social Psychology*, 1975, 32, 880-892.

108,   line 14 Pitz, G. F., Downing, L., and Reinhold, H., 'Sequential effects in the revision of subjective probabilities', *Canadian Journal of Psychology*, 1967, 21, 381-393.

109, line 9 Snyder, M., and Cantor, N., 'Testing theories about other people: remembering all the history that fits', unpublished manuscript: University of Minnesota, 1979.

110, line 4 The idea that inventing a story makes it difficult to get rid of a belief and the supporting experiments, some of which are described here, appear in Nisbett, R., and Ross, L., *Human Inference: Strategies and shortcomings of social judgment* (Englewood Cliffs: Prentice-Hall, 1980), pp 183-186.

110, line 19 Nisbett, R., and Ross, L., op. cit.

Chapter 12

114, line 2 Shapiro, D. A., and Shapiro, D., 'Meta-analysis of comparative therapy outcome studies: a replication', *Psychological Bulletin*, 1982, 92, 581-604.

115, line 19 For further evidence on the failure to take account of negative cases, see Ward, W. C., and Jenkins, H. M.. 'The display of information and the judgment of contingency', *Canadian Journal of Psychology*, 1967, 19, 231-241.

115, line 27 Smedslund, J., 'The concept of correlation in adults', *Scandinavian Journal of Psychology*, 1963, 4, 165-173.

117, line 6 Chapman, L. J., and Chapman. J. P., 'Illusory correlation as an obstacle to the use of valid psychodiagnostic signs', *Journal of Abnormal Psychology*, 1969, 74, 271-280.

121, line 10 Cox, J., and Tapsell, J., 'Graphology and its validity', paper presented at the Occupational Psychology Conference of the British Psychological Society, 1991.

121, line 16 Neter, E., and Ben-Shakhar, G., 'Predictive validity of graphological inferences: a meta-analysis', *Personality and Individual Differences*, 1989, 10, 737-745.

121, line 18 Ben-Shakhar, G., Bar-Hillel, M., Blui, V., Ben-Abba, E., and Hug, A., 'Can graphology predict occupational success?', *Journal of Applied Psychology*, 1989, 71, 645-653.

122, line 6 Taylor, S. E., and Fiske, S. T., Salience, attention and attribution: top of the head phenomena', in Berkowitz, L. (Ed.), *Advances in Experimental Social Psychology*, Vol 11 (New York: Academic Press, 1978).

122, line 20 Chapman, L. J., 'Illusory correlation in observational report', *Journal of Verbal Learning and Verbal Behavior*, 1967, 6, 151-155.

122, line 31 Hamilton, D. L., and Gifford, R. K., 'Illusory correlation in interpersonal perception: a cognitive basis of stereotypic judgments', *Journal of Experimental Social Psychology*, 1976, 12, 392-407.

Chapter 13

124, line 1 Most of this chapter is based on Eddy, D. M., 'Probabilistic reasoning in clinical medicine: problems and opportunities', in Kahneman, D., Slovic, P., and Tversky, A. (Eds), *Judgment under Uncertainty: Heuristics and biases* (Cambridge: Cambridge University Press, 1982).

130, line 10 Hoffman, P. J., Slovic, P., and Rover, L. G., 'An analysis of variance: models for the assessment of cue utilization in clinical judgment', *Psychological Bulletin*, 1965, 63, 338-349.

130, line 15 Christensen-Szalanski, J. J. J., and Bushyhead, J. B., 'Physicians' use of probabilistic information in a real clinical setting'. *Journal of Experimental Psychology: Human Perception and Performance*, 1981, 7, 928-935.

130, line 23 Paulos, J. A., *Innumeracy: Mathematical illiteracy and its consequences* (New York: Hill and Wang, 1988).

130, line 30 Egbert, L., Battit, C., Welch, C., and Bartlett, M., 'Reduction of postoperative pain by encouragement and instruction of patients', *New England Journal of Medicine*, 1964, 270

Chapter 14

132, line 9 The quotation was taken from Nisbett, R., and Ross, L., *Human Inference: Strategies and shortcomings of social judgment* (Englewood Cliffs: Prentice-Hall, 1980).

133, line 4 Nisbett, R., and Ross, L., op. cit.

133, line 13 For a critical review of studies of the effects of injested cholesterol see Totman, R., *Mind, Stress and Health* (London: Souvenir, 1990), from which, except where noted, the following studies were taken.

134, line 8 Booth-Kewley, S., and Friedman, H., 'Psychological predictors of heart disease: a quantitative review', *Psychological Bulletin*, 1987, 101, 343-362.

134, line 35 Huff, D., *How to Lie with Statistics* (London: Gollancz, 1954).

135, line 30 Bollas, C., *Forces of Destiny: Psychoanalysis and human idiom* (London: Free Association, 1989).

135, line 43 Smith, J. C., Glass, C. V., and Miller, J. I., *The Benefits of Psychotherapy* (Baltimore: Johns Hopkins Press).

136, line 15 Fisher, R. A., 'Lung cancer and cigarettes', *Nature*, 1958, 182, 108.

136, line 20 Doll, R., and Peto, R.. 'Mortality in relation to smoking: 20 years' observations on British doctors', *British Medical Journal*, 1976, 290, 1525-1536.

136, line 33 Eysenck, H. J., *Smoking, Health and Personality* (London: Weidenfeld, 1965).

136, line 40 Meehl, P., *Clinical vs. Statistical Prediction* (Minneapolis: University of Minnesota Press, 1955).

137, line 7 For tonsillectomy and other medical aberrations, see Malleson, A., *Need Your Doctor be so Useless?* (London: Allen and Unwin, 1973).

137, line 30 Tversky, A., and Kahneman, D., 'Causal schemas in judgments under uncertainty', in Kahneman, D., Slovic, P., and Tversky, A. (Eds), *Judgment Under Uncertainty: Heuristics and biases* (Cambridge: Cambridge University Press, 1982).

138, line 1 Walster, E., 'Assignment of responsibility for an accident', *Journal of Personality and Social Psychology*, 1966, 3, 73-79.

138, line 9 Piaget J., *The Moral Judgment of the Child* (London: Routledge and Kegan Paul, 1932).

139, line 5 Miller, A. G., Gillen, B., Schenker, C., and Radlove, S., 'Perception of obedience to authority', Proceedings of the 81st Annual Convention of the American Psychological Association, 1973, 8, 127-128.

139, line 12 Bierbrauer, G., 'Effect of set, perspective and temporal factors in attribution', unpublished doctoral dissertation, Stanford University, 1973.

139, line 24 Ross, L., Amabile, T. M., and Steinmetz, I. L., 'Social roles, social control, and biases in social-perception processes', *Journal of Personality and Social Psychology,* 1977, 35, 485-494.

139, line 34 For a discussion of the fundamental attribution error, see Nisbett, R., and Ross, L., *Human Inference: Strategies and shortcomings of social judgment* (Englewood Cliffs: Prentice-Hall, 1980), pp. 122-127.

139, line 43 Storms, M. D., 'Videotape and the attribution process: reversing actors' and observers' point of view', *Journal of Personality and Social Psychology*, 1973, 27, 165-175.

140, line 24 For evidence on the inconsistency of character traits, see Mischel, W., *Introduction to Personality*, fourth edition (New York: Holt, Rinehart and Winston, 1986).

141, line 29 Ross, L., Greene, D., and House, P., 'The false consensus phenomenon: an attributional bias in self perception and social perception processes', *Journal of Experimental Social Psychology*, 1977, 13, 279-301.

142, line 11 Schachter, S., and Singer, J., 'Cognitive, social and psychological determinants of emotional state', *Psychological Review*, 1962, 65, 379-399.

142, line 26 Cantor, J. R., Zillman, D., and Bryant, J., 'Enhancement of experienced arousal in response to erotic stimuli through misattribution of unrelated residual arousal', *Journal of Personality and Social Psychology*, 1975, 32, 69-75.

143, line 3 Weiss, J., and Brown, P., 'Self-insight error in the explanation of mood', unpublished manuscript, Harvard University, 1977.

Chapter 15

145, line 4 Kahneman, D., and Tversky, A., 'Subjective probability: a judgment of representativeness', in Kahneman, D., Slovic, P., and Tversky, A. (Eds), *Judgment Under Uncertainty: Heuristics and biases* (Cambridge: Cambridge University Press, 1982), pp 32-47.

146, line 1 Kahneman, D., and Tversky, A., 'On the psychology of prediction', *Psychological Review*, 1973, 80, 237-251

146, line 18 Tversky, A., and Kahneman, D., 'Extensional versus intuitive reasoning: the conjunction fallacy in probability judgement', *Psychological Review*, 1983, 90, 293-315.

148, line 2 Nisbett, R. E., and Lemley, R. N., 'The evil that men do can be diluted, the good cannot', unpublished manuscript, University of Michigan, 1979.

149, line 26 Tversky, A., and Kahneman, D., 'Causal schemata in judgments under uncertainty', in Fishbein, M. (Ed.), Progress in Social Psychology (Hillsdale, NJ: Lawrence Erlbaum, 1978).

150, line 5 Sutherland, N. S., 'Guilty by machine error', *New Scientist*, 30 January 1975, 262-265.

151, line 11 Casscells, W., Schoenberger, A., and Grayboys, T., 'Interpretation by physicians of clinical laboratory results', *New England Journal of Medicine*, 1978, 299, 999-1000.

151, line 21 Baron, J., Beattie, J., and Hershey, J. C., 'Heuristics and biases in diagnostic reasoning 11: Congruence, information and certainty', *Organizational Behaviour and Human Decision Processes*, 1989.

152, line 1 Paulos, J. A., *Innumeracy* (New York: Hill and Wang, 1988).

153, line 12 Kahneman, D., and Tversky, A., 'Subjective probability: a judgment of representativeness', *Cognitive Psychology*, 1972, 3, 430-454.

153, line 40 Tversky, A., and Kahneman, D., 'Introduction', in Kahneman, D., Slovic, P., and Tversky, A. (Eds), *Judgment Under Uncertainty: Heuristics and biases* (Cambridge: Cambridge University Press, 1982).

154, line 23 Borgida, E., and Nisbett, R. E., 'The differential impact of abstract vs concrete information on decisions', *Journal of Applied Social Psychology*, 1977, 7, 258-271.

154, line 24 Hamill, R., Wilson, T. O., and Nisbett, R. E, 'Ignoring sample bias: inferences about collectivities from atypical cases', unpublished manuscript, University of Michigan, 1979.

156, line 2 Paulos, J., op. cit.

Chapter 16

159, line 24 Tversky, A., and Kahneman, D., 'The framing of decisions and the psychology of choice', *Science*, 1980, 211, 453-458.

160, line 12 Tversky, A., and Kahneman, D., op. cit.

160, line 29 Wagenaar, W. A., *Paradoxes of Gambling Behaviour* (Hove: Lawrence Eribaum Associates, 1988).

161, line 9 Detambel, M. H., and Stolurow, L. M., 'Probability and work as determiners of multichoice behavior', *Journal of Experimental Psychology*, 1957, 53, 73-81.

161, line 20 Friedman, M. P., Burke, C. J., Cole, M., Keller, L., Millward, R. B., and Estes, W. K., Two choice behavior under extended training with shifting probabilities of reinforcement', in Atkinson, R. C. (Ed.), *Studies in Mathematical Psychology* (Stanford CA: Stanford University Press, 1964).

161, line 34 Tversky, A., and Kahneman, D., op. cit.

163, line 29 Kahneman, D., Knetsch, J. L., and Thaler, R., 'Fairness as a constraint on profit seeking: entitlements on the market', *American Economic Review*, 1986, 76, 728-711.

164, line 8 Elstein, A. S., Holzman, G. B., Ravitch, M. M., Metheny, W. A., Holmes, M. M., Hoppe, R. B., Rothert, M. L., and Rovner, D. R., 'Comparison of physicians' decisions regarding oestrogen replacement therapy for menopausal women and decisions derived from a decision analytic model', *American Journal of Medicine*, 1986, 80, 246-258.

164, line 27 Tversky, A., 'Intransitivity of preferences', *Psychological Review*, 1969, 76, 31-48.

165, line 17 Schwalm, N. D., and Slovic, P., 'Development and test of a motivational approach and materials for increasing use of restraint', final technical report PFTR-1100-82-3 (Woodland Hills, CA: Perceptronics Inc., 1982).

165, line 24 Tversky, A., Sattath, S., and Slovic, P., 'Contingent weighting in judgment and choice', *Psychological Review*, 1988, 95, 371-384.

166, line 2 Examples are from Thaler, R. H., 'Mental accounting and consumer choice', *Marketing Science*, 1985, 4, 199-214.

167, line 3 Loftus, E. F., *Eyewitness Testimony* (Cambridge, Mass: Harvard University Press, 1979).

167, line 32 On anchoring effects, see Tversky, A., and Kahneman, D., 'Judgement under uncertainty: heuristics and biases', *Science*, 1974, 185, 1124-1131.

168, line 15 Loftus, E. F., op. cit.

169, line 17 For this and the following estimates see Tversky, A., and Kahneman, D., 'Judgement under uncertainty: heuristics and biases', in Kahneman, D., Slovic, P., and Tversky, A. (Eds), *Judgment Under Uncertainty: Heuristics and Biases* (Cambridge: Cambridge University Press, 1982), pp. 3-20.

Chapter 17

172, line 6 Fischhoff. B., 'Hindsight ≠ foresight: the effect of outcome knowledge on judgment under uncertainty', *Journal of Experimental Psychology: Human Perception and Performance*, 1975, 1, 288-299.

173, line 28 Fischhoff, B., and Beth, R., '"I knew it would happen" remembered probabilities of once-future things', *Organizational Behavior and Human Performance*, 1975, 13, 1-16.

174, line 23 Quotation from Tawney taken from Fischhoff, B., 'For those condemned to study the past: heuristics and biases in hindsight', in Kahneman, D., Slovic, P., and Tversky, A. (Eds), *Judgment Under Uncertainty: Heuristics and Biases* (Cambridge: Cambridge University Press, 1982), pp. 335-351.

175, line 5 *The Independent*. See also Svenson, O., 'Are we all less risky and more skilful than our fellow drivers?', *Acta Psychologica*, 1981, 47, 143-148.

175, line 10 Ainslie, P. A., and Adams, J. K., 'Confidence in the recognition and reproduction of words difficult to spell', *American Journal of Psychology*, 1960, 73, 544-552.

175, line 14 Wright, G. N., Phillips, L. D., Whalley, P. C., Choo, G. T., Ng, K. O., Tan, I., and Wisudha, A., 'Cultural differences in probabilistic thinking', *Journal of Cross-Cultural Psychology*, 1978, 9, 285-299.

175, line 25 Fischhoff, B., Slovic, P., and Lichtenstein, S., 'Knowing with certainty: the appropriateness of extreme confidence', *Journal of Experimental Psychology: Human Perception and Performance*, 1977, 3, 552-564.

175, line 30 Oskamp, S., 'Overconfidence in case-study judgments', *Journal of Consulting Psychology*, 1965, 29, 261-265.

176, line 9 Fischhoff, B., Slovic, P., and Lichtenstein, S., op, cit. For a review of studies on overconfidence see Lichtenstein, S., Fischhoff, B., and Phillips, L. D., 'Calibration of probabilities: the state of the art', in Jungermann, H., and de Zeeuw, G. (Eds), *Decision Making and Change in Human Affairs* (Amsterdam: D. Reidel, 1977).

176,   line 23 For overconfidence in the professions, see e.g. Lusted, L. B., *Introduction to Medical Decision Making* (Springfield, Ill: Charles C. Thomas, 1968); and Dreman, D., *Contrarion Investment Strategy* (New York: Random House, 1979).

176,   line 39 Kahneman, D., and Tversky, A., 'Intuitive prediction: biases and corrective procedures', in Kahneman, D., Slovic, P., and Tversky, A. (Eds) *Judgment Under Uncertainty: Heuristics and Biases* (Cambridge: Cambridge University Press, 1982), pp. 414-421.

177,   line 13 Jenkins, H. H., and Ward, W. C., 'Judgment of contingency between responses and outcomes', *Psychological Monographs*, 1965, 79, 1, Whole No. 79.

177,   line 18 Goffman, E., *Interaction Ritual* (New York: Anchor, 1967).

177,   line 31 Koriat, A., Lichtenstein, S., and Fischhoff, B., 'Reasons for confidence', *Journal of Experimental Psychology: Human Learning and Memory*, 1980, 6, 107-118.

Chapter 18

179,   line 1 Except where otherwise noted, the analysis of the causes of risk is based on Slovic, P., Fischhoff, B., and Lichtenstein, S., 'Facts versus fears: understanding perceived risk', in Kahneman, D., Slovic, P., and Tversky, A. (Eds), *Judgment Under Uncertainty: Heuristics and Biases* (Cambridge: Cambridge University Press, 1982).

180,   line 41 Streff, F. M., and Getler, E. S., 'An experimental test of risk compensation: between subject versus within subject analyses', *Accident Analysis and Prevention*, 1988, 20, 277 287.

182,   line 16 For the analysis of the *Herald of Free Enterprise* disaster, see Wagenaar, W. A., 'Risk taking and accident causation', in Yates, J. F., *Risk-taking Behavior* (Chichester: John Wiley and Sons, 1992), pp 257-281.

183,   line 31 Slovic, P., Fischhoff, B., and Lichtenstein, S., 'Accident probabilities and seat belt usage: a psychological perspective', *Accident Analysis and Prevention*, 1978, 10, 281-285.

183,   line 33 Wagenaar, W. A., op. cit.

184,   line 15 The comparison of the dangers of nuclear power and fossil fuels is largely based on a report by the British Health and Safety Executive: *The Tolerability of Risk from Nuclear Power Stations* (London: HMSO, 1988).

186,   line 15 The data on X-rays were issued in a report by the Royal College of Radiologists summarised in *The Independent*.

Chapter 19

187,   line 24 Simon, H., *Models of Man: Social and Rational* (New York: John Wiley and Sons, 1957).

189,   line 1 Except where otherwise noted, the rest of this chapter is based on Kahneman, D., and Tversky, A., 'On the psychology of prediction', *Psychological Review*, 1973, 80, 237-251.

189,   line 29 Nisbett, R., and Ross, L., *Human Inference: Strategies and Shortcomings of Social Judgment* (Englewood Cliffs: Prentice-Hall, 1980).

190,   line 1 Baron, J., *Thinking and Deciding* (Cambridge: Cambridge University Press, 1988).

190,   line 9 Independent Research Services, 'Successful Personal Investing', unpublished, 1992.

190,   line 28 Kahneman, D., and Tversky, A., op. cit.

191,   line 25 Kahneman, D., and Tversky, A., op. cit.

192,   line 9 Kahneman, D., and Tversky, A., op. cit.

193,   line 4 Lichtenstein, S., Earle, T. C., and Slovic, P., 'Cue utilization in a numerical prediction task', *Journal of Experimental Psychology: Human Perception and Performance*, 1975, 104, 77-85.

193,   line 35 Fischhoff, B., 'For those condemned to study the past: heuristics and biases in hindsight', in Kahneman, O., Slovic, P., and Tversky, A. (Eds), *Judgment Under Uncertainty: Heuristics and Biases* (Cambridge: Cambridge University Press, 1982).

193,   line 5 Feller, W., *An Introduction to Probability Theory and Its Applications*, third edition, vol. 1 (New York: John Wiley and Sons, 1968).

194,   line 17 Kahneman, D., and Tversky, A., op. cit.

Chapter 20

196,   line 13 Eddy, D. M., 'Probabilistic reasoning in clinical medicine: problems and opportunities', in Kahneman, D., Slovic, P., and Tversky, A. (Eds), *Judgment Under Uncertainty: Heuristics and Biases* (Cambridge: Cambridge University Press, 1982).

197,   line 27 Quoted in Dawes, R. M., and Corrigan, B., 'Linear models in decision making', *Psychological Bulletin*, 1974, 81, 98-106. Except where otherwise stated, the remainder of this chapter is based on the above paper and on Dawes, R. M., 'The robust beauty of improper linear models in decision making', in Kahneman, D., Slovic, P., and Tversky, A. (Eds), *Judgment Under Uncertainty: Heuristics and Biases* (Cambridge: Cambridge University Press, 1982).

201,   line 18 Hess, F. H., 'Pupilometrics', in Greenfield, N., and Sternbach, R. (Eds). *Handbook of Psychophysiology* (New York: Holt, Rinehart and Winston).

202,   line 41 Goldberg, I. R., 'Man versus model of man: a rationale, plus some evidence for a method of improving on clinical inferences', *Psychological Bulletin*, 1970, 73, 422-432.

203,   line 22 Dreman, D., *Contrarian Investment Strategy* (New York: Random House, 1979).

206,   line 22 Schmitt, N., 'Social and situational determinants of interview decisions: implications for the employment interview', *Personnel Psychology*, 1976, 29, 79-101.

207,   line 11 Herriot. P., and Rothwell, C., 'Organizational choice and decision theory: effects of employers' literature and selection interview', *Journal of Occupational Psychology*, 1981, 54, 17-31.

207,   line 39 Einhorn, H. J., 'Expert measurement and mechanised confirmation', *Organizational Behaviour and Human Performance*, 1972. 7, 86-106.

208,   line 7 Harmon, P.. and King, D., *Expert Systems* (New York: John Wiley and Sons, 1989).

Chapter 21

212,   line 26 Baron, J., *Thinking and Deciding* (Cambridge: Cambridge University Press, 1988).

214,   line 14 Gardiner, P. C., and Edwards, W., 'Public values: multiattribute utility measurement for social decision-making', in Kaplan. M. F., and Schwartz, S. (Eds), *Human Judgment and Decision Processes* (New York: Academic Press).

215,   line 26 Hammond, K. R., and Adelman, L., 'Science, values, and human judgment', *Science*, 1976, 194, 389-396.

216,   line 4 Fogbeck, P. G., and Thornberg. J. R., 'Evaluation of a computerized Bayesian model for diagnosis of renal cysts versus tumour versus normal variant from exploratory arogram information', *Investigative Radiology*, 1976, 11, 102-111.

219,   line 5 Fischhoff, B., 'Cost-benefit analysis and the art of motorcycle maintenance', *Policy Sciences*, 1977, 8, 177-202.

219,   line 20 Fischhoff, B., op. cit.

219,   line 24 Health and Safety Executive, *The Tolerability of Risk from Power Stations* (London: HMSO, 1988).

221,   line 35 For a readable account of QALYs and associated approaches, see

Fallowfield, L., *The Quality of Life* (London: Souvenir Press, 1990) from which
the following examples are taken.
221, line 4 Christensen-Szalanski, J. J. J., 'Discount functions and the measurement
of patients' values: women's decisions during childbirth', *Medical Decision
Making,* 1984, 4, 47-58.

Chapter 22

224, line 1 Unless otherwise noted, the facts in this chapter are taken from Marks,
D., and Kamman, R., *The Psychology of the Psychic* (Buffalo, NY: Prometheus
Books, 1980).
224, line 7 The figures on astrology are based on polls, see Paulos, J. A., *Innumeracy*
(New York: Hill and Wang, 1988).
226, line 20 Ulrich, R. F., Stachnik, T. T., and Staintor, N. R., 'Student acceptance of
generalized personality profiles', *Psychological Reports*, 1973, 13, 831-834.
228, line 9 Hansel, C. E. M., *ESP and Parapsychology* (Buffalo, NY: Prometheus
Books, 1980).

Chapter 23

234, line 2 For a review see Baron, J., *Thinking and Deciding* (Cambridge:
Cambridge University Press, 1988), pp. 461-483.
234, line 19 Fong, G. T., Krantz, D. H., and Nisbett, R. E., 'The effects of statistical
training on thinking about everyday problems', *Cognitive Psychology*, 1986,
18, 253-292.
235, line 1 Lorrick, R. P., Morgan, J. N., and Nisbett, R. E., 'Who uses the norma-
tive rules of choice?'

index

Most names indexed are of people whose irrationality has been demonstrated, the remainder are the names of those who provided the demonstrations. Since awarding titles is irrational (see pages 79-80) none are given.

Obedience to Authority
Stanley Milgram
foreword by Jerome Bruner
2005 | paperback | 256 pages | ISBN 978-0-9530964-7-3

Volunteers are invited to a scientific laboratory under the pretence of participating in a study about the effects of punishment on learning. They are instructed by an experimenter to administer an electric shock of increasing intensity to a 'learner' every time he makes a mistake. How many, if any, would go right up the scale to 450 Volts?
The implications of Stanley Milgram's extraordinary findings are devastating. From the Holocaust to Vietnam's My Lai massacre, from Bosnia to Iraq's Abu Ghraib prison, Obedience to Authority goes some way towards explaining how ordinary people can commit the most horrific of crimes if placed under the influence of a malevolent authority.

'A masterpiece.' NEW STATESMAN

'Milgram's work is of first importance, not only in explaining how it is that men submit, but also in suggesting how better they may rebel.'
SUNDAY TIMES

STANLEY MILGRAM

The Individual
in a Social World

ESSAYS AND EXPERIMENTS
EDITED BY THOMAS BLASS

The Individual in a Social World
Stanley Milgram
edited by Thomas Blass
2009 | paperback | ISBN 978-1-905177-12-7

This third expanded and definitive collection of essays by Stanley Milgram, the creator of the iconoclastic 'Obedience Experiments' and the originator of the concept of 'six degrees of separation', familiarizes the reader with some of social psychology's more groundbreaking and exciting experiments. Milgram's lucid and entertaining style makes this essential reading not only for psychology students but anyone interested in the complexity of human nature.

Stanley Milgram was one of the world's most influential social psychologist and author of Obedience to Authority. Editor Thomas Blass, Ph.D., is a professor of social psychology at the University of Baltimore County and an expert on Stanley Milgram's life and work and the author of Milgram's definitive biography The Man who Shocked the World.

'Original, thought provoking and fascinating. Milgram was years ahead of his time, and this book should be read by every social scientist who is interested in behaviour beyond the laboratory.'
Richard Wiseman – author of Quirkology

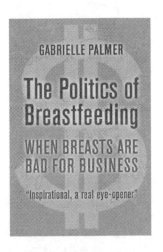

The Politics of Breastfeeding
When breasts are bad for business
Gabrielle Palmer

2009 | paperback | 464 pages | ISBN 978-1-905177-16-5

Every day more than 3,000 babies die from infections due to a lack of breastfeeding and the use of bottles, artificial milks and other risky products. In her powerful and provocative book Gabrielle Palmer describes the pressures on women, health workers and governments who are enmeshed in collusion with the sellers of infant feeding products. These companies invest in marketing strategies and clever promotion which help maintain practices that contribute to the suffering, illness and death of children in both poor and rich nations.

Gabrielle Palmer vividly describes the far-reaching consequences for health and well-being that the actions of large corporations have on global politics and the environment. With an engaging blend of facts, insight and anecdotes, she puts infant feeding fashions into their historic and economic contexts. An essential and inspirational eye-opener, The Politics of Breastfeeding challenges our complacency about how we feed our children and radically reappraises a subject which concerns not only mothers, but everyone: man or woman, parent or childless, old or young.

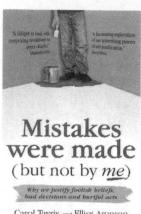

Mistakes were Made (but not by me)
Carol Tavris and Elliot Aronson

2008 | paperback | 304 pages | ISBN 978-1-905177-21-9

Why do people dodge responsibility when things fall apart? Why the parade of public figures unable to own up when they make mistakes? Why the endless marital quarrels over who is right? Why can we see hypocrisy in others but not in ourselves? Are we all liars?
Or do we really believe the stories we tell?
Backed by years of research and delivered in lively, energetic prose, Mistakes were made (but not by me) offers a fascinating explanation of self-deception – how it works, the harm it can cause, and how we can overcome it.

'Excellent.' THE GUARDIAN

'A brilliant new book.' THE TIMES

'By turns entertaining, illuminating and – when you recognise yourself in the stories it tells – mortifying.' THE WALL STREET JOURNAL